SPIRAL GUIDES

Travel With

D0420228

TUSCANY

Contents

the magazine 5

Finding Your Feet 35

Florence 49

Central Tuscany 87

Written by Tim Jepson
Verified and updated by Tim Jepson
Copy edited by Sheila Hawkins
American editor Tracy Larson

Produced by Duncan Baird Publishing Limited, London, England
for AA Publishing
Published in the United States by AAA Publishing,
1000 AAA Drive, Heathrow, Florida 32746
Published in the United Kingdom by AA Publishing

ISBN-13: 978-1-59508-184-1
ISBN-10: 1-59508-184-4

Cover design by permission of AA Publishing
Color separation by Leo Reprographics
Printed and bound in China by Leo Paper Products

10 9 8 7 6 5 4 3 2 1

A02693

the magazine

A Tuscan

It's hard to imagine a place where life's pleasures can be more easily or consummately gratified than Tuscany. What other region can boast Europe's greatest art, its loveliest countryside, some of its best food and wine, its most idyllic villas, and many of its most historic towns and villages?

Michelangelo, one of the finest artists and sculptors in art history, hailed from Tuscany

In Florence, Tuscany can claim Europe's premier artistic capital, and anywhere else, such a city would more than outshine its rivals. But in Tuscany even the lesser towns such as Siena, Lucca and Pisa – not to mention villages such as Pienza, Montalcino and San Gimignano – are places that would be the artistic envy of any country in the world.

Much the same can be said of Tuscany's landscapes, and in particular the timeless pastoral countryside with which the region is most closely associated: cypress-topped hills; silvery-grey olive trees; sun-dappled vineyards; poppy-strewn fields; elegant Renaissance villas; beautiful Italianate gardens; and lonely stone farmhouses.

Here again, however, the best-known images are merely the beginning, for Tuscany has a wealth of less celebrated but equally beguiling landscapes. In the north, for example, the Alpi Apuane are

Idyll

mountains of almost Alpine splendour; close by, the Orecchiella is an upland vastness of lonely peaks and ancient forests. In the region's heartland, Chianti is an enclave of vineyards and rolling wooded hills; to the east are the Mugello, Pratomagno and Casentino, high, wilderness areas that are Chianti's scenic equal yet remain all but unvisited.

If most of Tuscany's landscapes are familiar, then the names of some of its native sons are just as well known. Some of the greatest writers and artists of the last 1,000 years have hailed from this tiny corner of Italy. Among them are Michelangelo and Leonardo da Vinci, men of individual genius who would shine in any age; scientists such as Galileo Galilei; poets and writers such as Dante, Machiavelli, Boccaccio and Petrarch; sculptors such as Donatello; and a list of painters without compare – Botticelli, Giotto, Piero della Francesca, Uccello, Fra Angelico…

To these names must be added others from Tuscany's long history, which spans at least 3,000 years, from the ancient Etruscan tombs of southern Tuscany and the Roman ruins of Lucca and Volterra to the tangled affairs and burgeoning artistic and mercantile life of the region's medieval city states. The most resonant names are those of the Medici, the banking dynasty which dominated first Florence and then much of Tuscany for some 300 years.

In seeing the best of Tuscany, you are seeing the best – artistically, scenically and culturally – of Italy. Yet this is a region where the best is only the beginning – where there is so much to see, even the second rate is worth a special mention.

Tuscan-born Galileo Galilei founded modern science and astronomy with his experiments in the 16th century

Paradise *of* Exiles

A mixture of chance and cultural vigour gave rise to Tuscany's quartet of great medieval writers – Dante, Boccaccio, Petrarch and Machiavelli. More recently, however, it has been the lure of art, sun and other more hedonistic pleasures that has seduced foreign poets, artists, film-makers and other outsiders to this "paradise of exiles".

Different people express it in different ways, but the meaning is the same: Italy, and Tuscany in particular, has something the cold north lacks. The Scandinavians call it a "longing for figs"; the English poet Percy Bysshe Shelley yearned for a "beakerful of the warm south", and Lord Byron, ever mindful of amorous possibilities, observed: "What men call gallantry, and gods adultery, Is far more common where the climate's sultry."

Tuscany is full of the ghosts of writers, painters and others

Above: Petrarch was born in Arezzo and helped popularise the Tuscan dialect

drawn south by the siren call of art, history, beauty, scholarship, climate, health, landscape and romance. Indeed, it would almost be easier to list the literati who didn't visit, or settle here temporarily, than those who did.

Shelley was typical of the 18th- and 19th-century Grand Tourists, for whom life and education were considered incomplete without a ritualised cultural odyssey through the cities of Italy. In 1818 the poet came to "flee the shadows of his first marriage…the tumult of humankind, and the

wrote *The Decline and Fall of the Roman Empire*, made 12 tours of the gallery before even looking at a painting; Shelley ignored the paintings altogether.

The taste for the picturesque was also different. Today, San Gimignano's beauty and medieval towers make it the most visited village in Italy. In 1905, however, it appeared as the village of "Monteriano" in E M Forster's novel *Where Angels Fear to Tread*, where it stood as a symbol of the dirt, disease and drab poverty of rural Italy.

English poet Percy Bysshe Shelley made a second home in Tuscany

"a sunny place for shady people"

chilling fogs and rains of our own country." He found but brief respite, for Tuscany was to be his undoing – he drowned off the coast four years later and was cremated on a beach south of Livorno. Not before setting eyes on Florence, however, where he claimed never to have seen a city "so lovely at first sight." Many – but not all – exiles agreed, finding in Tuscany and its capital a foreign retreat close to perfection.

Past approaches to sightseeing, though, were very different. The Uffizi, for example, now renowned for Europe's greatest collection of Renaissance paintings, was visited mainly for its sculpture: Edward Gibbon, who

Tuscany: For and Against

"…the most enchanting place I know in the world." – Matthew Arnold, 1879

"A sunny place for shady people." – Sir Harold Acton, 1960

"Such dreary, uninteresting hillocks." – William Beckford, 1783

"…the fairest picture on our planet, the most enchanting to look upon, the most satisfying to the eye and the spirit." – Mark Twain, 1892

"…a pestilential place, smug little hills domed over with villas, and museums and churches that have been so much photographed and written about that one is fed up to the eyes with them long before one sets foot inside." – Violet Trefusis, 1921

A Tuscan Quartet

Dante Alighieri

Dante Alighieri was born in Florence in 1265. He served the city as a diplomat, but in 1302 was exiled – on trumped-up charges – and spent the years before his death drifting between cities across northern Italy. He died in 1321 in Ravenna, where he is buried. He is best known for his great epic poem, *La Divina Commedia* (*The Divine Comedy*), which helped secure the use of everyday Tuscan – the vernacular in which the poem is written – as a literary language. This language would eventually evolve into Italian as it is spoken today.

Francesco Petrarca

Francesco Petrarca, or Petrarch, was born in Arezzo in 1304 and died in 1375. A traveller and diplomat, he attended the papal court in Avignon, France, where he probably met Laura de Noves, the romantic inspiration for his *Canzoniere*, some of the finest sonnets ever written. Like his predecessor Dante and contemporary Boccaccio, Petrarch often wrote in Italian, but was also a member of the vanguard of writers who sought to revive Greek and Latin as literary languages, thus forming part of the upsurge in Classical scholarship that helped pave the way for the Renaissance.

Dante Alighieri, Italy's finest medieval poet

Petrarch's great love and inspiration, "Laura" was in fact a married woman who refused his advances, leaving the poet's love unrequited

Sleep, Eat – and Don't See the Sights

Not all Grand Tourists loved sightseeing. For Englishmen Thomas Gray and Horace Walpole, travelling together in 1741, it was not a priority. Describing their day, Gray wrote: "We get up at twelve, breakfast till three, dine till four, sleep till six, drink cooling liqueurs till eight, go to the bridge [Ponte Vecchio] till ten, sup till two, and so sleep till twelve again."

Boccaccio was the inspiration of English poet Chaucer

Giovanni Boccaccio

Giovanni Boccaccio (1313–75) was probably born in Paris, the illegitimate son of an Italian merchant. He grew up in Tuscany and Naples, settling in Florence in 1340. Here he met fellow writer Petrarch, with whom he shared an interest in reviving Greek and Latin as literary languages. His most famous work is *Il Decamerone* (*The Decameron*), which was written (in Italian) after the Black Death of 1348. It consists of 100 tales told by 10 people over 10 days as they seek to escape the pestilence raging in Florence.

Nicolò Machiavelli

Nicolò Machiavelli (1469–1527) has had a bad press. The term "Machiavellian", suggesting cunning and treachery, was actually coined by the French to denigrate all things Italian. Machiavelli himself was a Florentine diplomat, politician and bureaucrat. His book *Il Principe* (*The Prince*) was a masterpiece of political analysis, combining the study of historical cycles, political science and human nature, things which Machiavelli held to be immutable throughout history.

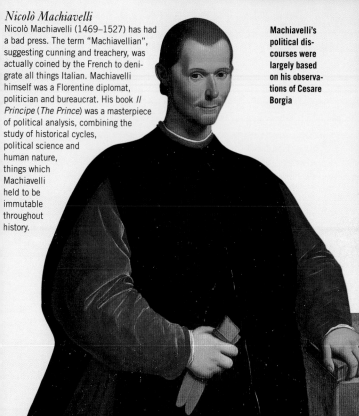

Machiavelli's political discourses were largely based on his observations of Cesare Borgia

Tuscany in Film

Tuscany's native soil may not have yielded any great Italian film directors – no Fellinis, Bertoluccis or Viscontis, for example – but its sublime historic towns and glorious landscapes have provided the locations for any number of well-known movies.

Tuscany has been used as the setting for films, both foreign and home-grown, since cinema's earliest days, but the films which started the industry's current love affair with the region were Merchant Ivory's *A Room with a View* in 1985, filmed in and around Florence, and Tarkovsky's *Nostalgia* (1983). Since that time, other films with Tuscan settings include: Kenneth Branagh's adaptation of Shakespeare's *Much Ado About Nothing* (1993); Bernardo Bertolucci's *Stealing Beauty* (1995); Antony Minghella's *The English Patient* (1996); Jane Campion's *The Portrait of a Lady* (1996) and Franco Zeffirelli's *Tea with Mussolini* (1998). Even more recently, much of the filming of *Hannibal* (2001), the sequel to psychological thriller *The Silence of the Lambs*, took place in Florence.

Above: Liv Tyler stars in *Stealing Beauty* (1996), which was set in Tuscany

Anthony Hopkins walks the streets of Florence in *Hannibal*, sequel to *The Silence of the Lambs*

How to Paint a Fresco

Painting in medieval Tuscany was not an easy business. As well as talent and inspiration, you had to be blessed with technical know-how and the ability to work at speed. You also had to confront the limitations of your medium, employ staff, satisfy patrons – and avoid falling off your scaffolding.

Most wall paintings in Tuscany from the 13th century onwards were frescoes, so-called because they were painted onto wet – or fresh (*fresco*) – plaster. Oil painting, a medium which allowed greater range of colour and effect, was practised in the 15th century but not mastered until the 16th century.

As a budding medieval Tuscan painter, therefore, you have to make do with a

An engraving by Albrecht Dürer showing an Italian fresco in progress

Above: *The Journey of the Magi* by Benozzo Gozzoli

Left: *The Death of St Francis* is part of Giotto's great fresco in Santa Croce in Florence

medium with many peculiarities and limitations.

To paint your fresco, you need a wall – usually in a church, villa or palace – and money from a patron such as the Church or a wealthy banker. You also need assistants to take care of all the peripheral chores, the first of which is to construct a scaffold on which you can work. You need to watch your step on this precarious work station – Michelangelo was injured when he fell off a platform in Rome's Sistine Chapel and Tuscan painter Barna da Siena died after falling from his scaffold.

Francesca's *Legend of the True Cross* in Arezzo's San Francesco church

...and Four Great Tuscan Fresco Cycles

Arezzo San Francesco. *The Legend of the True Cross* by Piero della Francesca (▶ 108).

Monte Oliveto Maggiore *Scenes from the Life of St Benedict* by Sodoma and Luca Signorelli (▶ 130).

San Gimignano Collegiata. *Scenes from the Old and New Testaments* by Bartolo di Fredi and Lippo Memmi (▶ 104).

Siena Palazzo Pubblico. *Allegories of Good and Bad Government* by Ambrogio Lorenzetti (▶ 94).

Allegories of Good and Bad Government by Lorenzetti

You can relax while an assistant applies the first of several layers of plaster to the wall: a layer known as the *arichio*, or *aricciato*, a rough coat of lime and sand. Then you can sketch or incise onto this the painting's basic composition and principal divisions. Note, however, that better painters than you – such as Giotto – often worked without sketches.

The next stage is a more detailed drawing in a red-earth pigment known as the *sinopia*, named after Sinope, the Greek city in Asia Minor which was believed to produce the finest of these pigments. Many Tuscan churches preserve these sketches, which are often revealed during restoration work.

Now the real problems begin. Wet plaster is essential to fresco, so you can only work on an area of wall small enough to be completed in a day (or before the plaster dries). You need to divide your painting into *giornate*, from the Italian *giorno*, meaning day, and each morning (or evening) instruct your assistant to apply a thin coat of wet finishing plaster (*intonaco*) to the *arichio* for the day's painting ahead. Once started, you have to work quickly and know exactly what you wish to paint – make a mistake, or take too long, and the *intonaco* has to be hacked off and a fresh layer applied.

Future scholars will be able to judge how quickly you worked, because at the end of each session you need to bevel the edge of the *intonaco* to prevent it from crumbling and provide a clean edge for the following morning's work. It is thus possible to make out a fresco's individual *giornate*, and how long the entire

artwork took to paint. Most Tuscan painters could create a figure in two days – one for the body and one for the head and shoulders. Masaccio, however, completed his entire *Expulsion of Adam and Eve* scene in the Brancacci Chapel in just four days (▶ 74).

Your skill in the use of colour will also be judged by future generations – and judged harshly, because the limitations of fresco means that it is difficult to mix colours. This restricts the range of colours available and makes effects of light and shade hard to achieve. Posterity will also spot any short cuts: if you use inferior or unsuitable pigments, for example, the colours will fade or change over time; add paint to a dry wall and the chances are it will flake off almost immediately.

Not that you are in bad company: no less an artist than Leonardo da Vinci, frustrated by fresco's limitations, painted much of his now almost ruined *Last Supper* in Milan on dry plaster with pigments of his own invention – with disastrous results.

How Fresco Works

A fresco relies for its longevity on a chemical reaction and, in particular, the drying and fixing qualities of plaster, a mixture of lime, water and sand. As plaster dries, carbon dioxide is absorbed from the air, converting the lime (calcium hydroxide) to calcium carbonate. This crystallises around the sand particles, binding them to the wall. If you add powdered and water soluble pigments to the wet plaster, the crystallisation process also fixes the particles of pigment and makes them resistant to further action by water.

Thereafter, only the crumbling of the plaster or the deterioration of the pigment will affect a fresco's appearance. If you apply oil pigment or water-based pigment to dry plaster, however, any moisture in the wall will quickly lift off the paint.

ECCENTRIC ARTISTS

Eccentric artistic behaviour is not just the preserve of modern painters. Tuscany had its share of unconventional artists: these are three of the strangest.

Jacopo Pontormo (1494–1556) was a strange, sensitive and solitary artist. He spent much of his career in a top-floor room that could only be reached by a ladder which he drew up behind him. His diaries record a daily obsession with his bowels and numerous minor ailments. He also had a morbid fear of death, yet was reputed to keep corpses in his bath to use as models. His work can be seen in the church of Santa Felicita in Florence.

Hermit and hypochondriac, Renaissance artist Jacopo Pontormo

Sodoma is the nickname of Antonio Bazzi (1477–1549), who came by his moniker after the Renaissance critic Giorgio Vasari claimed "he was always surrounded by young men, in whose company he took great pleasure." Sodoma claimed to have had three wives and 30 children, and kept a menagerie of "badgers, apes, cat-a-mountains, dwarf asses, horses and barbs to run races, magpies, dwarf chickens, tortoises, Indian doves…" as well as a talking raven.

Paolo Uccello (1396–1475) was a painter who became obsessed with the intricacies of perspective almost to the point of madness. Often he would lock himself away for weeks while grappling with a problem, a mania that left him close to ruin. In 1469 he wrote: "I am old, infirm and unemployed, and my wife is ill." Examples of his obsession can be seen in Florence in the Uffizi, the Duomo and Santa Maria Novella.

Paolo Uccello, whose search for perfection drove him to madness

At 3:25 pm on 7 January, 1990, the Leaning Tower of Pisa was closed to the public. A lean that had started in 1173 had finally tilted too far. Without radical intervention, said the scientists, the tower would collapse within 25 years. How had things come to such a pass – and what has been done to save one of Europe's most famous monuments?

The Leaning Tower

Fault for the Leaning Tower's lean lies with the 12th-century officials. They decided to build the tower, to act as a bell-tower for the nearby cathedral, on weak and sandy subsoil that had once been covered by the sea. One side of the site – the southern side – was softer than the other, causing the tower to sink almost from the moment it was begun in 1173.

Even as they built, medieval engineers tried to correct the lean, which by 1284 was already 90cm (35 inches) from the vertical, by altering the thickness of the marble used in construction and the angle at which they added the tower's upper levels. By 1350 however, when the tower was completed, the lean was 1.45m (4.75 feet) from the vertical. By 1990, when the tower was closed, it was 4.5m (14 feet) from the vertical, an angle of 5.5 degreees – and getting worse. Computer tests suggested that any angle above 5.44 degrees in such a tower should lead to its collapse.

Closing the tower was one thing, but deciding how to save the structure was another. Some 16 Italian government committees had already tried and failed to come up with a solution. Various panels of international experts, invited and otherwise, gave their opinions: the Japanese suggested building a completely new tower; the Russians favoured removing the base; and the Chinese recommended a second tower to act as prop.

While the experts bickered, a holding operation was put into place. Eighteen steel belts were fitted around the tower to prevent it from buckling and, in 1993, 661 tonnes of lead were attached to the tower's north side to balance its southward lean. After six months the tilt had been reversed – but by just 15mm.

The eventual solution – and the one that enabled the tower to be officially reopened in November, 2001 – was initiated in 1998. First, vast steel cables were slung around the tower and anchored in concrete piers as a precautionary measure. Then, a 70cm (27-inch) wedge of soil and clay was removed from beneath the tower's north side. Gradually the structure began to settle into the cavity. Within five months the tower had returned to the position it held in 1890; after three years it had recovered 14cm (5.5 inches) of its lean – well on the way to the engineers' eventual target of 42cm (16 inches). The "correction" is too small to be noticed by casual onlookers – the Leaning Tower will always lean – but for the monument, say scientists, it should mean salvation. But then scientists can be wrong…

In few other regions of the world does the simple act of eating and drinking conceal such a wealth of treats as it does in Tuscany. A holiday here can be made by an alfresco meal, a perfect espresso, a robust glass of Chianti or a sublime *gelato*.

eat drink an

In general, all Italians think the cuisine of their own region is the country's finest, and most are more than happy to put down the gastronomy of their neighbours. Tuscans, for example, are often referred to as *mangiafagioli*, or "bean-eaters", to sum up their supposedly simple cuisine.

Beans, to be fair, do feature in Tuscan cooking – *pasta e fagioli* (pasta and beans) is a rustic staple in much of the region. And it's true that much Tuscan cuisine has its roots in peasant tradition. But don't confuse simple with plain or uninspired. Tuscan cooking doesn't need to be over-elaborate because its native ingredients are so outstanding. Hams, salamis and cheeses, for example, are superb, and often feature as starters (*antipasti*) or as snacks in their own right. *Crostini* are also common –

Above: Enjoying an alfresco glass of wine in Montepulciano

Left: A Tuscan butcher's shop

small toasts spread with pâté, olive paste or other savoury garnishes. Other staples include superb olive oil (► 24–25), fine breads (often saltless) and – most importantly – the rich bounty of farm, field, forest and sea.

This bounty is the key to Tuscan cooking. Wonderful fresh fruit, mushrooms, herbs, legumes and vegetables are taken for granted. Better still, they are usually locally grown and only appear in shops, markets and on restaurant menus when they are fresh and in season. Spring yields asparagus and cherries, followed by apricots and peaches, while late summer and autumn see the arrival of figs, grapes and the first mushrooms, truffles and chestnuts.

Such ingredients are simply prepared and cooked, preserving flavours and freshness,

but they find their way into a wide range of dishes. Tuscans are fond of hearty soups, notably minestrone (ham and vegetable), *papa al pomodoro* (bread cooked in a rich broth and mixed with sieved tomatoes), and *ribollita* ("reboiled"), a thick vegetable soup that can be reheated and served over successive days. Two common pasta dishes are *pappardelle alla lepre* (large

A *gelateria* (ice-cream parlour) – is a mainstay of Tuscan life

be merry

Parmigiano-Reggiano is one of the many Italian cheeses on sale in Florence's Mercato Centrale

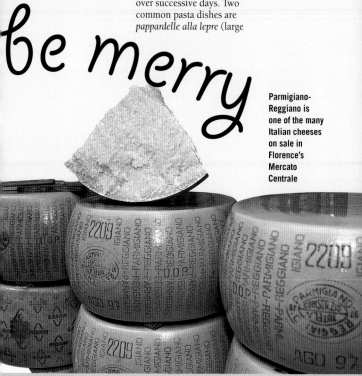

noodles with a hare sauce) and a pasta known as *pici* made from flour and water (and no egg). Game such as *cinghiale* (wild boar) is widely available in season, though the star of Tuscan meat dishes is *bistecca alla Fiorentina* (Florentine beef steak). Salad greens, plump tomatoes and a host of other vegetables accompany main courses.

Desserts are perhaps the one area where the Tuscan culinary repertoire disappoints, though some regional specialities are winners, notably Siena's *panforte*, a rich

The French Debt

In 1534, Caterina de' Medici married Henri Valois, the future King Henri II of France. When she moved from Italy to France she insisted on taking with her a retinue of Florentine chefs, and it is this event which forms the basis of the Florentines' claim that it was they who invented French cuisine. If this sounds far-fetched, then just consider the similarity between classic "French" dishes such as *vol au vents* (*turbanate di sfoglia* in Florence) and *canard à l'orange* (duck in orange sauce), which is a variation on Florence's *papero alla melarancia*. Caterina is also credited with introducing the French to napkins and forks.

cake of cloves, crystallised fruit, chocolate and nuts made since the 13th century. Not that sweet-toothed Tuscans need worry when they have something as good as the local *gelato* to fall back on.

Local cheeses are also outstanding – in particular the sheep's milk cheese (*pecorino*), produced in the region around Pienza.

Tuscan Wines

Tuscany has a wealth of wines, all based on the Sangiovese grape and its various hybrids, but certain names stand out and are usually a reliable indicator of quality. Don't pay too much heed to the official classification system – indicated by the letters "DOC" (*Denominazione di Origine Controllata*) or "DOCG" on

The vineyards around the village of San Gimignano are prolific wine producers

some bottles – as this no longer guarantees quality. Indeed, many producers do not apply for its classification and produce superlative wine under the "humblest" of labels, *Vino da Tavola* (Table Wine).

Chianti There are hundreds of Chiantis, good and bad. Some of the better versions are made by producers in the Gallo Nero (Black Cockerel) consortium. Fontodi, Felsina and Isole e Olena are also good names.

Super Tuscans This generic name for red wines is made by producers using new methods and new mixes of grape varieties. Prices are high. Top names include Sassicaia, Querciagrande, Olmaia, Tignanello, Ceparello and the wines of Carmignano.

Montalcino This village produces two main red wines: the expensive Brunello di Montalcino and its cheaper (but less aged) cousin, Rosso di Montalcino.

One of many Tuscan red wines, produced in the vineyards around Pienza

or *frullati* (milkshakes made with fresh fruit and sometimes ice-cream).

Sundown Popular apéritifs include Campari soda, which comes ready mixed in a distinctive triangular bottle (ask for *un Campari bitter* if you want the real thing); Cynar, an artichoke-based drink; and the non-alcoholic Crodino. Gin and tonic is *gin tonic*, ice is *ghiaccio* and a slice of lemon is *un spicchio di limone*.

After dinner Popular Italian digestifs include *grappa*, a clear (but occasionally flavoured) spirit, and the dark, herby *amaro* (literally "bitter") – Averna is a good brand. Sweeter drinks are Limoncello (lemon-based), Amaretto (almond) and Sambuca (similar to anise). Vin Santo – an amber-coloured dessert wine – is also popular.

Tuscany's three great virtues combined: stunning Florence architecture, superb coffee and warm summer sun

Il Poggione is a good producer of Brunello and Rosso.

Vino Nobile This so-called "King of Wines" produced around Montepulciano is a fuller, stronger red than Chianti. Producers include Avignonesi, Poliziano, Fattoria del Cerro and Cantucci.

Vernaccia Made since at least the 13th century in San Gimignano and said to have been Michelangelo's favourite wine, today it is too often an insipid wine aimed at tourists. Producers such as Teruzzi e Puthod, Panizzi and Falchìni make good versions.

Drinking All Day

Morning Breakfast means *cappuccino* or *caffè latte* and perhaps a fresh fruit juice (*spremuta*) or bottled juice (*succo di frutta*).

Noon Cooling drinks in the heat of the day include cold milky coffee (*caffè latte freddo*), cold tea with lemon (*tè freddo*), lemon soda (*limonata*), *granita* (crushed ice with a coffee or other flavoured syrup), and *frappé*

Olive Oil –Tuscany's Amber Nectar

It's hard to imagine Tuscan cooking without olive oil, and harder still to imagine the Tuscan landscape without its familiar groves of silvery-grey olive trees. More recently, the business of producing and buying olive oil has become imbued with something of the mystique that surrounds the production of wine.

Accepted wisdom has it that the best olives come from trees that are at least 50 years old, and that groves should be planted away from the fluctuating temperatures and increased moisture levels of the coast. At the same time they can't be planted too high – temperatures much below about 18°F will kill olive trees, as happened in a notorious winter in 1985, when many thousands of trees across central Italy were ravaged by temperatures as low as -4°F.

Olives are harvested between late October and January. The tell-tale signs are the green nets around trees and groups of workers shaking the branches with long sticks to loosen their fruit. In smaller, more conscientious estates, the olives will be picked early in the season by hand to avoid bruising, which imparts a bitter taste to the eventual oil. To produce the best oil, olives should be pressed within 36 hours of picking.

Most industrially refined oils, which means most oils available in supermarkets, will have been rendered bland by large-scale production. And note that the terms "virgin" or "extra virgin" mean little these days – an oil must have less than 0.1 per cent acidity to be "extra virgin", but low acidity alone does not guarantee a good flavour and minute differences in acidity are imperceptible in terms of taste.

To be sure of a good oil you need to buy from small producers or single estates that use small-scale (and expensive) methods. Traditionally, olives are washed, ground to a pulp between stone mills, heated slightly to release the oil, kneaded and then spread on woven mats. These mats are stacked on top of each other around a central pole and squeezed in a press. The resulting liquid is then spun in a centrifuge to separate the

oil. The paste residue is known as *sansa* and can be used as fuel or subjected to chemical solvents that extract more oil.

These days, however, small producers are increasingly turning to the "continuous cycle" method of production. Here, olives and pulp are treated in sterile, temperature-regulated stainless-steel containers, which means machinery can be scrupulously cleaned between batches of olives, thus avoiding contamination. Some of the best oil is also now made from olives that are finely chopped instead of being pressed, allowing the oil to drain away by gravity.

Below right: From the branch of the distinctive silver-leafed olive tree…

Below left: …to luscious, plump olives on sale in food shops

Siena's Palio

A Day at the

The Palio has often been condemned for being dangerous for both horse and rider

It has been a hotly contested event for centuries

The term "sporting event" comes nowhere near to describing the spectacle or the great traditions and historic rivalries of Tuscany's most celebrated pageant.

The race, which has been run almost without interruption for 700 years, involves representatives of Siena's *contrade*, the medieval parishes into which the city has been divided since the 13th century. Once there were 42 such parishes, today there are just 17, but the ancient bonds and rivalries are as strong as ever. Each *contrada* has a church, a baptismal fountain, a social club, flag and teams of *alfieri* (flag-throwers) and *tamborini* (drummers). Allegiance to the

Races

Twice a year, Siena's Piazza del Campo is the stage for a bareback horserace. The prize is modest and the race short. Yet the Palio is one of the most vivid and fiercely contested sporting events in Europe.

Preparations go on for months beforehand. Skulduggery is common and in the days before the race both horses and riders are watched for signs of betrayal. Divine assistance is also sought, horses being marched up the aisles of *contrada* churches to be blessed. Betting is widespread.

Pageants in medieval dress precede the race, which takes place at 7 pm. National television broadcasts the event, while in Siena the Campo is filled to bursting. The race is hectic and often dangerous – no race is complete without at least one call for its abolition. The only rule is that riders must not interfere with each other's reins.

The winning *contrada* celebrates with a vast banquet and revels in its triumph for weeks, while defeated parishes prepare for one more 90-second contest in Tuscany's very own day at the races.

contrada of your birth is absolute. Centuries of feuds and long-forgotten snubs come to a head in the Palio, when 10 of the *contrade* are chosen by lot each year to enter the race.

Once the event was held in the city's streets, but since 1656 it has followed a three-lap circuit of the Campo. The prize has always been the same, however – the embroidered banner (*pallium*) which gives the race its name. The contest is dedicated to the Holy Virgin and held on or around feast days associated with the Madonna – 2 July (the Feast of the Visitation) and 16 August (the day following the Feast of the Assumption).

A drummer boy performs at the Palio, representing his own *contrada*

Tuscany's *Weird* and *Wonderful*

Mummified saint See the wizened but uncorrupted corpse of St Zita, the 13th-century patron saint of maid-servants, in the church of San Frediano, Lucca (➤ 161).

Roll out the barrel One of Tuscany's strangest festivals revolves around the Bravio delle Botti, a barrel-rolling contest held in Montepulciano on the last Sunday in August between the town's eight parishes (➤ 135).

Saintly relics Some of the most revered of Tuscany's many relics are kept in Florence's Museo dell'Opera del Duomo (➤ 72). Among them are reputedly nails from the True Cross, the jaw of St Jerome, a finger belonging to St John the Baptist, St Philip's arm, and one of the arrows used in the attempted martyr-dom of St Sebastian.

Steaming square One of Tuscany's most evocative sights is the main square in the village of Bagno Vignoni – not a square at all but a large natural hot spring enclosed in a Renaissance pool. On cool days the "square" steams to magical effect (➤ 143).

Tower-top tree Tuscany's most bizarrely placed tree is a holm oak that sprouts oddly from

A contestant in the Bravio delle Botti barrel-rolling contest in Montepulciano

Steaming hot springs in Bagno Vignoni

road and is occasionally open to the public (tel: 0564 895122; www.nikidesaint phalle.com for the current opening times).

Spooky tombs Drive along the road between the villages of Sorano and Sovana in southern Tuscany close to the Lazio border and you will see thousands of tiny niche tombs cut into the living rock. The honeycomb of tombs dates from Etruscan times and is more than 2,000 years old (▶ 145).

Tilted but not toppled Pisa's Leaning Tower is such a familiar sight to modern-day visitors that it is easy to forget just how strange it is that a

the roof of the 44m (144-foot) high Torre Guinigi in Lucca (▶ 156).

Tarot Garden Tuscany's strangest and most compelling modern sculpture is found in the Gaudí-inspired Giardino dei Tarocchi, or Tarot Garden, close to the hamlet of Pescia Fiorentina between Chiarone and Capalbio in the region's southwest corner.

Begun in 1976, it is the work of the sculptress Niki de Saint Phalle, and consists of more than 20 vast sculptures based on the major cards of the Tarot. The garden can be seen from the

The holm oak flourishing on a medieval tower in Lucca – like the landscape turned upside down

tower of this weight and size can lean by so much – almost 5m (16 feet) from the vertical – and still remain standing. Work is on-going to prevent further tilting (► 18).

Fabbriche di Careggine was revealed after Lago di Vagli was drained

St Catherine's reliquary in San Domenico in Siena

Sunken village Beneath the Lago di Vagli in the Alpi Apuane region lies the sunken village of Fabbriche di Careggine, which was engulfed when the artificial lake was created. Most eerie of all, the village "reappears" every 10 years when the lake is emptied for maintenance – the next sighting is scheduled for 2014 – but the village's former church tower is some-times visible above the water.

The lake lies 15km (9 miles) west of Castelnuovo di Garfagnana (► 170).

Lost her head You can admire a reliquary containing the head of St Catherine, patron saint of Italy, in the church of San Domenico in Siena (► 100). You would be able to see the rest of her body, were it not for the fact that her remains were dismembered by heretics after her death. Her limbs are now held in reliquaries all over Italy.

Wax horrors Florence's most macabre museum display is found alongside the Palazzo Pitti at the Museo Zoologica La Specola (Via Romana 17, tel: 055 228 8251, open Thu–Tue 9–1, moderate). It consists of hundreds of anatomical waxworks: lovingly and exactly crafted limbs, eyes, skulls, organs and numerous full-sized "corpses", splayed or dissected to reveal every physical detail down to the tiniest capillary.

Best of...

Best Views

In Florence, climb the Campanile or the cathedral dome for great city views (➤ 61), or walk to San Miniato al Monte for views of the city and Tuscan hills (➤ 75). In Siena, climb the Torre del Mangia (➤ 92) for views of the Campo and beyond, or walk to Santa Maria dei Servi for distant views of the countryside. Note that the Museo dell'Opera del Duomo has a secret little Sienese viewpoint (➤ 97). The Torre Grossa and Torre Guinigi offer good views of San Gimignano and Lucca respectively (➤ 105 and 161). For sweeping views of southern Tuscany visit Montalcino's Fortezza (➤ 138), climb to the Fortezza Medicea in Cortona (➤ 112), walk Pienza's walls (➤ 133) or drive to the top of Monte Amiata (➤ 143).

Best Abbeys

Two abbeys stand out among Tuscany's many monastic buildings: Sant'Antimo (➤ 139) and Monte Oliveto Maggiore (➤ 130).

Siena's spectacular Campo, Tuscany's finest medieval square

The peaceful setting of Sant'Antimo Abbey

Best Scenic Drives

Drives which offer pretty views include the SS222 road, the **Chiantigiana** between Florence and Siena (► 181); the **SS68 road from Colle di Val d'Elsa and Volterra** (► 115); any of the mountain roads in the **Alpi Apuane and Orecchiella** (► 169–71); the **SS63 road** from Montecatini Terme to San Marcello Pistoiese; **the SS46 road** from San Quirico d'Orcia to Pienza (► 132); and the road numbers SS70, **SS71 and SS556** in the Casentino region in north-west Tuscany between Arezzo (► 108), Dicomano and Pontassieve.

Best Market

There's really no contest here: the **Mercato Centrale in Florence** is Europe's largest covered food market selling every Tuscan delicacy you can imagine (► 71).

Best Piazzas

First prize surely goes to the **Campo in Siena** (► 92), home of the Palio race, though the Campo dei Miracoli or Piazza del Duomo in Pisa, home to the Leaning Tower as well as the Duomo, comes a close second (► 164). The **Piazza Grande in Arezzo** (► 109) captivates by virtue of its steep slope, while the square of the same name in Montepulciano pleases on its own account, with lovely outdoor cafés (► 135). **Piazza San Michele in Foro in Lucca** owes its beauty to the church of the same name at its heart (► 156). **Bagno Vignoni's** tiny main square is not a square at all, but a natural hot spring (► 143).

Best Ice-Cream

Vivoli in Florence has been renowned for years as the purveyor of some of Tuscany's best – some would say Italy's best – *gelato* (► 81).

Best Evening Strolls

The quiet streets of almost any Tuscan hill town offer fine places to stroll as the sun goes down. Especially memorable is the promenade along the walls from **Piazza Dante in Pienza** (► Inside Info, page 132); the Passeggiata del Prato in Cortona; and a walk in **Florence's Giardino di Boboli** (► 74).

The Giardino di Boboli in Florence is ideal for a quiet stroll

Best Beaches

The **Marina di Alberese**, still relatively uncommercialised, is reached from Rispecia, 6.5km (4 miles) south of Grosseto in southwest Tuscany. The nearby beach in the **Parco Naturale della Maremma** is also superb, but access is via a special bus from Alberese, 8km (5 miles) southwest of Rispecia. North of Grosseto, paths lead to beaches off the coast road to Castiglione della Pescaia. Of the developed resorts in the north, **Viareggio** has the best beach (► 168); farther south there are resorts at Punta Ala and stretches of sand on the Tombolo di Giannella and di Feniglia near Orbetello.

The popular, chic beach resort of Viareggio

- Florence was the birthplace of Carlo Lorenzini in 1826, a writer less well known than his creation – Pinocchio.

- The Florentine flood of 1966 killed 39 people, made 14,000 families homeless, destroyed 15,000 cars and damaged more than 1.5 million books and manuscripts. In some places, the waters rose 6m (19 feet) above street level.

- The Medici family symbol – six or more balls on a shield – is still common on buildings or works of art across Tuscany – but nobody knows its original meaning.

Did You Know?

- Two ancient columns flank the east doors of Florence's Baptistery. Their polished surface was supposed to foretell acts of treason, for which reason the Pisans deliberately ruined them before giving them to Florence as a gift.

- A statute in medieval Florence made it compulsory to issue three loud warning cries before emptying a chamber-pot directly into the street.

- Until 1750, Florence's calendar began on 25 March, the Feast of the Annunciation, the date of the incarnation of Christ.

- Florence's medieval council members, the Priori, enjoyed the services of a professional joke-teller, the Buffone.

- Michelangelo claimed his sculpting skill came from ingesting the milk of his wet-nurse, a woman from the marble town of Carrara.

- Pistoia owns the *cintola* (girdle) that the Virgin Mary is said to have thrown to Thomas the Apostle at the moment of her Assumption. It is displayed five times a year.

- Two of Florence's most famous "medieval" church façades – those of the Duomo and Santa Croce – actually date from the 19th century.

- Galileo dropped balls of different weight from the Leaning Tower of Pisa in order to disprove Aristotle's theories on the acceleration of falling bodies.

- Rivalries between Tuscan towns are summed up in a proverb: *"meglio un morto in casa che un Pisano all'uscio"* – "better a death in the family than a Pisan on the doorstep." It was coined in Lucca but adapted for other cities.

- Florence was the capital of Italy between 1865 and 1870.

Pinocchio dolls on sale on a Tuscan street stall

Finding Your Fe

First Two Hours

Arriving By Air

You have four options if you are flying to Italy for a Tuscan holiday.

- **Rome** has the most international connections, but it is approximately a three-hour drive to Florence or Pisa from the Italian capital (slightly less to southern Tuscany).
- **Pisa** is served by several major European scheduled and charter airlines and lies about an hour by road or train from Florence; it also leaves you well placed for Siena, Chianti and the west and north of the region.
- **Bologna**, in the region of Emilia-Romagna to the north of Tuscany, also has an international airport. It is about 80 minutes by road or rail to Florence, but the journey is more complicated and leaves you less well placed than Pisa for the rest of Tuscany.
- **Florence** has a small airport which makes the most convenient entry point for the Tuscan capital and the central and eastern parts of the region, although at present its modest size means it is only served by a handful of small international airlines.

From Rome

Rome's airport is officially called Leonardo da Vinci (tel: 06 65 951; www.adr.it) but is better known by its colloquial name, **Fiumicino**.

- **Car rental** desks lie within walking distance of the main arrivals terminal, near the airport railway station for trains to central Rome (► 38). Take the underpass or the raised, covered walkway across the parking area outside the main terminal towards the railway station and follow the appropriate signs.
- **By car from Rome Airport** Follow signs for "Roma" (Rome) on the motorway spur between the airport and city outskirts and, after 11km (6.5 miles), watch for signs to "Firenze" (Florence) and the Grande Raccordo Anulare (GRA), the main Rome ring road: be prepared, as the junction comes suddenly. Follow the GRA clockwise for about 35 to 45 minutes to junction 10 (Firenze-A1); from here it is 240km (149 miles) to Florence on the A1 toll motorway. If you are heading for western Tuscany, leave the motorway spur earlier, following signs for Civitavecchia and the SS1 Via Aurelia, the main west-coast route to Grosseto and Pisa.
- **By train from Rome Airport** For trains to Florence, Pisa or Arezzo, first take the **airport shuttle train to Termini**, Rome's main railway station. Shuttles leave roughly every 30 minutes and the journey takes 30 minutes. Buy tickets for the shuttle from the office to the right of the station concourse as you face the platforms. You can also buy tickets here for the main leg of your journey, which avoids long queues at Termini.
- **Trains for Florence** These leave at least every hour from Termini. The quickest trains (Eurostar and InterCity services) make the journey in less than two hours – the slowest take up to four hours. Remember you will need to pay supplements for InterCity and Eurostar trains, and don't forget to validate your tickets before travelling (► 40).

From Pisa

Pisa's **Galileo Galilei Airport** (tel: 050 849300 for flight information or 050 849111 for the switchboard; www.pisa-airport.com) lies about 95km (59 miles) west of Florence. It is served by many major **European scheduled** and **charter companies**. The arrivals area has a small tourist office, a ticket office for Trenitalia (FS) trains (see below), and **car rental desks**, which are found immediately on exiting Customs.

■ **By car from Pisa** The airport lies close to major dual-carriageway and motorway links to Livorno (the A12 south), Viareggio and Lucca (the A12 north) and the A11 to Florence by way of Empoli (connections to Siena). The network of roads is confusing, however, so pay careful attention to the signs outside the airport.

■ **By train from Pisa** About six **direct train services** daily links Pisa Aeroporto (Pisa Airport) with Florence's main railway station, Santa Maria Novella. Journey time is 1 hour 20 minutes. Most trains stop at Empoli for connections to Siena. An hourly shuttle train runs from the airport station to Pisa Centrale, Pisa's main station, where you can connect with more services to Florence (and also trains to Lucca and other Tuscan towns). Buy through tickets to Florence's main station at the airport ticket office, located just outside the customs area.

■ **By bus** Visitors with valid boarding passes for Ryanair, easyJet, Thomsonfly or Travia flights can use the Terravision buses (tel: 06 3212 0011; www.terravision.it) to Florence's Santa Maria Novella. Buses meet incoming flights 8:40 am–10:35 pm. Journey time is 70 minutes. Tickets cost €7.50 (€13.50 return) and can be bought at the Terravision desk in Arrivals or (returning from Florence) at the BOPA Agency on platform 5 at Santa Maria Novella station. Buses leave from in front of the staiton for Pisa airport 5:50 am–7:30 pm.

From Florence

Florence airport is officially called Amerigo Vespucci (tel: 055 315874, 7:30 am–11 pm for information; 055 306 1702 for 24-hour information on international flights; 055 306 1700 for domestic flights; www.safnet.it), but is also known by its colloquial name of **Peretola**. It lies just 4km (2.5 miles) northwest of central Florence. Several **small scheduled and charter companies** have direct flights from European cities, including Meridiana (tel: 020 7839 2222; www.meridiana.it) from London Gatwick (two to three flights daily). The tiny arrivals area has a small visitor information desk (tel: 055 315874; daily 7:30 am–11:30 pm) and a handful of desks for the major **car rental firms**.

■ **Taxi to Florence** Taxis (white in Florence) are the **most expensive** but most convenient way to reach central Florence from the airport. Journey time is about 15 minutes in light traffic. Cabs wait outside the airport's small arrivals area and by the almost adjacent departure terminal. Expect to pay in the region of €18–€20, plus surcharges for any baggage in the boot, travel on Sundays or public holidays, and travel between 10 pm–6 am.

■ **By bus to Florence** Take the **ATAF-SITA "Vola in bus" service**. Tickets can be bought on board and cost €4. There are departures daily every 30 minutes between 5:30 am and 8:30 pm, and hourly after 8:30 pm. Buses depart from outside the arrivals area and arrive at the city's main bus terminal on Via Santa Caterina da Siena, three minutes' walk west of Santa Maria Novella railway station. For information, contact ATAF (tel: 800 424500; www.ataf.net) or SITA (tel: 800 373760; www.sita-on-line.it Phone lines are open Mon–Fri 8 am–7 pm, Sat–Sun 8 am–1 pm).

■ **By car to Tuscany** Peretola Airport lies alongside a 10km (6-mile) spur of the A11 motorway, which runs west to link with the main A11-A1 motorway junction between Prato and Florence. From here there are onward links to north, west and south Tuscany.

From Bologna

Bologna's **Guglielmo Marconi Airport** (tel: 051 647 9615; www.bologna-airport.it) lies 105km (65 miles) northeast of Florence and caters for both **scheduled services** (Alitalia, Air France, British Airways, SAS, Lufthansa) and **charter** and **low-cost airlines**. All major **car rental firms** have booths inside Terminal A (Arrivals).

- **By car from Bologna** The main route to Tuscany is the A1 motorway south, which crosses the A11 Lucca–Florence motorway between Prato and Florence. Note that the A1 is a **busy road**, and has many twists and tunnels along its route over the Apennine mountains between Bologna and Florence.

- **By train from Bologna** For trains from Bologna Centrale, the main railway station, you need to take a taxi or the "Aerobus" **shuttle bus** (tel: 051 290 290) from the airport. Aerobus services leave roughly every 20 minutes (7.45 am–11:45 pm) from outside Terminal A. Journey time to the station is about 25 minutes and tickets cost €4.5. Fast and frequent trains (two to three every hour) run from Bologna Centrale straight to Florence. The journey takes just over an hour. Again, you must remember to validate tickets in platform machines before travelling (➤ 40).

Arriving By Train

- Florence is one of the **main arrival points** for trains from Europe, with direct rail links with Paris, Frankfurt and other major European cities. The city's main station, Santa Maria Novella, is located close to the heart of the Tuscan capital, within easy walking distance of the Piazza del Duomo (➤ 59) and Piazza della Signoria (➤ 64).

- Some **international train links** to Rome also follow Italy's main coast route, stopping at Pisa.

- For more information on **Italian train services** contact the state railway, the Ferrovie dello Stato, or FS (tel: 848 888088; www.fs-on-line.it or www.trenitalia.it; open daily 7 am–9 pm).

Getting Around

The ideal way to explore Tuscany is by car, but it is also possible to see virtually all of the region's main highlights by bus or train. Cars can be rented from Pisa, Florence, Rome and Bologna airports (➤ 36–38), or from international or local companies in most of the area's cities and larger towns. Driving and parking, however, can be difficult in towns and cities, especially in Florence and Siena, where much of the centre is closed to traffic.

By Car

To drive in Italy you need a **full driver's licence**, a copy of which also needs to be translated into Italian unless you have a pink European Union driving licence. **Translations** are available from Italian State Tourist Offices or driving organisations in your country of origin. If you bring a foreign-registered car into Italy, you must also carry the vehicle's **registration** and **insurance documents**.

- **Car rental** To rent a car in Italy you must be over 21 and possess a full valid driver's licence (see above). It is often **cheaper** to rent a car when you book your holiday as part of a "fly-drive" package to the region – ask for details from your travel agent or holiday company. Cars can also be booked through the central telephone numbers or websites of the major rental companies in your country of origin before leaving. In Tuscany, ask for details of local companies at tourist offices or look in the *Pagine Gialle* (Yellow Pages) under *Autonoleggio* (car rental).

Driving Essentials

- Driving is **on the right** and you should give way to traffic from the right unless there are signs to the contrary.
- Road signs are **blue**, but **green** on motorways (*autostrade*).
- The wearing of seat belts is **compulsory** in front and back seats.
- Unless indicated otherwise, the **speed limit** is 50kph (31mph) in urban areas, 90kph (56mph) outside urban areas on secondary roads, which are known and signed as *nazionale* (N) or *strada statale* (SS), 110kph (68mph) on dual-carriageways (*superstrade*) and 130kph (80mph) on motorways (*autostrade*).
- **Tolls** are payable on motorways (*autostrade*). Collect a ticket from the automated machines at your entry junction and present the ticket at the manned booths at your departure junction.
- In rural areas in Tuscany you will also often encounter hard-packed **gravel roads** known as *strade bianche* (white roads). These are marked on maps and intended (and suitable) for cars.
- Petrol is *benzina*, diesel is *gasolio*. Petrol stations follow shop hours (closed daily 1–3:30 pm) and many close all day on Sunday. Motorway petrol stations, however, are open all day, seven days a week. Smaller rural petrol stations may not accept payment by credit card. Many stations have automatic dispensers for use in closed periods which take euro notes.
- The best Tuscan **map** is the green Touring Club of Italy (TCI) 1:200,000 Toscana sheet (No D39), widely available in local Tuscan bookshops or in larger bookshops in the UK and abroad.
- It is often difficult to find a **car-park** (*parcheggio*) or parking place in Tuscany's towns and cities. This is especially true of Florence and Siena. **Metered parking** (*parcometro*) is now common. It is often wiser to park on the outskirts and take a local bus to the centre, or to make day-trips to Florence by train. Never leave luggage or valuables unattended in cars.
- If your car breaks down, switch on the hazard warning lights and place a red warning triangle (provided with rental cars) about 50m (55 yards) behind your vehicle. Call the **emergency breakdown number** (tel: 116) and give the operator your location and the car's make and registration number. Many car rental companies often have their own arrangements in the event of vehicle breakdown; enquire at the time of booking.
- In the event of an **accident**, place a red warning symbol (see above) 50m (55 yards) behind the car. Call the emergency services (tel: 113), police (tel: 113) or breakdown services (tel: 116). Do not admit liability or make potentially incriminating statements. Ask witnesses to remain on the scene, exchange names, addresses and insurance details with any other drivers involved, and make a statement to the police.

By Train

Trains provide **quick and efficient links** to a large number of Tuscan towns and cities. Connections south from Florence's Santa Maria Novella station run to Arezzo and Cortona, with a branch line link from Arezzo to Poppi and Stia in the heart of the Casentino region. Connections west from Florence link to Prato, Pistoia, Lucca and Viareggio, with a scenic branch line from Lucca running north through the Garfagnana region to Aulla. Another line west from Florence runs to Empoli (and Pisa) and then south to Siena, continuing through beautiful countryside to Buonconvento and Grosseto near the coast. Italy's main **west-coast line** from Rome to Genoa runs the length of the Tuscan coast, linking Pisa and other minor centres.

■ Italy has several types of trains. The fastest are **InterCity** and **Eurostar**. The latter usually need to be booked in advance on Friday and Sunday (a reservation is "*una prenotazione*"), but in practice you can book seats up to a few minutes before departure. Both types of trains generally run only on major routes such as Florence–Rome, Rome–Bologna or Rome–Pisa–Genoa. Slower trains which stop at more stations are known as *espressi* (ES), *diretti* (Dir), *regionali* (Reg) or *inter-regionali* (IR).

■ **Rail tickets** (*biglietti*) can be bought at stations, some travel agents and – for certain shorter journeys such as Florence to Siena – newspaper kiosks. They are issued in first- (*prima*) and second- (*seconda*) class categories. A single ticket is "*andato*", a return is "*andato e ritorno*".

■ On key fast trains such as InterCity (IC) or Eurostar trains (see above) a **supplement** (*supplemento*) is payable on each fare. These should be bought at the same time as buying a ticket as they are more expensive if you buy them on the train.

■ Whatever type of train you take, it is vital to **validate your ticket** by inserting it immediately before travel into small machines (usually yellow or gold in colour) in ticket halls and on platforms. Failure to do so will result in a large on-the-spot **fine** from ticket inspectors.

■ **Rail passes** are available for non-resident visitors, but are not really cost-effective over the short distances you'll travel in Tuscany. For details of purchasing the passes in the UK contact The Travel Bureau (0800 698 7545; www.thetravelbureau.co.uk).

■ Ticket offices and platforms always have two **timetables**: *Arrivi* (Arrivals), which are usually white, and *Partenze* (Departures), which are usually yellow: be sure to consult the right one. If you intend to use trains extensively, the small *Pozzorario* timetable is invaluable: it is available to buy from most newspaper kiosks.

By Bus

Town and city buses are known as ***autobus***, while long-distance inter-town buses are known as ***pullman*** or ***corriere***. Inter-town buses link main centres such as Florence, Pisa, Lucca and Siena to a large number of out-of-the-way towns and villages. Services are reliable and inexpensive, though often there are only a handful of departures to smaller centres. The train is almost always quicker when you have a choice of transport between larger towns.

■ **City buses** Most Tuscan towns and cities are small enough to negotiate on foot. The only place where you might need to take a bus is Florence. The city's distinctive orange buses are run by **ATAF** (tel: 800 424500; daily 7 am–8 pm; www.ataf.net). Tickets must be bought before boarding the bus from shops and bars displaying ATAF stickers, from automated machines, or from the ATAF office near the east entrance to the Santa Maria Novella railway station. Depending on price, tickets are valid for either one or three hours (€1–1.80) from when you validate them by stamping them in the small machines on board buses. You can also buy **one-, two- and three-day passes** (€4.50/7.60/9.60) from the same outlets, which are validated in a similar way. Special small **electric buses**, which run on four loop routes (A, B, C and D), can be most useful for exploring or seeing the city.

■ **Inter-town buses** Towns and cities rarely have a special bus terminal (Florence is a notable exception). Instead, buses often leave from a town's main or other large square, a major street or from outside the local railway station. Ask at tourist offices if in doubt. Tickets must generally be bought before boarding the bus and, in larger towns such as Siena or

Lucca, can be obtained from dedicated ticket offices. Elsewhere, tickets are usually available from the railway station bar or newspaper kiosk or a shop or major bar on or near the square or street used by departing buses. Inter-town buses are **almost always blue** in colour.

Tourist Information Centres

Arezzo

- Piazza della Repubblica 22; tel: 0575 377678; www.apt.arezzo.it; open Mon–Sat 9–1, 3–6:30/7, Sun 9–1, May–Sep.

Cortona

- Via Nazionale 42; tel: 0575 630352; www.cortona.net; open Mon–Sat 9–1, 3–7, Sun 9–1, May–Sep; Mon–Fri 9–1, 3–6, Sat 9–1, Oct–Apr.

Florence

- Via Cavour 1r; tel: 055 290832/290833; open Mon–Sat 8:30–6:30, Sun 8:30–1:30.
- Borgo Santa Croce 29r; tel: 055 234 0444; open Mon–Sat 9–7, Sun 8:30–1:30, May–Sep; 9–1:30, Oct–Apr.
- Piazza della Stazione 4a; tel: 055 212245; open Mon–Sat 9–7, Sun 8:30–1:30.

Lucca

- Porta di San Donato, Piazza San Donato, off Piazzale Giuseppe Verdi; tel: 0583 5831500 or 0583 442944; www.luccaturismo.it or www.comune.lucca.it; open daily 9–7, Mar–Oct; 9–5:30, Nov–Feb.

Montepulciano

- Via Gracciano del Corso 59r; tel: 0578 757341; www.comune.monte pulciano.si.it or www.prolocomontepulciano.it; open Mon–Sat 9:30–12:30, 3–7, Sun 9:30–12:30, Apr–Oct; Mon–Sat 9:30–12:30, 3–6, Sun 9:30–12:30, Nov–Mar.

Pienza

- Palazzo Comunale, off Piazza Pio II, Corso Rossellino 59; www.comunedipienza.it; tel: 0577 749071; open Mon–Sat 10–1, 3–7.

Pisa

- Piazza Vittorio Emanuele II 16; tel: 050 42291; open Mon–Fri 9–7, Sat 9–1
- Piazza del Duomo (Campo dei Miracoli); tel: 050 560464; open daily 9:30–6:30.

San Gimignano

- Piazza del Duomo 1; tel: 0577 940008; www.sangimignano.com; open daily 9–1, 3–7, Mar–Oct; 9–1, 2–6, Nov–Feb.

Siena

- Campo at Piazza del Campo 56; tel: 0577 280551; www.terresiena.it; open Mon–Sat 9–7.

Admission Charges
The cost of admission for museums and places of interest featured in the guide is indicated by the following price categories.
Inexpensive under €4 **Moderate** €4–€6.50 **Expensive** over €6.50

Accommodation

Tuscan towns and villages generally have a wide range of accommodation, but prices in main centres such as Florence and Siena are higher than in much of Italy. You'll need to book well in advance in the main centres, especially between June and September, but in the countryside you also have access to less busy farm-stay and other rural accommodation known as *agriturismo*. It is also worth noting that many hotels, particularly in smaller towns, close in January, February and August.

Grading

- Every Italian hotel (*albergo*) is graded by the state from **1- to 5-star** (5 being luxury). The old *pensione* (*locanda*) classification, which referred to a simple hotel or set of rooms, sometimes with a restaurant, no longer exists, but you may still see 1-star hotels calling themselves *pensione*.
- The criteria used to award stars are usually based on the **number of facilities** offered rather than the standard of those facilities, the service or other qualitative aspects. Invariably, 1-star hotels are budget options, and often have shared bathrooms or only a handful of rooms with private bathrooms; 2-star hotels have private bathrooms; and rooms in 3-star hotels usually have telephones and TVs. Most 4-star hotels represent a jump in price and quality – you should expect something a little special in such establishments, both in the presentation of the rooms and the public areas. Luxury 5-star hotels, of which Tuscany has a handful, are a class apart. New bed-and-breakfast establishments outside these classifications are increasingly common.

Agriturismo

- *Agriturismo* is the name given to **rural accommodation** in Italy. It is becoming very popular, with much choice in many parts of rural Tuscany. Occasionally the accommodation may be part of a working farm, estate or vineyard, though often the rooms or apartments are purpose-built and away from the main property. Many offer activities, notably horse-riding, and many – unlike town hotels – have swimming pools.
- Prices are competitive when compared with most hotels, and though rooms are usually simple, they are invariably clean and modern. Some places, however, require a **minimum stay** of two or more days in high season, though many offer discounted rates for longer stays. Many also have multi-room accommodation, making them ideal for families.
- Listings of such properties are still rather haphazard, but most **local tourist offices** have details of *agriturismo* accommodation in their immediate vicinity. Often, though, you will stumble across such places by chance while touring the countryside – most are signposted using a standardised yellow sign.

Location

- It pays to stay in the **centre** (*centro*) of Tuscan towns and cities. You will be close to all the sights and often in an attractive medieval or Renaissance quarter of the city; on the **outskirts** (*la periferia*), you will invariably be in less characterful hotels and more modern surroundings. This said, parking can be a real problem in larger and busier towns, especially Florence and Siena, where a peripheral hotel – or one in the countryside nearby – can be an advantage. Some town hotels will have **private parking** (*parcheggio privato*), but it is likely to have limited spaces.

- In **Florence**, the main concentrations of inexpensive hotels are in the streets east of the station – Via Faenza, Via Nazionale and Via Fiume – and the far less convenient streets around the Piazza della Libertà on the northeast edge of the city centre. You'll need to take a bus or taxi into the centre if you're staying in the latter. The former are far more convenient but, as in most cities, the railway station district is relatively unappealing (though rarely dangerous).

Noise
- This **can be a problem** in Tuscan towns, even in smart hotels, and it can be worth asking for a room at the back of a hotel or looking onto a central courtyard or garden, as on summer nights – unless there's air-conditioning – you'll need to have windows open.
- Visitors are often surprised at how noisy it can be in the Tuscan countryside and its small villages: church bells, busy main squares or streets, barking dogs, cockerels, teenagers revving scooters and the like can all be a problem for light sleepers. **Ear plugs** are the perfect solution.

Prices
- Prices for each room (*camera*) in a hotel are **fixed by law** and must be displayed in the reception area and in bedrooms. They may **vary within a hotel**, so look at a selection of rooms.
- Prices should also include any **taxes**, but watch out for **surcharges**, notably over-priced breakfasts (*prima colazione*), which may or may not be included in the room rate: where it's optional, it's invariably cheaper and more fun to have breakfast in a bar. Good buffet-style **breakfasts** are becoming more widespread in better hotels, but a Tuscan hotel "breakfast" generally still means just a bread roll, jam and coffee.
- Hotels may also add surcharges for **air-conditioning** (*aria condizionata*) and garage facilities.

Prices
The following symbols refer to the average cost of a double room.
€ under €100   €€ €100–€175   €€€ over €175

Booking Accommodation
- Book all hotels **in advance** year-round in Florence and Siena. Neither city has a low season to speak of, though the quietest months are November, January and February. Easter and June to September are always busy.
- Book well ahead in smaller towns if you are visiting at a time that coincides with a **major festival or cultural event**.
- **Reservations** should be made by phone and followed by a faxed or e-mail confirmation. It is also an idea to reconfirm bookings a couple of days before arrival. A double room with twin beds is *una doppia*, and *una matrimoniale* for a double bed. A single room is *una singola*.
- Hoteliers are **obliged to register** guests, so on checking in you must hand in your passport. It's returned in a few hours or on the day of departure.
- **Check-out times** range from around 10 am to noon.

Villas and Apartments
- Several companies based in the UK offer villas and apartments to rent throughout Tuscany. The following are a selection of the best:
  Cottages to Castles, offering around 50 villas and houses throughout Tuscany (tel: 01622 775217; www.cottagestocastles.com)

Magic of Italy, both villas and booking facilities for transport and events
(tel: 0870 888 0220; www.magictravelgroup.co.uk)
Simply Travel, more villas and a tempting brochure (tel: 020 8541 2211;
www.simplytravel.com)
Traditional Tuscany, interesting and good-value properties from apartments to palaces (tel: 01553 810003; www.traditionaltuscany.co.uk)
Tuscany Now, some of the best villas in the region, with prices to match
(tel: 020 7684 8884; www.tuscanynow.com)
Individual Italy, villas (tel: 08700 772772; www.individuality.com)

Food and Drink

Eating and drinking in Tuscany can be every bit as memorable as the region's
historic towns and sublime countryside (► 20–25). Restaurants range from
temples of gastronomic sophistication to simple one-roomed *trattorie* with
unpretentious home-style cooking and rustic decor. Towns and cities also
boast a broad range of cafés and bars, good for everything from a breakfast
cappuccino to a snack lunch or hunk of bread and cheese washed down with
a glass of wine.

Eating Places

The differences between the types of restaurant in Tuscany are becoming
increasingly blurred. A *ristorante* (restaurant) used to refer to somewhere
smart and expensive; a *trattoria* was simple and cheap; an *osteria* even
more so; and a *pizzeria* a no-frills place to fill up on pizza and little more.

■ The old-fashioned *trattoria*, at least in cities and larger towns, is fast
  disappearing, to be replaced by a more modern and informal type of
  eating venue (often called an ***osteria***) with young owners and younger
  attitudes to style and cuisine. The term ***ristorante*** can now be applied to
  just about any eating establishment, and ***pizzerias*** – while often still fairly
  utilitarian – now usually also serve a range of pastas, salads and other
  main courses.

■ These changes are also true of restaurants in the more popular Tuscan
  towns and villages, where the influx of visitors has led to a proliferation of
  eating establishments. **Quality**, however, can be poor in some of the more
  obvious tourist traps – set "tourist menus", for example, are invariably
  bad value. But wherever you are, the chief thing to remember is that
  price and appearance are no guarantee of quality – smart interiors often
  mean nothing in Florence and Siena, and you can frequently eat excellent
  food at fair prices in humble-looking places in cities or in the countryside.

■ Other terms you may come across are ***enoteca***, which means wine bar.
  This usually indicates a place to buy wine by the glass or bottle and the
  chance to eat a limited selection of light meals or snacks. A ***fiaschetteria***
  or ***vinaio*** is similar, but often much simpler; these establishments were
  once found in many Tuscan towns, but today they're a dying breed. The
  same cannot be said of the ***gelateria***, or ice-cream parlour, a mainstay
  of just about every Italian town and city.

Eating Hours

■ **Bars** open from 7 am or earlier for breakfast (*colazione* or *prima
  colazione*), which generally consists of coffee (*cappuccino* or *caffè latte*)
  and a plain or filled sweet croissant (*brioche*).

- **Lunch** (*pranzo*) starts around 12:30 pm and finishes at about 2 pm, although most restaurants stay open a little later.
- **Dinner** (*cena*) begins at about 8 pm, although many restaurants open before this to cater for tourists used to dining earlier. Bars that are busy in the day usually close at around 8 or 9 pm, but in larger towns there are often late bars aimed more at the nocturnal visitor. An *enoteca* usually follows bar opening times, but some may close in the afternoon.

Meals

- Italian meals start with hors d'oeuvres, or *antipasti* (literally "before the meal"), and are followed by a **first course** (*il primo*) of pasta, soup or rice.
- The main, or **second course** (*il secondo*) is the meat (*carne*) or fish (*pesce*) course, and is accompanied by vegetables (*contorni*) or salad (*insalata*) which are usually served (or eaten) separately.
- **Desserts** are *dolci*, and may be accompanied by, or offered as an alternative to fruit (*frutta*) and cheese (*formaggio*). Ice-cream (*gelato*) from a *gelateria* makes a good alternative to desserts, which in all but the top restaurants are often uninspiring.
- Meals are **accompanied** by bread (*pane)* and mineral water (*acqua minerale*), for which you pay extra. Ask for mineral water to be fizzy (*gassata*) or still (*non gassata*).
- Meals can be **followed** by grappa, a bitter digestif such as *amaro*, an *espresso* coffee, or an infusion tea such as camomile. Note that Italians *never* drink *cappuccino* after dinner.
- You need not eat every course – at lunch and in all but the grandest restaurants it is acceptable to **order a pasta and salad** and little more. More expensive and popular restaurants, however, may take a dim view of this in the evening.

Cafés and Snacks

- In cafés and bars it costs less to **stand at the bar** than sit at a table. Pay for what you want first at the separate cash desk (*cassa*) and then take your receipt (*scontrino*) to the bar and repeat your order. You cannot pay at the bar.
- If you **sit at a table**, a waiter will take your order. It's not acceptable to pay and then sit down – a waiter will quickly appear to move you on. If you do pay to sit, however, you can remain almost as long as you wish.
- Cafés and bars are excellent sources of **sandwiches** (*tramezzini*), filled rolls (*panini*) and sometimes light meals. Also look out for small shops or bakeries selling **pizza by the slice** (*pizza al taglio*).

Set Menus

- If possible, steer clear of restaurants full of foreigners and those that offer a **menù turistico** (tourist menu). The latter may appear to be inexpensive and guarantee what you'll pay, but portions are often meagre, wine (if offered) unexceptional, food quality poor, and dishes plain – usually a pasta with simple tomato sauce and grilled chicken with a salad or single side dish.
- In more expensive restaurants, **un menù degustazione** or **menù gastronomico** provides a selection of the restaurant's best dishes – a good option if you can't decide what to choose from the à la carte menu.

Paying and Tipping

- The **bill** (*il conto*) should be a formal itemised receipt – if it appears on a scrawled piece of paper the restaurateur is breaking the law and you are entitled to demand a proper receipt (*ricevuta*).

■ Most eating places charge *pane e coperto*, a **cover charge**. The authorities are trying to stamp this out but if it's included you must pay it.

Prices
The following prices refer to a three-course meal for one with wine
€ under €26   €€ €26–€52   €€€ over €52

Etiquette and Smoking

■ Foreign visitors often don't dress up to eat out, but Italians generally make more of an effort – **"smart casual"** is a good rule of thumb, though aim to be more elegant (jacket and tie for men) in top restaurants such as Florence's Enoteca Pinchiorri (➤ 79).

■ Smoking is still acceptable **but a ban** has recently been introduced in public places, including bars and restaurants. It is not always observed.

Shopping

Tuscany offers a wealth of good shopping. Across the region you'll find a wide variety of shops selling mouth-watering food, wine and local craft objects, while Florence and Pisa have numerous luxury and other shops selling top designer clothes, exquisite shoes, fine leatherware, jewellery, rich fabrics, artisan and craft items, and a host of paintings, prints and antiques.

Florence

Florence is the place to go for serious shopping. A wealthy city, its chief strengths for shoppers are luxury goods, especially leather and high-quality shoes and clothes. Much the same goes for other large Tuscan towns, notably Pisa and Lucca, but none have quite the choice and variety of the region's capital.

■ The main **designer shops** lie in the west of the city on Via de' Tornabuoni and nearby streets such as Via della Vigna Nuova.

■ **Leather shops** are found across the city, but the most popular area is in the Santa Croce district.

■ **Jewellers** occupy the Ponte Vecchio, their traditional home since the 16th century, though you'll also find jewellery stores on most busy city streets.

■ The same is true of artisans' workshops and shops selling **crafts** – everything from furniture to beautiful marbled paper. There are concentrations of such shops in the Oltrarno, especially on or near Via Maggio, and on Via della Porcellana in the west of the city.

■ Via Maggio and its surrounding streets also contain many of Florence's leading **antiques shops** and commercial **art galleries**, though such shops are also dotted elsewhere across the city centre.

■ The city centre is also where you'll find the majority of bookshops, kitchenware and household goods shops – another area in which Italy excels, with wonderful designer gadgets – and **department stores**, of which Coin is the best (➤ 83).

Tuscany

Food and wine are good buys across the region, but check import **restrictions** on meat and other products if you wish to take purchases home: safe items include pasta, wine, olive oils and most cheeses.

- **Specialities** of the region include the wines of Chianti, Montalcino and Montepulciano, the oils of Lucca, Pienza's sheep's milk cheese (*pecorino*), the honey of Montalcino and spicy *panforte* cake from Siena.
- Other notable buys are **craft items**, such as the alabaster ware of Volterra, glassware from Colle di Val d'Elsa and the marble artefacts of Carrara.

Markets

You can buy perfectly good produce in most neighbourhood food stores (known as *alimentari*), but for the best selection of gourmet and other provisions, and for plenty of local colour, head for town markets.

- In **Florence** the best market for food is the wonderful Mercato Centrale near San Lorenzo (▶ 71). The streets around San Lorenzo are also filled with a general market, a good place to buy inexpensive clothes, bags and souvenirs. Other less well-known markets include Sant'Ambrogio, northeast of Santa Croce, and the small flea market, or Mercato dei Pulci, in the Piazza dei Ciompi.
- Most smaller towns hold markets **once a week**, which tend to be general markets – Florence's biggest such market is held in the Parco delle Casine near the River Arno to the west of the city centre every Tuesday (8–1). Few visitors come here, and prices for goods of all descriptions are highly competitive.

Opening Times

- Most stores in smaller towns and villages are traditionally open **Tuesday to Saturday** about 8 or 9 to 1 and 3:30 or 4 to 8. Most stores close on Monday morning or one other half-day a week.
- Many of Florence's shops, however, are beginning to **open all day** (known as *orario continuato*), which generally means Tuesday to Saturday 9 or 10 to 7:30 or 8. Some shops, notably the city's major department stores, also open on Sunday.

Credit Cards

Credit cards are accepted in most large shops, but cash is still preferred in smaller stores: check before making any major purchases. Note that non-European Union visitors can take advantage of tax-free shopping on a variety of goods: many shops are members of the **Tax-Free Shopping System** and will guide you through the necessary procedures.

Entertainment

Tuscany offers a broad spectrum of entertainment, from the music and cultural festivals of Florence and other large towns to the plethora of smaller pageants and festivities (*festa* or *sagra*) held across the region to celebrate a local saint's day, a prized local delicacy or an historical event from a town or village's past. Nightlife in the conventional sense – clubs, bars, live music and such like – is mostly restricted to Florence, though larger cities such as Pisa, Lucca and Siena also have a smattering of late-night entertainment. Most of the region's cultural entertainment is easily accessible to visitors, except for theatre and cinema, where most presentations and productions are in Italian.

Information

Your first ports of call for information on cultural events should be the internet (▶ 188), or tourist offices in individual towns.

- Tourist offices in larger places such as Florence and Siena (► 41) generally have details of all **major cultural festivals** in the region, and may be able to provide programmes and advice on how to book tickets or obtain further information. They may also have details of the region's smaller festivals, though often you stumble across these almost by accident: most *feste* or *sagre* are advertised in advance on **posters** in and around the villages in which they are to take place.
- Also consult visitors centres for details of **local nightlife**, as new clubs and bars open and close regularly or may lose their fashionable "club of the moment" status as trends change.
- Alternatively, consult the **listings section** of Florence and Tuscany's main daily newspaper, *La Nazione*, which has listings of numerous events and festivals: scan its different regional sections for details of events in your area. In Florence you can also buy the monthly *Firenze Spettacolo*, a detailed listings magazine. It contains a section in English, but the layout is such that you should be able to understand the information even if you don't speak Italian. The magazine is available from many newsstands and bookshops such as Feltrinelli (► 82).

Tickets

Tickets for events in Florence can be obtained from individual box offices or through **Box Office**, the city's central ticket agency, which has outlets at Via Alamanni 39 (tel: 055 210804; www.boxol.it) and Chiasso dei Soldanieri 8r, off Via Porta Rossa, on the corner with Via de' Tornabuoni (tel: 055 219402).

Festivals

The key festivals in Florence and Tuscany are detailed below, but remember that there are many minor and more specialised events, information on which can be obtained from visitor centres. **Holy Week** (Easter) sees special services and processions held in churches across the region.

- The most famous event in Tuscany is Siena's **Palio** horse race, which takes place twice-yearly on 2 July and 16 August (► 26).
- The **Scoppio del Carro** concludes Florence's Easter Sunday ceremonies, when a cart of flowers and fireworks is lit at noon by a mechanical dove that "flies" along a wire from the altar of the cathedral to the piazza.
- May and June see the prestigious **Maggio Musicale** arts and music festival in Florence, with orchestral concerts and dance and drama performances.
- The most vivid of Florence's city festivals is the **Calcio Storico**, consisting of three fast and furious soccer games played in traditional medieval dress; the first takes place the day after the feast of St John (► 190), and other dates are picked from a hat on Easter Sunday. The games take place in Piazza Santa Croce or Piazza della Signoria.
- Key summer events in **Pisa** are the Regatta di San Ranieri, a costumed boat race and colourful procession (16–17 June), and the Gioco del Ponte, a mock battle in period costume on the third Sunday of June.
- **Lucca** has medieval pageants on the third Sunday of July (the Festa di San Paolino) and on 14 September (the Festa della Croce), when the *Volto Santo* relic is paraded through town by torchlight.
- **Arezzo's** main event is a medieval joust, the Giostro del Saraceno, held on the first Sunday of September.
- **Montepulciano** hosts a Baccanale festival of wine, food and song on the next to last Saturday in August, to celebrate the grape harvest for the local Vino Nobile wine.

Florence

Getting Your Bearings

Florence is Europe's greatest artistic city, a focal point for the Renaissance, one of history's most dramatic periods of creative endeavour, and home to magnificent paintings, sculptures and architecture spanning almost 1,000 years.

To suggest that you can see the best of Tuscany's capital in two days may sound far-fetched, but it can be done. Ideally you would stay in the city overnight, although if you are visiting between Easter and October accommodation needs to be booked well in advance. The best way to visit Florence is by train – most Tuscan centres are linked to the regional capital by rail (➤ 39).

Florence is a city of art and architecture. Some of the best is in Piazza del Duomo, one of two main squares: here you'll find the cathedral, Baptistery and Campanile (bell-tower), while nearby are two major museums, the Museo dell'Opera del Duomo and the Museo Nazionale del Bargello. A short walk away lies Piazza della Signoria, Florence's second square, dominated by the Palazzo Vecchio, the seat of government.

★ Don't Miss

2 Galleria dell' Accademia ➤ 54
5 Cappelle Medicee ➤ 55
6 Santa Maria Novella ➤ 57
7 Piazza del Duomo ➤ 59
10 Museo Nazionale del Bargello ➤ 62
13 Piazza della Signoria ➤ 64
14 Santa Croce ➤ 66
15 Galleria degli Uffizi ➤ 68

Previous page: Florence's celebrated cathedral dome

Right: The River Arno and its bridges, including the famous Ponte Vecchio

0   500 metres
0   500 yards

At Your Leisure

Giardino dei Semplici

CAVOUR

1 Museo di San Marco

V. RICASOLI

GUELFA VIA

Palazzo Medici-Riccardi

V. GINO CAPPONI

2 Galleria dell'Accademia

PIAZZA DELLA SANTISSIMA ANNUNZIATA

V. DEI SERVI

VIA DEGLI ALFANI

azza l uomo

8 Museo dell' Opera del Duomo

PINTI

BORGO

9 Museo di Firenze com'era

BORGO DEGLI ALBIZI

n- ele

10 Museo Nazionale del Bargello

V. DELLA ONDOTTA

PIAZZA SAN FIRENZE

V. GIUSEPPE VERDI

Piazza della Signoria

Galleria degli Uffizi

V. DE' BENCI

VIA DE' CORSO DEI TINTORI

14 Santa Croce

LUNGARNO GENERALE DIAZ

San Miniato al Monte **20**

BARDI

LUNGARNO SERRISTORI

Nearby is the Galleria degli Uffizi, home to many of the world's most important Renaissance paintings. East of Piazza della Signoria stands Santa Croce, the most compelling of Florence's many churches, narrowly outranking Santa Maria Novella, a church in the west of the city crammed with frescoes.

In the Oltrarno area, reached via the celebrated Ponte Vecchio, are the paintings and frescoes of the Palazzo Pitti and Cappella Brancacci. Two Michelangelo highlights north of the river are his statue of David in the Galleria dell' Accademia and a series of sculptures in the Cappelle Medicee.

This said, not all your time need be spent admiring art. Florence has some superb shopping, from designer names to colourful markets (➤ 82), and there are excellent bars, cafés and restaurants. You can also enjoy gardens, notably the Giardino di Boboli, and the simple charm of medieval and Renaissance streets.

The very best of Florence can just about be seen in two days, but you will need to keep a close eye on the opening times of various sights to avoid disappointment.

Florence in Two Days

Day One

Morning

Start the day booking tickets for the next day for the Galleria degli Uffizi, then go to the **❶ Museo di San Marco** (➤ 71) for paintings by Fra Angelico (above). Stroll the short distance to the **❷ Galleria dell'Accademia** (➤ 54) to see Michelangelo's famous *David*. Then go to the **❸ Palazzo Medici-Riccardi** (➤ 71) for superb frescoes by Benozzo Gozzoli.

Lunch

On the way to the Mercato Centrale, stop off at **Zà-Zà** for lunch (➤ 80) or have a picnic with ingredients from the Mercato.

Afternoon

Explore the **❹ Mercato Centrale** (➤ 71) before visiting the **❺ Cappelle Medicee** and San Lorenzo area (➤ 55). Then pay a visit to the superb church of **❻ Santa Maria Novella** (➤ 57, left) for some quiet time at the end of the day before heading back to your hotel.

Day Two

Morning

Make your way to the **7 Piazza del Duomo** (► 59) and climb the Campanile or cathedral dome for some great views. Then see the cathedral – it opens later than the Campanile and dome – but note that the Baptistery (left) is closed in the morning, so return later today. Then go to the **8 Museo dell'Opera del Duomo** (► 72) and the **10 Museo Nazionale del Bargello** (► 62, *Pitti Tondo* by Michelangelo, right).

Lunch

Walk to **13 Piazza della Signoria** (► 64) to have lunch (below), which you might take as a snack in Rivoire (► 81) – an expensive option. Or you could try the more reasonable Cantinetta dei Verrazzano (► 79).

Afternoon

Devote most of the afternoon to the **15 Galleria degli Uffizi** (► 68), but also take time to see **14 Santa Croce** (► 66), being sure to leave enough time to see the church and Cappella dei Pazzi before they close. Treat yourself to a *gelato* from Vivoli (► 81): Baldovino (► 78) or Cibreo (► 79) are good choices for dinner close to Santa Croce, but you'll need to book ahead.

❷
Galleria dell'Accademia

Tucked away in the north of the city, the Galleria dell' Accademia, or simply Accademia, as it is more commonly known, is slightly off the city's main tourist track. Yet a visit here is unmissable, if only to see one of Florence's finest artistic treasures – Michelangelo's famous statue of *David*.

Michelangelo's *David* greets visitors to the Accademia

As soon as you enter the Accademia you are greeted by the sight of Italy's most celebrated statue – Michelangelo's *David*. It was commissioned in 1501 by the Opera del Duomo, responsible for the upkeep of the cathedral. Several artists, including Leonardo da Vinci, had already tried to work with the same block of marble – a thin and cracked piece of stone believed to be too poor quality for sculpture, which had been quarried from the Apuan mountains north of Pisa some 40 years earlier.

The 26-year-old Michelangelo managed to confound his contemporaries by transforming the stone into a masterpiece in just three years. After months of wrangling, the sculpture was eventually raised in Piazza della Signoria, where it remained until moved to its present home in 1873. The fact that the statue was intended as an outdoor piece explains some of its deliberate distortions – the overlong arms and over-sized head and hands were designed to emphasise its monumentality.

Also in the Accademia, don't miss Michelangelo's statues of *St Matthew* (1504–8) and the *Four Slaves* (or *Prisoners*), the latter unfinished. Other rooms contain paintings by artists such as Filippino Lippi and Fra Bartolomeo.

TAKING A BREAK

Try the **Gran Caffè San Marco** in Piazza San Marco (tel: 055 215833), a few minutes' walk north of the Accademia.

🕇 199 D5 ✉ Via Ricasoli 60 ☎ 055 238 8609 or 055 294883 to pre-book tickets 🕐 Tue–Fri 8:15–6:50 (last ticket 6:05) 💷 Expensive

Cappelle Medicee

The Cappelle Medicee (Medici Chapels) comprise the Medici family's mausoleum. Many of the dozens of tombs here are either insignificant or overly grandiose, but three merit special attention, thanks to the fact that they are graced by a trio of outstanding sculptures by Michelangelo.

The chapels fall into three sections, the first of which you come to immediately beyond the ticket hall: a low, dimly lit **crypt**, the resting place of many of the less important Medicis. From here, steps lead to the **Cappella dei Principi**, a cavernous hall decorated in coloured marble that contains the tombs of the Medici's six grand dukes, the last of the Medici to rule Florence before the dynasty died out in 1743. The building was begun in 1604 and was to be the most expensive project ever undertaken by the family: it was still draining Medici coffers when Gian Gastone, the last grand duke, died.

The highlight, however, is the **Sagrestia Nuova** (New Sacristy), which was designed by Michelangelo and contains three groups of sculpture by the artist. It was commissioned in 1520 by Pope Leo X, himself a Medici, as a mausoleum for Lorenzo the Magnificent and Lorenzo's brother, Giuliano. Ironically, their tombs were never completed and the pair lie buried close to Michelangelo's unfinished sculpture of *Madonna and Child* (1521). More ironic still, the tombs that were completed are those of two of the most feckless of the Medici: Lorenzo de' Medici (1533), grandson of Lorenzo the Magnificent, and Giuliano de' Medici, Lorenzo the Magnificent's third son. Lorenzo is shown as a man of thought,

The Medici

The Medici dominated Tuscan life for almost four centuries. The founding father of the family's banking business was Giovanni de Bicci de' Medici (1360–1429), who secured the lucrative papal account. His son, Cosimo the Elder (1389–1464) consolidated the family's position and became a patron of the arts, as did his grandson, Lorenzo the Magnificent (1449–92). In the 16th century two members became popes and the Florentine Medici became Grand Dukes of Tuscany. The line died out in 1743.

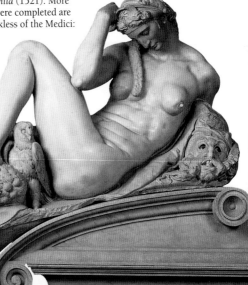

Michelangelo's "Night" on Giuliano's tomb

with two allegorical figures symbolising "Dawn" and "Dusk". Giuliano is posed as a man of action, accompanied by figures representing "Day" and "Night".

The Cappella dei Principi contains the tombs of six Medici Grand Dukes

TAKING A BREAK

The nearby **Mercato Centrale** has several small bars (▶ 71), while to the south the best bet is the **Caffè Gilli** on Piazza della Repubblica. Other nearby recommendations are **Zanobini** or the **Casa del Vino** (▶ 81).

✚ 198 C4 ✉ Piazza Madonna degli Aldobrandini 6 ☎ 055 238 8602
🕐 Tue–1st, 3rd and 5th Sun and 2nd and 4th Mon of month 8:15–4:50; public holidays 8:15–1:50 🚌 1, 6, 17 to Via Cavour 💶 Expensive

---

CAPPELLE MEDICEE: INSIDE INFO

Top tips The Medici Chapels quickly become crowded, so arrive early if possible. Or you can **pre-book an entry ticket** by calling 055 294883.
• Watch out for **pickpockets** if you explore the busy general market in the streets around San Lorenzo and the Cappelle Medicee.

In more depth The Cappelle Medicee form part of the 4th-century **San Lorenzo church**, the Medici's former parish and one of Florence's oldest and most important religious buildings. The present church was designed in the 15th century by Brunelleschi. Donatello was partly responsible for the church's two bronze pulpits.

❻

Santa Maria Novella

Florence's two great churches sit like sentinels on opposing sides of the city: Santa Croce(► 66), built by the Franciscans, in the east and Santa Maria Novella, the work of the Dominicans, in the west. Santa Maria may lack Santa Croce's hallowed tombs and monuments, but it wants for nothing in size or wonderful fresco cycles and other notable works of art.

The church was begun in 1246 and largely completed by 1360. Only its façade remained unfinished, until a textile merchant, Giovanni Ruccellaia, commissioned Leon Battisti Alberti to finish the work in 1456. The sponsor's Latin name can be seen across the façade, along with his emblem, the billowing "Sail of Fortune". The sun at the top is the symbol of the Dominicans.

A Trick of the Eye

Inside, the church's vast interior is given an added sense of scale by a **trick of perspective** – the pillars of the nave are set progressively closer together towards the high altar. Skilful use of perspective also accounts, at least in part, for the effect of the church's most celebrated painting, **Masaccio's** *Trinità* (1427),

Santa Maria Novella's ornate 15th-century façade

on the left (north) wall between the second and third pillars. It was one of the first Renaissance paintings in which the laws of perspective were mastered.

Further Artworks

Less influential but no less impressive paintings are found in the chapels close to the high altar. In the first, on the right as you face the altar, is a fresco cycle by Filippino Lippi on the **Life of St Philip the Apostle** (1489–1502). The **tomb** (1491–5) **of Filippo Strozzi**, the wealthy banker who commissioned the frescoes, is a delicate work by Benedetto da Maiano, to the rear of the chapel.

The chancel is swathed with even more striking **frescoes** (1485–90) by Domenico Ghirlandaio. Their many panels purport to show scenes from the Life of St John the Baptist (right and rear walls) and the Virgin, but most are vignettes of 15th-century Florentine life.

To the left of the chancel lies the **Cappella Strozzi**. The frescoes (1350–57) are the work of Nardo di Cione and show *Paradiso* (left) and *Inferno* (right), inspired by Dante's poem (► 10). The chapel's altarpiece (1357) is the work of Nardo's brother, Andrea (Orcagna).

The three-dimensional effect of Masaccio's *Trinità*

TAKING A BREAK

Try **Belle Donne** for a light lunch (► 79) or **Caffè Amerini** (► 80) to the south for a good café.

Santa Maria Novella
🔶 198 B4 🖂 Piazza Santa Maria Novella ☎ 055 215918 🕐 Mon–Thu & Sat 9–5, Fri & Sun 1–5 🚌 1, 14, 17, 22, 23 💷 Inexpensive

Museo di Santa Maria Novella
🔶 198 B4 🖂 Piazza Santa Maria Novella ☎ 055 282187 🕐 Mon–Thu, Sat 9–5, Fri, Sun and public holidays 9–2 🚌 1, 14, 17, 22, 23 💷 Inexpensive

SANTA MARIA NOVELLA: INSIDE INFO

Top tip Santa Maria lies close to Florence's **main railway station**, so make it the first or last thing you see if you're coming to the city by train.

In more depth To the left of Santa Maria as you face the church lies the entrance to the **Museo di Santa Maria Novella**. Its highlights are a cloister painted with faded frescoes by Paolo Uccello and the Cappellone degli Spagnoli, the latter painted with stunning frescoes on a vast scale (1367–9) by the otherwise little-known Andrea da Firenze.

7

Piazza del Duomo

Piazza del Duomo forms a magnificent stage for the Duomo (cathedral), the Baptistery and the Campanile, the cathedral's bell-tower. On its eastern flank it also plays host to the Museo dell'Opera del Duomo, a museum of impressive paintings and sculptures collected over the centuries from the piazza's principal buildings.

The Duomo

Florence's majestic and multicoloured Duomo was begun in 1296, when it replaced an earlier 7th-century church, Santa Reparata, on the same site. Its construction, however, has been an on-going process: Filippo Brunelleschi's magnificent **dome**, one of the miracles of medieval engineering, was only completed in the late 1460s, while the richly embellished façade was added as recently as 1887. The highlight of the visit is the dome, which you can reach from a separate entrance midway down the right (south) side of the nave. It's a long and rather

The 15th-century dome of Florence's cathedral is one of the wonders of medieval engineering: even today many of its building techniques are not fully understood

claustrophobic ascent of more than 400 steps, but the views of Florence are breathtaking. Inside, the cathedral's **interior** appears austere at first glance, but hidden in the half-gloom are several outstanding paintings and works of art. The key paintings are all on the left (north) wall: *Dante with the Divine Comedy* (1465) by Domenico di Michelino and, to its left, two equestrian portraits: *Sir John Hawkwood* by Paolo Uccello (1436) and *Niccolò da Tolentino* by Andrea del Castagno (1456).

The Baptistery

Piazza del Duomo's second major set piece is the **Baptistery** (*Battistero*), Florence's oldest surviving building. No one is sure of its precise origins – ancient chroniclers believed it was a 1st-century Roman temple to Mars. In truth, it probably dates

from the 8th or 9th century, while the exterior's striking marble decoration was added between 1059 and 1128. The Baptistery's **exterior** highlights are three sets of doors: the south doors (1328–36) designed by the Pisan sculptor Andrea Pisano; the north doors (1403–24) designed by the Florentine Lorenzo Ghiberti, who won a famous competition to create the doors in 1401; and the east doors (1425–52), also crafted by Ghiberti, which Michelangelo considered so beautiful he reputedly called them the Gates of Paradise. Note that the doors' panels are copies – the originals are displayed in the Museo dell'Opera.

The Baptistery's **interior** is equally captivating. A glance upward from the comparatively plain walls – ringed by granite columns removed from Florence's ancient Roman Capitol – reveals a glorious 13th-century mosaic ceiling decorated with episodes from the lives of Christ, Joseph and St John the Baptist. To the right of the distinctive apse (*scarsella*) on the

Spectacular mosaic images of Christ keep watch over the Baptistery's interior

north wall lies the **Tomb of Baldassare Cossa**, the work of Donatello and his pupil Michelozzo. Its incumbent was an "antipope" and a friend of the Medici family, who died in Florence in 1419.

The Campanile

It is unlikely you'll have the legs to climb both the cathedral dome and the 85m (278 foot) Campanile, built between 1334 and 1359. However, the **views** from the top of the latter's 414 steps are as good, if not better than those from the cathedral dome, if only because they include views of the dome itself and the Baptistery's distinctive octagon way below. The bell-tower was designed by Giotto, better known as a painter, and adorned with 14th- and 15th-century reliefs by Andrea Pisano, Luca della Robbia, Donatello and assistants.

The duomo's façade was built with white and pink Tuscan marble

TAKING A BREAK

Ignore the cafés on the piazza; go to **Caffè Italiano** (► 81).

Duomo ➕ 199 D4 ✉ Piazza del Duomo ☎ 055 230 2885 🕔 Mon–Wed, Fri 10–5, Thu 10–3:30, Sat 10–4:45 (last Sat of month 10–3:30), Sun 1:30–4:45 🚌 A, 1, 6, 14, 17, 23 💷 Free

Dome
➕ 199 D4 ✉ Piazza del Duomo ☎ 055 230 2885 🕔 Mon–Fri 8:30–7 (last ticket 6:20), Sat 8:30–5:40 (8:30–4, 1st Sat of month); closed public and religious holidays 🚌 A, 1, 6, 14, 17, 23 💷 Moderate

Baptistery
➕ 198 C4 ✉ Piazza del Duomo–Piazza di San Giovanni ☎ 055 230 2885 🕔 Mon–Sat noon–7, Sun 8:30–2 🚌 A, 1, 6, 14, 17, 23 💷 Inexpensive

Campanile
➕ 198 C4 ✉ Piazza del Duomo ☎ 055 230 2885 🕔 Daily 8:30–7:30 (last ticket 6:50), Apr–Oct; daily 9–5 (last ticket 4:20), Nov–Mar 🚌 A, 1, 6, 14, 17, 23 💷 Moderate

PIAZZA DEL DUOMO: INSIDE INFO

Top tips Avoid the often considerable **crowds and lines** for the dome and Campanile by visiting them as early as possible.
• The **Baptistery** is closed every morning until noon except on Sunday, when it opens at 8:30.
• The **Campanile and dome** open earlier than the main body of the cathedral, so save time by climbing one or the other (or both) before visiting the Duomo.

In more depth The Museo dell'Opera del Duomo (► 72) contains Florence's finest collection of **medieval and Renaissance sculpture** after the Museo Nazionale del Bargello (► 62).

🔟

Museo Nazionale del Bargello

The Museo Nazionale del Bargello began life as a palace and prison, but today has Europe's finest collection of Italian Renaissance sculpture, with exceptional works by Donatello, Michelangelo and many others. It also has a beautiful but little-known collection of ceramics, carpets, glassware, textiles, tapestries, ivories and other decorative arts.

The building in which the museum is housed is the Palazzo del Bargello, a superb medieval palace begun in 1255 as the seat of the Podestà, Florence's chief magistrate. It took its present name in 1574, when the Medici abolished the post of Podestà and made the building over to the Bargello, or chief of police. It opened as a museum in 1865.

Giambologna's much imitated figure of Mercury, cast in bronze and flowing with movement

Priceless sculptures in the Bargello's *loggia*

Immediately past the ticket office you enter a single room of sculpture that would be the envy of most entire museums. Pride of place goes to works by Michelangelo, of which the most eye-catching is the drunken figure of *Bacchus* (1496–7), carved when the sculptor was 22 years old. Other works by the master include the *Pitti Tondo* (1504), a delicate, shallow relief showing the Madonna and Child; a figure of **David** or **Apollo** (1530–2) – critics are unsure of the intended identity; and a portrait of *Brutus* (1539–40), the only portrait bust Michelangelo completed. In the same room, look out for 16th-century works by Benvenuto Cellini, a flamboyant sculptor and goldsmith, and Giambologna, in particular the latter's lithe figure of *Mercury* (1564).

From this first room you walk into the Bargello's central **courtyard**, formerly a place of execution. Climb the courtyard staircase to a *loggia*, dotted with a menagerie of 16th-century bronze animals by the French-born sculptor Giambologna.

Turn right at the *loggia* and you enter the **Salone del Consiglio Maggiore**, containing the cream of Florence's early Renaissance sculpture. Its most celebrated works are a diverse selection of masterpieces by Donatello, notably an androgynous bronze statue of David (1430–40), an earlier marble *David* (1408), an heroic *St George* (1416), the Cupid-like figure *Amor-Atys* (1430–40) and a portrait bust of soldier Niccolò da Uzzano. The panels of *The Sacrifice of Isaac* were submitted by Ghiberti and Brunelleschi in the 1401 competition to design the Baptistery doors (➤ 60).

Other fascinating collections in the museum include fine displays of Islamic art, ivories and miniature bronzes.

TAKING A BREAK

Walk a few minutes south from the Bargello on Via del Proconsolo to the **Bar San Firenze**, housed in a 15th-century *palazzo* (Piazza San Firenze 1r; tel: 055 211426; closed Sun in winter).

✚ 199 D3 ✉ Via del Proconsolo 4 ☎ 055 238 8606 ⏰ Tue–Fri, 2nd and 4th Sun of month, 1st, 3rd and 5th Mon of month 8:15–1:50 (last ticket 1:20), Sat 8:15–6:50 🚌 A, 14, 23 💶 Moderate

---

MUSEO NAZIONALE DEL BARGELLO: INSIDE INFO

Top tip Allow as long, if not longer, to admire the Bargello's **decorative arts** as much as its sculpture.

In more depth The 10th-century **Badia Fiorentina abbey** lies directly opposite the Bargello. Although it has erratic opening hours, it is worth trying to get in to admire a painting of the *Apparition of the Virgin to St Bernard* (1485) by Filippino Lippi, 15th-century sculptures by Mino da Fiesole and a fresco cycle on the Life of St Benedict (by an anonymous hand) in the abbey cloister (entered by a door to the right of the high altar).

⓭

Piazza della Signoria

The second of Florence's great squares has long had a civic rather than religious focus. As well as being home to the impressive Palazzo Vecchio, the city's main seat of government for more than 700 years, it is notable for its range of captivating fountains and monumental sculptures commissioned over the centuries by Florence's rulers.

Piazza della Signoria dates from the 13th century, when the city set aside land here for the Palazzo dei Priori (1299–1315), a council chamber which eventually became the present-day Palazzo Vecchio. The piazza was enlarged and adapted several times over the centuries, hence its irregular shape. Major changes were made in the 14th century to accommodate the Loggia della Lanzi (also known as the Loggia dei Signori) on its southern flank, and again in 1560, when Cosimo I de' Medici created the palace which later would house the Uffizi gallery, which took its name from the offices (*uffizi*) in the building.

Bandinelli's *Hercules and Cacus* in the Piazza della Signoria

Statues and Fountains

The square's **statues and fountains** run along its eastern flank. From left to right as you face them they are an equestrian monument of Cosimo I de' Medici (1594–8) by Giambologna and the Fontana del Nettuno (1563–75), or Fountain of Neptune, by Bartolomeo Ammanati, in which the central figure is again an idealised portrait of Cosimo I de' Medici. Then come two copies of work by Donatello: *Il Marzocco* (1418–20), a representation of the Marzocco (lion), Florence's heraldic symbol, and *Judith and Holofernes* (1456–60). The originals of both these works are in the Palazzo

---

PIAZZA DELLA SIGNORIA: INSIDE INFO

Top tips Visit the **church of Orsanmichele** (➤ 72) as you walk between Piazza del Duomo and Piazza della Signoria on Via dei Calzaiuoli.
• A **"Carnet" ticket** valid for a year entitles you to 50 per cent off the admission charge to the Palazzo Vecchio and other sights.
• **Free pamphlets** in English are available from the ticket office.

In more depth The Sala degli Gigli is named after its decorative lilies (*gigli*) and features a carved ceiling (1472–6) by Giuliano and Benedetto da Maiano and a fresco cycle by Ghirlandaio. Added attractions in the Palazzo Vecchio include a Multimedia Area, **Children's Museum** and the **"Secret Passageways"** tour.

Vecchio. The final major sculptures are a copy of Michelangelo's *David* (➤ 54) and the figures of *Hercules and Cacus* (1534) by Baccio Bandinelli, designed as a companion piece for *David*.

Walk to your right and wander around the **Loggia dei Lanzi**, an airy arched space built in 1376 to protect the city's dignitaries from the elements during processions and ceremonials. The most outstanding of its statues are Benvenuto Cellini's bronze *Perseus* (1545), shown holding the severed head of Medusa, and Giambologna's three-figured *Rape of the Sabine* (1583) – the name of the latter is misleading, for the sculptor intended it to be a study of old age, male strength and female beauty.

Palazzo Vecchio

The Palazzo Vecchio opens with an exquisite main **courtyard** (1553–74), the work of Giorgio Vasari, followed on the first floor by the huge **Salone dei Cinquecento**, once the palace's main council chamber. The latter features the Studiolo di Francesco I (1569–73), a study created for Cosimo I's son, and Michelangelo's *Victory* (1525). Other highlights include rooms filled with **frescoes and sculptures**, notably the Cappella di Eleonora, the Sala dell'Udienza and Sala dei Gigli.

Part of Ammanati's Fontana del Nettuno (Fountain of Neptune)

TAKING A BREAK

The Palazzo Vecchio has a **café** in the Quartiere degli Elementi and Terrazza di Saturno on the second floor. **Rivoire** is a famous old café with outside tables on Piazza della Signoria (➤ 81); it's expensive, but worth the price to enjoy one of Tuscany's great squares at your leisure.

Palazzo Vecchio
🚩 199 D3 ✉ Piazza della Signoria ☎ 055 276 8325; www.palazzovecchio.it. Reservations for Secret Passageways tours and sessions in the Children's Museum ☎ 055 276 8224; www.museo ragazzi.it (same hours as Palazzo) 🕐 Palazzo Vecchio: Mon–Wed, Fri, Sat 9–7, Thu and Sun 9–2 (last tickets 30 minutes before closing). Secret Passageways: consult tourist office or Palazzo Vecchio ticket office for current details or tel: 055 276 8465 🚌 B to Piazza della Signoria or A to Via della Condotta 💶 Moderate. Expensive if joint ticket with Cappella Brancacci

🔟4️⃣

Santa Croce

Santa Croce is arguably Florence's most important church. It is noted both for its many outstanding works of art – including spectacular fresco cycles by Giotto and other medieval masters – as well as for the fact that many of the city's most illustrious citizens, including Michelangelo, Galileo and Machiavelli, lie buried within its walls. It was built for the Franciscans and intended as a riposte to Santa Maria Novella, the church of the Dominican order, the Franciscans' rivals.

Santa Croce was probably designed around 1294 by Arnolfo di Cambio, the architect responsible for Florence's cathedral and Palazzo Vecchio. Much of the money for the church's many tombs and decorated chapels came from wealthy Florentines, bankers in particular. They were eager to be buried alongside the humble Franciscans to assuage the stigma associated with usury, or lending money with interest, a practice then considered a sin by the Church.

Herod's Banquet by Giotto is one of the masterpieces of Santa Croce

Famous Residents

It was not only bankers who were buried here, however: the first tomb on the right (south) wall as you enter belongs to **Michelangelo**. He is buried close to the entrance at his own request, apparently so that the first thing he glimpsed when he rose from his tomb on the Day of Judgement would be Brunelleschi's cathedral dome. Almost alongside it is a memorial to **Dante**, the Florentine poet who died and is buried in Ravenna on Italy's Adriatic coast. A short distance away is the tomb of Machiavelli, while the tomb of scientist **Galileo** lies on the opposite wall, again close to the church entrance.

Frescoes and Tombs

The church's key works of art are two **fresco cycles by Giotto** in the two chapels to the right of the high altar: the Cappella Bardi, which is adorned with *Scenes from the Life of St Francis* (1315–20), and to its right, the Cappella Peruzzi, decorated with *Scenes from the Life of St John and St John the Baptist* (1326–30). Other major **14th-century cycles** by Taddeo and

SANTA CROCE: INSIDE INFO

Top tip Pause for a moment on entering Santa Croce to take in its **scale** and magnificent wooden ceiling.

In more depth To the right of Santa Croce as you face its façade is the entrance to the **Museo dell'Opera di Santa Croce** (church museum) and Cappella dei Pazzi (1429–70), the church's former chapter house. The museum has works of art by Donatello and Cimabue, while the Cappella is one of the finest small architectural and decorative ensembles of the early Renaissance. It was designed by Brunelleschi, architect of the cathedral dome, and decorated by Luca della Robbia, Desiderio da Settignano and others.

Agnolo Gaddi, followers of Giotto, grace the Cappella Castellani and Cappella Baroncelli, adjacent chapels in the right (south) transept.

Don't miss some of the other **14th-century frescoes** around the chancel and in the rooms off the right transept, or the two influential **Renaissance tombs** that stand on opposite sides of the church close to the top of the nave. The first of these, on the right (south) side, belongs to the humanist scholar Leonardi Bruni (1146–7), and is the work of Bernardo Rossellino; the second (1453) by Desiderio da Settignano – who was much influenced by Rossellino's work – contains another eminent humanist scholar, Carlo Marsuppini.

TAKING A BREAK

Piazza Santa Croce has plenty of **cafés**, but the nearby *enoteca* **Baldovino** (▶ 78) is a far more distinctive place for a drink or snack. While in the vicinity of Santa Croce, be sure to buy a *gelato* from the famous **Vivoli** *gelateria* (ice-cream parlour), considered by many to be the best in Italy (▶ 81).

Santa Croce
➕ 199 E3 ✉ Piazza Santa Croce ☎ 055 244619 🕐 Mon–Sat 9:30–5:30, Sun 1–5:30, (8 am–1 pm for worship only) 🚌 B, 23 💶 Moderate (includes Museo dell'Opera di Santa Croce)

Museo dell'Opera di Santa Croce–Cappella dei Pazzi
➕ 199 E2 ✉ Piazza Santa Croce 16 ☎ 055 244619 🕐 Opening times as for Santa Croce 🚌 B, 23 💶 Moderate (includes church of Santa Croce)

[15]

Galleria degli Uffizi

The Galleria degli Uffizi, more commonly known simply as the Uffizi, not only houses the world's greatest collection of Italian Renaissance art, but also a host of outstanding paintings from other periods and other European countries.

The immense palace housing the Uffizi art gallery was built in 1560 by Giorgio Vasari as a suite of offices (*uffizi*) for Cosimo I de' Medici. The paintings themselves formed the lion's share of the **Medici's private collection**, acquired over many centuries but left to Florence – on condition they never left the city – by Anna Maria Luisa, sister of the last Medici Grand Duke, Gian Gastone Medici.

The collection ranges over 45 rooms and comprises more than 2,000 paintings on display, with some 1,800 other works of art kept in storage. Many of the most famous works – the Italian paintings of the Renaissance and medieval period – are found in the first 15 or so rooms. Be prepared for throngs of

Paolo Uccello's
Battle of San Romano
(*c*1456)

people in this area, particularly around the works of Botticelli in Rooms 10–14.

This said, you shouldn't skip some of the early masterpieces in your hurry to reach these rooms. The three pictures which open the gallery proper in Room 2 all depict the *Maestà*, or "Madonna in Majesty". They are by three of the greatest painters of the 13th century: the Sienese master Duccio and the Florentine-based Giotto and Cimabue.

Pre-book your entry to the Uffizi to avoid a long wait to get in

Other highlights in Rooms 3–6 include paintings by Sienese artists, notably a sublime *Annunciation* (1333) by Simone Martini and works by Pietro and Ambrogio Lorenzetti, two painters who probably died in the Black Death, the plague epidemic that ravaged Tuscany in 1348. Also look out for the intricately detailed and beautifully coloured *Adoration of the Virgin* by Gentile da Fabriano (1423) and *Coronation of the Virgin* (1413) by Lorenzo da Monaco.

Room 7 has works by early Renaissance masters such as Piero della Francesca, Masaccio and Paolo Uccello – the latter's *Battle of San Romano* (c1456) is outstanding for its perspective. The room is outshone by Rooms 10–14, however, where you'll see Sandro Botticelli's celebrated *Primavera* (1478) and *The Birth of Venus* (1485), paintings which drew on classical myth rather than religion for their themes and imagery. Room 15 has two paintings by Leonardo da Vinci – the *Annunciation* and *Adoration of the Magi*. He was born in Vinci, a village in the hills west of Florence.

Highlights in the remaining rooms are many. Look out in particular for the *Medici Venus* (Room 18), considered one of the most erotic works of the 3rd century; the 1490 *Sacred Allegory* (Room 21) by the Venetian Giovanni Bellini; the 1505 *Doni Tondo* (Room 25), the Uffizi's only painting by Michelangelo; Raphael paintings in Room 26; the *Venus of Urbino* (1538), an infamous nude by Titian in Room 28; and the paintings of Van Dyck, Caravaggio, Rubens, Rembrandt and others in the last six rooms.

The stunning architecture of the Uffizi's elegant salons is almost as impressive as its exhibits

TAKING A BREAK

The gallery has a good **café-bar**, but you could also visit the **Rivoire** (► 81) on nearby Piazza della Signoria to enjoy a relaxed coffee on its terrace. Alternatively, try **Caffè Italiano** (► 81).

➕ 198 C3 ✉ Loggiata degli Uffizi 6, off Piazza della Signoria ☎ 055 238 8651 🕐 Tue–Sun 8:15–6:50 (last tickets 6:05). Closed Mon. Corridoio Vasariano tours: times vary, but usually twice weekly Wed and Fri. Booking obligatory (tel: 055 265 4321) 🚌 B or 23 💶 Expensive; Corridoio: expensive

---

GALLERIA DEGLI UFFIZI: INSIDE INFO

Top tips The Uffizi will be busy whatever day or month of the year you visit. To avoid a long wait to get into the gallery **pre-book a ticket and entry time by credit card** (tel: 055 294883; Mon–Fri 8–6:30, Sat 8:30–12:30 or online www.week-endfirenze.com). You will receive a reservation number for the day and time of entry. Tickets are held at the meeting point for advance reservations to the left of the main gallery entrance. A small booking fee is charged.
• The Uffizi's pre-booked phone and online entry service is available for Florence's **state museums**, including the Cappelle Medicee, Galleria dell'Accademia, Palazzo Pitti (Galleria Palatina), Museo Nazionale del Bargello and Museo di San Marco.
• If you have time, try to **make two visits** to the Uffizi: one to see the Italian paintings in Rooms 1–15; a second to view the other Italian and foreign paintings in the remaining 30 or so rooms.

In more depth You can visit the **Corridoio Vasariano**, an extraordinary corridor lined with paintings, built by Giorgio Vasari in the 16th century to link the Uffizi with the Palazzo Pitti (► 75). Part of its route runs over the Ponte Vecchio.

At Your Leisure

❶ Museo di San Marco

This museum lies to the north of Florence's other main attractions, but of all the city's "second" sights, it is the one most worth visiting. A former Dominican monastery, it is almost entirely given over to the paintings of Fra Angelico, a monk and former prior here, and one of the finest early Renaissance painters. In the main gallery off the old cloister, the Ospizio dei Pellegrini, the highlights are the San Marco Altarpiece (1440) and *Madonna dei Linaiuoli* (1433). Don't miss Domenico Ghirlandaio's *Last Supper* (1480) in the Refettorio Piccolo (Small Refectory). On the first floor you are greeted by Angelico's lovely *Annunciation*, a prelude to a succession of tiny monastic cells, each of which has a fresco by Angelico or his assistants painted as aids to devotion. Also here is a majestic library, built with funds from Cosimo de' Medici from 1441 to 1444.

🔁 199 D5 ⊠ Piazza San Marco 1
☎ 055 238 8608 ⏰ Tue–Fri 8:15–1:50 (last ticket 1:20), Sat 8:15–6:50, plus 8:15–1:50 1st, 3rd and 5th Mon of month and 8:15–6:50, 2nd and 4th Sun of month
🚌 1, 5, 17 to Piazza San Marco; 11 from San Marco to city centre 🎫 Expensive

❸ Palazzo Medici-Riccardi

This palace belonged to the Medicis while they were at the height of their powers. Completed for Cosimo the Elder in 1462, it remained the family home until 1540, when Cosimo I de' Medici moved to the Palazzo Vecchio.

While the palace retains it daunting exterior, only one small fragment of splendour survives inside – the tiny Cappella dei Magi, frescoed by Benozzo Gozzoli in 1460. The theme of the three main paintings is the Magi, but Gozzoli also incorporated contemporary details, not least portraits of the Medici clan and aspects of 15th-century Florentine processions.

🔁 198 A4 ⊠ Via Cavour 3 ☎ Pre-booked entry 055 276 0340 ⏰ Mon, Tue, and Thu–Sun 9–7 (last ticket 6:30)
🚌 1, 6, 17 to Via Cavour and all services to Piazza del Duomo 🎫 Moderate

❹ Mercato Centrale

Florence's vast covered food market – the largest such market in Europe –

Plump Italian tomatoes on sale at the Mercato Centrale

first opened in 1874. Since then it has been beguiling Florentines and foreigners alike with its array of fruit, vegetables, hams, cheese, olive oils and countless other gastronomic treats. Its stalls are a wonderful source of picnic provisions or gifts, or visit simply for the sights and smells. The market is easily seen in conjunction with San Lorenzo (➤ 84) and the Cappelle Medicee (➤ 55).

➕ 198 C5 ✉ Piazza del Mercato Centrale ⊙ Mon–Sat 7–2 (winter also Sat 4–8) 🚍 1, 6, 7, to Via Cavour and services to Piazza del Duomo 💷 Free

🔟 Museo dell'Opera del Duomo

The Opera del Duomo ("Work of the Duomo") was a body founded in 1296 to look after the Duomo, Baptistery and Campanile (➤ 59). Since 1891, its headquarters east of the cathedral have provided the home for this now modern museum, filled with works of art donated or removed for safekeeping from the piazza's buildings over a period of 700 years. Its highlights are mainly medieval and Renaissance sculptures, but it also contains a wealth of paintings, gold and silverware, illustrated manuscripts and other artefacts. Its most celebrated treasure is a statue of the Pietà (1550–3) by Michelangelo, but other fine works include Donatello's *Mary Magdalene* (1453–5), Lorenzo Ghiberti's restored bronze panels from

the Baptistery's east doors and most of Andrea Pisano's and della Robbia's bas-reliefs from the Campanile.

➕ 199 D4 ✉ Piazza del Duomo 9 ☎ 055 230 2885 ⊙ Mon–Sat 9–7:30, Sun 9–1:40 🚍 14, 23 💷 Moderate

🟧 Museo di Firenze com'era

The "Museum of Florence As It Was" is a tiny, little-visited gem just a couple of minutes' walk east of the Museo dell'Opera del Duomo. The museum takes only moments to see, but contains 12 of the most charming paintings in Florence (1555) of the villas owned by the Medici, by Flemish artist Justus Utens (died 1609). Also noteworthy is the *Pianta della Catena* (Chain Map), an 1887 copy of a 1470 bird's-eye view of Florence.

➕ 199 D4 ✉ Via dell'Oriuolo 24 ☎ 055 261 6545 ⊙ Mon–Wed, Fri–Sun 9–2 🚍 A to Borgo degli Albizzi or A, 14 or 23 to Via del Proconsolo 💷 Inexpensive

🟧 Orsanmichele

The church of Orsanmichele is often missed by tourists, situated as it is on the Via dei Calzaiuoli, but it is easily visited as you walk between the

A copy of Verrocchio's St Thomas outside Orsanmichele

Piazza del Duomo (▶ 59) and Piazza della Signoria (▶ 64). The fortress-like building takes its name from a 7th-century oratory built in the garden of a Benedictine abbey. The oratory was replaced in 1280 by a grain market and by the present structure in 1380.

The building's artistic importance stems from the early 15th-century statues arranged around 14 exterior niches. These were commissioned by Florence's major medieval guilds – each figure represents an individual guild's patron saint. They demonstrate some of the most important sculptures of their day and were produced by many of the period's most important artists – Donatello, Ghiberti, Michelozzo, Brunelleschi and Verrocchio. Many of the works are now copies, the originals having been removed for safe-keeping to museums such as the Bargello (▶ 62).

Inside, the church walls are decorated with faded medieval frescoes that also depict the guilds' patron saints. The nave is dominated by a sumptuous tabernacle (1355–9) by Orcagna, which encloses a painting of the *Madonna delle Grazie* (1347) by Bernardo Daddi.

➕ 198 C3 ✉ Via dei Calzaiuoli–Via dell'Arte della Lana ☎ 055 284944 🕐 Daily 9–noon, 4–6. Closed 1st and last Mon of month 🚌 A and services to Piazza del Duomo 🎟 Free

The Ponte Vecchio's arcaded shops are reflected in the Arno River at sunset

🄵 Santa Trinità

The 11th-century church of Santa Trinità is relatively unassuming to look at, its late 16th-century facade concealing a mostly Gothic interior that was remodelled between 1300 and 1330. Its real worth lies in its side chapels, several of which contain compelling works of art. The Cappella Sassetti, the second chapel to the right of the high altar, contains a fresco cycle of *Scenes from the Life of St Francis* (1483–6) by Ghirlandaio. The same artist was responsible for the chapel's altarpiece, *The Adoration of the Shepherds* (1485), a consummate Renaissance fusion of Christian and pagan classical imagery. The fourth chapel on the right (south) side of the church contains a fresco cycle by Lorenzo Monaco of *Scenes from the Life of the Virgin* (1420–5).

➕ 198 B3 ✉ Piazza Santa Trinità ☎ 055 216912 🕐 Mon–Sat 8–noon, 4–6, Sun 4–6 🚌 A, B, 6, 11, 36, 37 🎟 Free

🄶 Ponte Vecchio

Florence's most famous bridge has occupied its site close to the Arno's narrowest point in the city since about 1345. Earlier bridges here included a Roman bridge and two wooden medieval bridges swept away in floods of 1117 and 1333. The present bridge only narrowly escaped a similar fate in the great flood of 1966, and in 1944 it was the only bridge in the city not blown up by the Nazis as they sought to slow the advance of the United States Fifth Army.

The Ponte Vecchio's picturesque overhanging stores and workshops date from the bridge's earliest days (previous bridges here had similar shops). They were originally the domain of butchers and fishmongers, attracted by the convenience of being able to tip their rubbish in the river – the open space that still exists at the centre of the bridge was created for this purpose. Later, the bridge was taken over by tanners, who used the river to soak their hides, and later still by jewellers and goldsmiths. Descendants of these jewellers still operate from the bridge.

🚹 198 C3 ⊠ Via Por Santa Maria–Lungarno degli Acciaiuoli 🕐 Daily 🚌 B, 6, 11, 36, 37 💶 Free

🔢 Cappella Brancacci

Florence has many fresco cycles, but two are particularly alluring. In northern Florence, Gozzoli's Palazzo Medici-Riccardi frescoes appeal for their narrative verve (▶ 71); in the Oltrarno district, it is the frescoes of the Cappella Brancacci that draw the largest crowds. Here the appeal is the paintings' innovation and the seminal place they hold in the development of Florentine Renaissance art.

One of many shaded walkways in the Giardino di Boboli

The frescoes occupy part of Santa Maria del Carmine, an otherwise uninspiring church, and were commissioned in 1424 by Felice Brancacci, a wealthy diplomat and silk merchant. They were begun by Masolino da Panicale (1383–1447) and his assistant Masaccio (1401–28). Two years into the project, Masolino was called to Budapest, as official painter to the Hungarian court. In his absence, Masaccio's genius flourished. Masolino returned in 1427, but a year later was called to Rome, Masaccio died and, in 1436, Brancacci was exiled by the Medici. Work only resumed in 1480, when Filippino Lippi completed the cycle, working so closely to his predecessors' style that his contribution was only recognised in 1838.

The frescoes' narrative power, perspective and realism were unlike anything seen before in Florence.

🚹 198 A3 ⊠ Piazza del Carmine 🕿 055 238 2195 or 276 8224; pre-booked entry 055 294 883 🕐 Mon and Wed–Sat 10–5, Sun 1–5 💶 Moderate; ticket with Palazzo Vecchio: expensive

🔢 Giardino di Boboli

The Giardino di Boboli (Boboli Garden), is central Florence's principal garden and the only significant open space in which you can escape the city streets. Set behind the Palazzo Pitti, it was begun in 1549 when Cosimo I de' Medici acquired the palace. It was opened to the public in 1776. In high summer it can look parched and worn, but at other times the tree-shaded walkways, formal gardens, parterres, lawns, fountains, grottoes and statues are a delight. There is a café in the garden, but this is also a pleasant place for a picnic.

🔀 198 B1 ✉ Entrances off Piazza de' Pitti and Piazzale di Porta Romana
☎ 055 265 1816/1838 🕐 Tue–Sun, 8:15–6:30, Apr–May and Sep–Oct; 8:15–5:30, Mar; 8:15–7:30 (last ticket 6:30), Jun–Aug; 8:15–4:30, Nov–Feb. Also open 2nd and 3rd Mon of month
🚌 D, 11, 36, 37 💶 Inexpensive

🄳 Palazzo Pitti

The long-forgotten Pitti family may have begun this huge Oltrarno palace in 1458, but after it was bought by Cosimo I de' Medici in 1549 it was for many years the Medici family's main Florentine home. Today it plays host to several museums, with two of particular note. The Museo degli Argenti is devoted primarily to silverware (*argento*) but also contains countless precious objects accumulated by the Medici over the centuries. The Galleria Palatina contains hundreds of priceless paintings from the Medici collection, making this Florence's second-ranking art gallery after the Uffizi (➤ 68). Works by Raphael and Titian are the collection's real treasures, but there are also canvases by Filippino Lippi, Caravaggio and other leading names.

🔀 198 B2 ✉ Piazza de' Pitti
☎ 055 238 8614 🕐 Galleria Palatina: daily 8:15–6:50 (last ticket 6:05)
🚌 D 💶 Expensive

🄴 San Miniato al Monte

The church of San Miniato is the most outlying of all Florence's major sights, yet it is also one of the most beautiful. You can take a bus or follow a pretty uphill walk from close to the Ponte Vecchio, which offers memorable views.

San Miniato is one of Tuscany's finest Romanesque buildings. It was begun in 1013 on the site of an earlier chapel to St Minias, martyred in Florence around AD 250. The façade was completed in 1207 – note the statue of an eagle clutching a bale of cloth, symbol of the Cloth Merchants' Guild, responsible for the church's upkeep. Inside, the marble pavement dates from 1207, as do the pulpit, screen and apse mosaic. Walk down to the crypt with its tiny columns and admire the fresco by Spinello Aretino of *Scenes from the Life of St Benedict* (1387) in the chapel right of the apse.

🔀 198 E1 ✉ Via del Monte alle Croci–Viale Galileo Galilei ☎ 055 234 2731
🕐 Daily 8–12:30, 3–7, Apr–Sep; daily 8–12:30, 2:30–4:30 or 6 pm rest of year. Closed for services 🚌 12 or 13 💶 Free

The 13th-century apse mosaic is one of many outstanding works of art in San Miniato al Monte

Where to... Stay

Florence has numerous hotels, from simple 1-star rooms with shared bathrooms to luxury villas. However, for most of the year you need to book ahead, especially in the mid-price 1- and 2-star options and be aware that Florence is more pricey than the rest of Tuscany.

Alessandra €€

Noise shouldn't be a problem at this central 2-star hotel, thanks to its position on a quiet back street between the Ponte Vecchio and church of Santa Trinita. Rooms are bright and airy with wooden floors, but only around half have private bathrooms (for which you pay more): about the same proportion have TVs and air-conditioning.

➕ 198 C3 ⊠ Borgo SS Apostoli 17
☎ 055 283438; fax: 055 210619;
www.hotelalessandra.com ⊘ Closed two weeks in Dec

Bellettini €

The Bellettini stands out in its 2-star class, its only rival the similarly priced Casci. The 27 rooms are plain but clean, but all have telephones and air-conditioning and around half have TVs. Better still, the atmosphere is welcoming, the breakfasts better than average, and the location – on a small street just west of the Cappelle Medicee – central and convenient.

➕ 198 C4 ⊠ Via dei Conti 7
☎ 055 213561; fax: 055 283551;
www.hotelbellettini.com

Brunelleschi €€€

The 4-star, 87-room Brunelleschi has an excellent position in a quiet back street between the Duomo and Piazza della Signoria. A wonderful conversion of an historic site, it was designed by leading Italian architect Italo Gamberini and is built around a Byzantine chapel and the 5th-century Torre della Pagliazza, one of the city's oldest-known structures. A small in-hotel museum is devoted to some of the Roman and other archaeological treasures unearthed during construction. Rooms and common areas combine a modern feel with features retained or copied from the original buildings, notably the exposed brickwork.

➕ 198 C4 ⊠ Via dei Calzaiuoli–Piazza Santa Elisabetta 3
☎ 055 27 370; fax: 055 219653;
www.hotelbrunelleschi.it

Casci €

The Casci is one of the best 2-star hotels in Florence, thanks to its position (just north of Piazza del Duomo), the warm welcome of its multilingual family owners, a good buffet breakfast, the fair prices and the range of clean and pleasant rooms. All 25 rooms have TVs and only a handful face onto the Via Cavour (these have double-glazing).

➕ 199 D5 ⊠ Via Cavour 13 ☎ 055 211686; fax: 055 239 6461;
www.hotelcasci.com

Firenze €

The 1-star Firenze has 57 rooms so there's a good chance of finding space here when other places are full. The rooms in question are plain and uninspiring, but well kept, and almost all have private bathrooms and TVs. The location is first-rate, on a small square almost midway between the Duomo and Piazza della Signoria.

✚ 199 D4 ☒ Via del Corso–Piazza dei Donati 4 ☎ 055 214203; fax: 055 212370; www.albergofirenze.org

Gallery Hotel Art €€€

This stylish 4-star hotel is unlike almost anything else in Florence. It has a sleek, minimalist look – dark wood, neutral colours and modern art displayed in the reception and the 65 rooms. There is a small, stylish bar and a comfortable lounge area. The position is very convenient, in a small, quiet square next to the Ponte Vecchio.

✚ 198 C3 ☒ Vicolo dell'Oro 5 ☎ 055 27 263; fax: 055 268557; www.lungarnohotels.com

Helvetia & Bristol €€€

The 18th-century Helvetia & Bristol may have rivals for the title of "best hotel in Florence" but none can really compete with the historic pedigree and panache of this 5-star retreat. It's located between Via de' Tornabuoni and Piazza Strozzi in the west of the city centre, and past guests have included Pirandello, Stravinsky, De Chirico and Bertrand Russell. The award-winning décor of the common areas, 34 rooms and 18 suites is mostly old-world – antiques, rich fabrics, and period paintings – but the facilities and service are modern and efficient. A first choice if money is no object.

✚ 198 C4 ☒ Via de' Pescioni 2 ☎ 055 288353; fax: 055 288353; www.hotelhelvetiabristolfirenze.it

Hermitage €€

You need to book early to have any chance of securing one of the 28 rooms at this charming 3-star hotel. It owes its popularity to the amiable service, the good facilities (several bathrooms have Jacuzzis) and a superb position almost overlooking the Ponte Vecchio. Not all rooms have river or bridge views, however, and those that do can be noisy: if this is a concern, request a court-yard room. In summer, you can take breakfast on the delightful roof terrace.

✚ 198 C3 ☒ Vicolo Marzio 1–Piazza del Pesce ☎ 055 287216; fax: 055 212208; www.hermitagehotel.com

Loggiato dei Serviti €€€

Well to the north of Piazza del Duomo, this isn't the best located of Florence's 3-star hotels, but there are few complaints about its style. The 25 rooms and 4 suites vary in size and decoration, but all have a serene and minimal look – reminiscent of the building's original 16th-century role as a Servite monastery. The mood is lightened by fabrics, paintings and antiques. All rooms have televisions and air-condition-ing. You can choose between rooms that look out over Brunelleschi's piazza or the gardens of Accademia delle Belle Arti.

✚ 199 D5 ☒ Piazza SS Annunziata 3 ☎ 055 289592; fax: 055 289595; www.loggiatodeiservitihotel.com

Maxim €

The friendly and well-run Maxim is only 2-star, so don't expect too many frills, but its location next to the Duomo could hardly be better. There are 22 rooms, with a choice of private or shared bathrooms: try for the quieter rooms looking onto the central courtyard.

✚ 198 C4 ☒ Via dei Calzaiuoli 11 (with lift) and Via de' Medici 4 (stairs) ☎ 055 217474; fax: 055 283729; www.hotelmaximfirenze.it

Morandi alla Crocetta €€

This 3-star gem bears the cultivated stamp of its ex-pat owner, Kathleen Doyle. The hotel's 10 rooms all boast antiques, prints and polished wood floors; the nicest room has fragments of fresco from the mona-stery that once occupied the site. East of Piazza SS Annunziata, the location isn't very convenient, but you'll still have to book in advance.

✚ 199 E5 ☒ Via Laura 50 ☎ 055 234 4747; fax: 055 248 0954; www.hotelmorandi.it

Where to...
Eat and Drink

Prices
Expect to pay for a three-course meal for one with wine

€ under €26	€€ €26–€52	€€€ over €52

Opening times can vary based on several factors – the time of year, the arrival and departure time of the last customer, or simply the whim of the owners. Most cafés open about 7 am and close in the early evening. Wine bars open about 10 am or noon and close for a couple of hours in the afternoon before opening again in the early evening.

The area around Santa Croce has some of the city's best eating and drinking options. These include the two best restaurants, Cibreo (▶ 79) and Enoteca Pinchiorri (▶ 79), but also a variety of mid-price choices. You can eat in lively, modern surroundings – notably in Baldovino (▶ right), or the simple trattoria-style Benvenuto (▶ 79).

Northern Florence is an area of inexpensive cafés and restaurants, due in part to a large student population and the shoppers and market traders of the Mercato Centrale.

In western Florence, Rose's (▶ 80), Caffè Amerini (▶ 80) and Belle Donne (▶ 79) are all good places for lunch. The Oltrarno has several popular and relatively inexpensive bars, cafés and restaurants, especially on and around Piazza Santa Spirito, Piazza de' Pitti and Piazza del Carmine.

RESTAURANTS

Angiolino €–€€

An Oltrarno *trattoria* of the old school, Angiolino has one of Florence's prettiest interiors: strings of tomatoes and plump pumpkins adorn the bar at the entrance, while dried flowers and chillies hang from the old brick-vaulted main dining room. Red-checked table-cloths and wicker-covered wine bottles complete the picture. The food consists of simple dishes that never stray far from the Tuscan mainstream.

✛ 198 B3 ⬜ Via di Santo Spirito 36r
☎ 055 239 8976 ⬤ Daily
12:30–2:15, 7:30–10:30

Baldovino €–€€

If you're in a dilemma over where to eat lunch or dinner close to the church of Santa Croce, look no further than Baldovino. An informal combination of modern and traditional, the restaurant has been one of Florence's great successes of recent years, if only because of its welcoming owner, Scotsman David Gardner. As a foreign restaurateur, Gardner has managed to satisfy a demanding Florentine clientele by mixing good food – Tuscan classics, Neapolitan pizzas plus innovative salads and other non-Italian novelties – with a bright décor, young staff and a convivial, cosmopolitan atmosphere. Booking is strongly advised, especially if you want to go on a Friday and Saturday.

A sister *enoteca* (wine bar) lies just across the street if you simply want a snack, coffee or a glass of wine.

✛ 199 E3 ⬜ Via San Giuseppe 22r
☎ 055 241773 ⬤ Daily 11:30–2:30,
7–11:30. Closed Mon, Nov–Mar

Beccofino €–€€

Success often breeds success, and this has certainly been the case with Beccofino, opened in the Oltrarno by David Gardner of Baldovino. The ingredients here are similar: a welcoming modern atmosphere; good, fairly priced modern Italian food; and a modern, if rather plain setting that combines comfort with architectural and designer panache (the building was previously a mosque and art gallery). There's also an outside terrace, plus a wine bar with a choice of snacks and wines by the glass.

➕ 198 B3 ⊠ Piazza degli Scarlatti 1, off Lungarno Guicciardini ☎ 055 290076 ⓦ Restaurant: Mon–Sat 7–11.30 pm, Sun 12:30–3, 7–11.30. Wine bar: Mon–Sat 7 pm–midnight, Sun 12:30–3:30, 7–midnight

Belle Donne €

On entering Belle Donne you are immediately struck by the huge piles of fruit, vegetables and flowers laid out in almost sculptural arrangements. The place is small, turnover quick and the setting informal – you share wooden tables with fellow diners, eat off paper tablecloths and choose from a list of daily Florentine specials chalked up on a blackboard.

➕ 198 B4 ⊠ Via delle Belle Donne 16r ☎ 055 238 2609 ⓦ Daily noon–3, 7–11. Closed for a period in Aug

Benvenuto €–€€

Don't expect too much of this place and you won't be disappointed. This is a basic *trattoria* with no-nonsense food and décor, but it has been serving dependable Tuscan staples for as long as anyone can remember. It's popular with everyone.

➕ 199 D3 ⊠ Via della Mosca 16r, corner Via de' Neri ☎ 055 214833 ⓦ Mon–Sat noon–2:30, 7–10.30

Cantinetta del Verrazzano €

This is a superb place for a snack or light meal, just a few paces from Via dei Calzaiuoli. All manner of sandwiches and other tasty delights (most of them baked on site) are presented under a huge display. You can buy food to take away or have a drink or meal at the tables in the café-wine bar. The place is owned by the Castello di Verrazzano estate, one of Chianti's leading vineyards, so the wine here is also good.

➕ 198 C3 ⊠ Via dei Tavolini 18–20r ☎ 055 268590 ⓦ Mon–Sat 8 am–9 pm

Cibreo €€

Many rate Cibreo Florence's best restaurant, thanks to its imaginative interpretations of traditional Florentine "peasant" food. The dining area is simple – rustic tables and plainly painted walls – and the service and atmosphere are informal. Prices are set for each course, regardless of what you order (and include service), but be sure to leave room for one of the excellent desserts. You can eat at lower prices in the adjoining "trattoria", the Vineria Cibreino, but the atmosphere is somewhat muted. Don't forget the other parts of the Cibreo "empire" – the delicatessen and café (▶ 81). Book in advance for the restaurant.

➕ 199 E3 ⊠ Via de' Macci 118r ☎ 055 2341100 ⓦ Tue–Sat 12:50–2:30, 7.30–11:15. Closed Aug

Enoteca Pinchiorri €€€

An *enoteca* is usually an inexpensive wine bar: not here, although there is plenty of wine – some 80,000 bottles of Italian, French and other vintages, including some of the world's rarest (the cellar is one of the best in Europe). In fact, this is Florence's best and most expensive restaurant, award-winning for many years. The prices for the refined and elaborate Italian and international food are very high, while the service and surroundings are formal (men should wear a jacket and tie). The Florentine gastronomic treat.

➕ 199 E3 ⊠ Via Ghibellina 87 ☎ 055 242777; www.pinchiorri.it ⓦ Lunch: Thu–Sat 12:30–2. Dinner: Tue–Sat 12:30–2, 7:30–10. Closed Mon and Aug

Mario €

Mario is a Florentine institution which makes few concessions to stylish dining. It's a basic eatery just north of the Mercato Centrale that provides cheap, authentic and good-quality Tuscan food (lunch only) to students, shoppers and market traders. You'll find tripe on Mondays and Thursdays, fish on Fridays and just one choice of dessert week-round – *cantucci con vin santo* (biscuits with a dessert wine). It's good in a rough-and-ready sort of way, but if you want a little more style, look into Za-Za a couple of doors away (▶ right).

🕂 **198 C5** ⊠ **Via Rosina 2r–Piazza del Mercato Centrale** ☎ **055 218550** 🕲 **Mon–Sat noon–3**

Osteria dei Benci €€

This place epitomises Florence's new breed of bright and informal restaurants, and is distinguished by a single attractive dining room painted in warm colours and crowned by a pretty medieval brick vault. The staff are young, the service is charming and relaxed, and the Tuscan food well prepared and imaginative without being too daring. Menus change regularly to take account of seasonal availability of fresh produce.

🕂 **199 D3** ⊠ **Via de' Benci 13r** ☎ **055 234 4923** 🕲 **Mon–Sat 1–2:45, 7:30–10:45**

Rose's €

There may come a time when you want a change from the classic Florentine restaurant or café and its terracotta floors, wooden beams and regional cooking. In this respect, Rose's is a breath of fresh air: a modern and stylish bar-restaurant that wouldn't be out of place in New York or Sydney. The food is diverse and includes *sushi* – served in the evening in a separate room to the left of the bar – or inventive sandwiches and snacks at lunch. It makes a great place for lunch, but you could also come here for morning coffee, afternoon tea, an early evening apéritif or even a late snack and nightcap.

🕂 **198 B3** ⊠ **Via del Parione 26r** ☎ **055 287090** 🕲 **Mon noon–4, Tue–Sat 12:30–3, 7:30–midnight, Sun 7:30–midnight.**

Zà-Zà €

Until recently, few people – save those in the know – took much notice of Za-Za, a low-key and long-established place close to the Mercato Centrale. Then it was patronised by King Juan Carlos of Spain, US actor Bill Cosby, and models Naomi Campbell and Linda Evangelista. Now you'll have to wait for a table at busy times. You can see the appeal: low prices – several set-price menus; a rustic dining room of dark stone walls lined with old photographs; and good, basic food – try the hot *antipasti* (starters) or the *crostini* (toasts) with Taleggio cheese, oil, pepper and vinegar.

🕂 **198 C5** ⊠ **Piazza del Mercato Centrale 26r** ☎ **055 215411** 🕲 **Daily 11–11**

Caffè Amerini €

Like the nearby Rose's, Caffè Amerini is a little different to most Florentine eating places. While it has the familiar medieval brick-arched vaults of many of the city's bars and restaurants, its paint-effect walls and oddball furniture provide a modern and slightly eccentric edge to a place that is patronised by everyone from shoppers and tourists to students and genteel old ladies. It's a cosy and easy-going retreat in which you could happily spend an hour or two with a book on a rainy afternoon. It's also good for breakfast or lunch – simply point out which of the sandwiches, salads or other snacks you want from the glass-fronted bar just inside the door and then take a seat to be served. You pay only a small premium for sitting down.

🕂 **198 B3** ⊠ **Via della Vigna Nuova 61r** ☎ **055 284941** 🕲 **Mon–Sat 8–8**

Caffè Cibreo €

It's hard to think of a prettier café in Florence than Caffè Cibreo, whose lovely wood-panelled interior dates from 1989, but could just as easily be 200 years older. Although it's some way from the centre, it's convenient if you're visiting the Sant'Ambrogio market or church. As an added incentive, the snacks and cakes (including a famed chocolate torte) come from the celebrated kitchens of the co-owned Cibreo restaurant nearby (▶ 79). There's outside seating in summer, but the street is not particularly attractive.

➕ 199 E3 ✉ Via Andrea del Verrocchio 5r ☎ 055 234 5853 🕐 Tue–Sat 8 am–1 am

Caffè Italiano €

This stylish café remains something of a well-kept secret, despite its position just off the busy Via dei Calzaiuoli. You can stand in the pretty, wood-panelled bar downstairs or relax in the cosy little hideaway of dark wood and red velvet

seats upstairs. Light lunches are served between 1 pm and 3 pm.

➕ 199 D3 ✉ Via della Condotta 56r ☎ 055 291082 🕐 Mon–Sat 8 am–8:30 pm, Sun 1–8:30

Caffè Pitti €

Piazza Pitti in front of the Palazzo Pitti offers several café options, of which this – the southernmost in the square – with its pretty and old-fashioned interior, is the best.

➕ 198 B2 ✉ Piazza de' Pitti 9r ☎ 055 239 9863 🕐 Daily 11 am–2 am. May close Mon in winter

Casa del Vino €

Unsurprisingly, the "House of Wine" is a place to drink or buy wine. It's often busy, due to its location close to the Mercato Centrale, but usually with locals. You can buy wine by the bottle to take out, or wash down crostini (toasts) or panini (rolls) at the bar with wines by the glass.

➕ 198 C5 ✉ Via dell'Ariento 16r ☎ 055 215 609 🕐 Mon–Fri 9:30–7, Sat 10–3

Hemingway €

Off Piazza del Carmine, Hemingway is unlike anything else in Florence, thanks to its specialities. You can choose from many different tea flavours, sample more than 20 types of coffee, try a tea-based cocktail or gorge on the sensational, award-winning cakes and chocolates (the owners belong to the Compagnia del Cioccolato, a chocolate appreciation society). More conventional drinks and food are also available. Unusually, it is also a non-smoking café.

➕ 198 A3 ✉ Piazza Piattellina 9r ☎ 055 284781 🕐 Tue–Thu, Sun 4:30 pm–1 am, Sat 4:30 pm–2 am

Le Volpi e L'Uva €

A first-rate wine bar in a small square just across the Ponte Vecchio. There are 50 or so wines by the glass, with many unusual vintages, which change every few days. The snack food is also good.

➕ 198 C2 ✉ Piazza dei Rossi 1r, off Piazza di Santa Felicita ☎ 055 239 8132 🕐 Mon–Sat 10–9

Rivoire €

It's hard to resist settling down at one of Rivoire's outside tables, if only because they overlook the Piazza della Signoria. When the café was founded in 1872 it specialised in hot chocolate, but these days teas, coffee and most other drinks are also available. Prices are high, however, and the sandwiches and other food average, but it's worth it at least once just for the view.

➕ 198 C3 ✉ Piazza della Signoria 5r ☎ 055 214412 🕐 Tue–Sun 8 am–midnight

Vivoli €

A Florentine institution that has been in the same hands for three generations. It once held the unofficial title of the best ice-cream in Italy and you'll still have to go a long way to find gelati, sorbets or frozen yoghurts quite as good. It lies in a side street just west of Piazza Santa Croce, off Via Ghibellina.

➕ 199 D3 ✉ Via Isole delle Stinche 7r ☎ 055 292334 🕐 Closed Mon

Where to... Shop

Florence is an excellent place to shop for food, wine and designer, luxury and leather goods. It also has several good markets. Chic designer stores are on Via de' Tornabuoni and the surrounding streets. Borgo Ognissanti also has smarter stores and individual designers' "ateliers", as well as artisans' furniture and other workshops tucked into Via del Porcellana. Shopping in northern Florence is dominated by two markets, the Mercato Centrale and San Lorenzo, but in eastern and central Florence only one or two key streets have many shops – Via dei Calzaiuoli and Borgo degli Albizzi. Some of the more off-beat shops lie in the Sant' Ambrogio district, which also has a good market, and the streets around Santa Croce. The Oltrarno district has food and other stores designed to serve locals, but also the art and antiques shops concentrated on Via Maggio and its surrounding streets.

BOOKS

Feltrinelli

Feltrinelli belongs to a modern, Italy-wide chain. Invariably busy, its floors are filled not only with Italian titles, but a sprinkling of English and other foreign-language books – though the sister store, Feltrinelli Internazionale at Via Cavour 12–20r, is a better bet for such titles. This branch just west of the Duomo has a good selection of guides and maps in English and Italian.

➕ 198 C4 🖾 Via Cerretano 30r ☎ 055 238 2652; www.feltrinelli.it ⏰ Mon–Sat 9–8, Sun 10–1, 3–8

CLOTHES AND ACCESSORIES

Armani

Giorgio Armani's flagship Florentine store is on Via de' Tornabuoni: the cheaper Emporio Armani outlet is on Piazza degli Strozzi.

➕ 198 B3 🖾 Via de' Tornabuoni 48r ☎ 055 219 041; www.armani.com ⏰ Mon 3–7, Tue–Fri 10–7, Sat 10:30–7:30

➕ 198 C3 🖾 Piazza degli Strozzi 14–17r ☎ 055 284315 ⏰ Mon 3:30–7:30, Tue–Sat 10–2, 3:30–7:30

Gucci

The famous Gucci label was founded at this Florentine address, which still acts as a prestigious showroom for the revitalised company's clothes, shoes and accessories. Prices are high, but quality and cutting-edge style are assured.

➕ 198 C3 🖾 Via de' Tornabuoni 73r ☎ 055 264011 ⏰ Mon–Sat 10–7, Sun 2–7

Prada

Prada may have Milanese roots, but Florentines happily patronise the shop of what is currently the most fashionable of all designer labels.

➕ 198 C3 🖾 Via de' Tornabuoni 51–53r ☎ 055 283439; www.prada.it ⏰ Mon 3–7, Tue–Sat 10–7

Pucci

The aristocratic Marchese Emilio Pucci made his name in the 1950s and '60s with his bright and distinctive printed silks. His star waned somewhat until the 1990s, when the same silks again became fashionable. Today, Pucci is the doyen of Florentine designers and is much fêted in the city's fashion circles. In addition to this shop, there is a showroom just north of the Duomo at Via dei Pucci 6.

➕ 198 B3 ⊠ Via de' Tornabuoni 20–22r ☎ 055 294028; www.emiliopucci.com
🕐 Mon 3:30–7:30, Tue–Sat 10–1, 3:30–7:30

DEPARTMENT STORE

COIN

COIN offers the best one-stop shopping in Florence, partly because of its central location and partly because the quality of clothes, linens and other household goods is generally outstanding. Clothes include own-label and designer items, Italian classics for men and women, and younger, more modern fashion items in a dedicated area on the ground floor. Kitchenware can be found in the basement. Open on Sunday – useful if you're in Florence for a long weekend.

➕ 198 C3 ⊠ Via dei Calzaiuoli 56r ☎ 055 280531; www.coin.it
🕐 Mon–Sat 10–8, Sun 11–8

FOOD AND WINE

Pegna

Florentines have been visiting this temple to fine food just south of the Duomo since 1860. Here you can buy cheese, salami, coffee, tea, olive oil, wine, chocolates and other treats from Italy and around the world.

➕ 199 D4 ⊠ Via dello Studio 26r ☎ 055 282701/2; www.pegna.it
🕐 Mon–Tue, Thu–Sat 9–1, 3:30–7:30, Wed 9–1. Closed Sat pm, open Wed pm in summer

Stenio del Panta

This delicatessen just west of the Mercato Centrale has been in business for several generations. It sells a wide range of food, but is best known for its preserved fish (salt cod and tins of sardines, anchovies and the like). You can also buy sandwiches with a filling of your choice.

➕ 198 C4 ⊠ Via Sant' Antonino 49r ☎ 055 216 889 🕐 Mon–Sat 9–7:30, Sun 10–1

HOUSEHOLD GOODS

Bartolini

Founded in 1921, Bartolini has since become such a fixture that locals refer to the shop's street junction as the "angolo Bartolini" ("Bartolini corner"). It sells just about every item of kitchenware you could wish for, as well as fine china, porcelain and glassware from some of the best names worldwide.

➕ 199 D4 ⊠ Via dei Servi 30r ☎ 055 289223; www.dinobartolini.it
🕐 Mon 3:30–7:20, Tue–Sat 9–12:30, 3:30–7:30

La Ménagère

Founded in 1901 and run by the same family since 1921, this shop offers several floors of superb glassware, china, furniture and many other unusual items for the home and office.

➕ 198 C4 ⊠ Via de' Ginori 8r ☎ 055 213875 🕐 Mon 3:30–7:30; Tue–Sat 9–1, 3:30–7:30

Raspini

Raspini offers a range of designer and other clothes, including less expensive "diffusion" lines by the major names in fashion. The main store is in Via Roma, but there are two others, including a children's store.

➕ 196 A1 ⊠ Via Roma 25r ☎ 055 213077 🕐 Mon–Sat 10:30–7:30, Sun 2–7, Dec–Oct (phone for times in Nov)

JEWELLERY

Lapini

This historic shop is a cut above Florence's many jewellers. The stones and metals are of the highest quality, and often have unusual designs (modern and traditional). The shop also sells watches.

➕ 198 C3 ⊠ Borgo San Frediano 50r ☎ 055 213276 🕐 Mon–Fri 3:30–7:30

Torrini

It's hard to argue with the reputation or quality of a jeweller which first registered its trademark – a half clover-leaf with spur – as long ago as 1369. It is still one of the best places in Florence to buy jewellery; gold in particular, though other metals and designs are also available.

🞧 199 D4 ⊠ Piazza del Duomo 10r ☎ 055 2302401 🅖 Mon 3–7:30, Tue–Sat 9:30–1:30, 3–7:30

MARKETS

Mercato Centrale

Florence's vast indoor market is a wonderful place to stock up on picnic provisions or gifts (▶ 71).

🞧 198 C5 ⊠ Piazza del Mercato Centrale 🅖 Mon–Sat 7–2; winter also Sat 4–8

San Lorenzo

The market fills the area outside the church of San Lorenzo, as well as smaller side streets in the vicinity. Many stalls sell similar products – mid-price leather jackets, shoes, ties, handbags, luggage and T-shirts. The quality of the leatherware, coats and jackets in particular, can be good, but with high prices given that this is a market. You may be able to haggle, but be warned that the stallholders here are a pretty hard-nosed bunch.

🞧 198 C4 ⊠ Via dell'Ariento–Piazza di San Lorenzo–Via Canto de' Nelli 🅖 Daily 7 am–8 pm

PAPER AND STATIONERY

Pineider

Pineider is Italy's – and possibly Europe's – ultimate stationers. Founded in 1774, its customers over the years have included Napoleon, Stendhal, Puccini, Lord Byron, Shelley and Maria Callas. All have been beguiled by the exquisite pens, diaries and other associated items – Elizabeth Taylor once ordered blue-violet stationery to match her eyes.

🞧 198 C3 ⊠ Piazza della Signoria 13r ☎ 055 284655; www.pineider.com 🅖 Tue–Sat 10–1:30, 2:30–7:30

PERFUMES AND TOILETRIES

Farmacia di Santa Maria Novella

One of Italy's most famous pharmacies, this wonderful old shop occupies a 13th-century chapel in the Santa Maria Novella complex – complete with frescoes, old pharmacy equipment and wooden cabinets. It was created in 1612 by Dominican monks to sell the elixirs, ointments and other products conjured from their workshops and medicinal gardens. Most of the toiletries are still made along the traditional lines, such as the fine pot-pourris of flowers from the Florentine hills and Aqua di Santa Maria Novella, a toilet water known for its calming properties. All the products are lovingly packaged, making this an excellent place for gifts to take home.

🞧 198 B4 ⊠ Via della Scala 16 ☎ 055 216276; www.smnovella.it 🅖 Mon–Sat 9:30–7:30, Sun 10:30–6:30. Closed public holidays and 2 weeks in Aug

PRINTS AND ENGRAVINGS

Giovanni Baccani

Many stores in Florence sell prints and engravings, but few are quite as alluring as this beautiful old shop founded in 1903. There's a huge selection of framed and unframed prints at prices to suit every budget.

🞧 198 B3 ⊠ Via della Vigna Nuova 75r ☎ 055 214467 🅖 Mon 3:30–7:30, Tue–Sat 9–1, 3:30–7:30

SHOES

Ferragamo

The famous Salvatore Ferragamo was born in Naples and made his name making shoes for Hollywood stars. His descendants still run the company, and this shop also has a top range of clothes and accessories, as well as the most up-to-date collection of beautiful shoes.

🞧 198 C4 ⊠ Via de' Tornabuoni 16r ☎ 055 292123; www.salvatore ferragamo.it 🅖 Mon–Sat 10–7:30

Where to...
Be Entertained

Tickets for many musical and other events in Florence can be obtained from individual box offices or through **Box Office**, a ticket agency with outlets at Via Alamanni 39 (tel: 055 210804) and Chiasso dei Soldanieri 8r, off Via Porta Rossa on the corner with Via de' Tornabuoni (tel: 055 219402; www.boxol.it).

INFORMATION

For details on events and entertainment listings in Florence, ► 48.

CLASSICAL MUSIC

The **Teatro Comunale** (Corso Italia 16; tel: 055 27791) is Florence's main theatre and auditorium, and stages performances of its own and visiting companies. The main season for concerts, opera and ballet runs from January to April and September to December. The Teatro also hosts performances of the annual music festival, Maggio Musicale. Tickets and information from the box office (Tue–Fri 10-4:30, Sat 10–1, tel: 055 213535; www.maggiofiorentino.com). Tickets can also be bought from Box Office (left) or Charta call centre (tel: 199 112 112 in Italy, 0424 600 458 outside Italy).

Tuscany's regional orchestra, the **Orchestra della Toscana** (Via Verdi 5, tel: 055 2340710 or 055 2342722; www.orchestradella toscana.it) usually performs during its main December to May season at the nearby **Teatro Verdi** (Via Ghibellina 99–101; tel: 055 212320; www.teatroverdifirenze.it). Buy tickets from the Teatro Verdi box office or the Box Office agency. Florence's city orchestra, the **Filarmonica di Firenze "Giacchino Rossini"** performs at several venues during its January to February season, but also presents a series of outdoor concerts in the Piazza della Signoria during the summer months. Consult visitor centres for further details (► 41).

The **Orchestra da Camera Fiorentina** (Via Enrico Poggi 6; tel: 055 783374; www.orchafi.it) holds concerts in the church of Orsanmichele (► 72); tickets and information from the above number, from Box Office, or from Orsanmichele. The **Amici della Musica** music association (Via Pier Capponi 41, tel: 055 608420 or 055 607440; www.amicamusica.fi.it) organises concerts at the beautiful Teatro della Pergola, northeast of the Duomo (Via della Pergola 18; tel: 055 226 4316; www.pergola.firenze.it). Built in 1656, it is reputedly Italy's oldest surviving theatre.

Churches such as San Lorenzo and the Duomo also sometimes host concerts – for details check with visitor centres or keep a look out for posters outside the venues.

JAZZ

The informal **Jazz Club** (Via Nuova de'Cacciani 3; tel: 055 247 9700; closed Mon and Jun–Sep) has live jazz most nights; it is located in a side street a block south of Via degli Alfani at the corner of Borgo Pinti. You need to buy "membership" as a formality to enter the club, which is based in a medieval cellar.

NIGHTCLUBS

Meccanò (Viale degli Olmi 1; tel: 055 331371; open Wed, Fri–Sat 11:30 pm– 6 am) in the Casine park is the city's most famous disco. People come from across Tuscany for a night out here, so it's likely to be crowded, though in summer the action spills outdoors: dress is fairly smart and the music is commercial pop. More central dance clubs include the **Blob Club** (Via Vinegia 21r; tel: 055 211209; open daily 6 pm–3 am), just east of the Palazzo Vecchio, with a small dance floor: it is very popular, especially with Florentine students.

In the west of the city, **Space Electronic** (Via Palazzuolo 37; tel: 055 293082; open daily 10 pm–2 am or later) is a vast disco – it claims to be Europe's largest – and good if all you want to do is dance and aren't too bothered by a lack of cutting edge music or style. Much the same can be said about **Yab** (Via Sassetti 5r; tel: 055 215160; open Mon, Wed–Sun 9 pm–4 am; may close Jun–Jul/Aug), which generally pursues a more adventurous music policy than its rivals, but also operates an insidious "card" system whereby admission is usually free, but you have to spend a minimum amount on drinks (recorded on your card): fail to spend enough and you have to pay up before leaving.

You'll hear occasional live jazz at **BZF** (pronounced Bizzeffe), a mixture of bar, restaurant, bookshop, gallery and internet point (Via Panicale 61r, tel: 055 2741009; wwwbzf.it; open Tue–Sat 11 am–midnight, Sun noon–midnight) just north of the Mercato Centrale.

One of the hippest bars and clubs is **Angels** (Via del Proconsolo 29–31; tel: 055 2398762; www.ristoranteangels.it; open daily noon–3 for light lunch, 7 pm–11 pm (bar till 1 am). An American-style bar and chic restaurant, dress up for this stylish place.

BARS

To start or finish the evening quietly, try the **Art Bar** (Via del Moro 4r; tel: 055 287661; open Mon–Thu 7:30 pm–1 am, Fri–Sat 7:30 pm–2 am), a discreet little bar popular with Florentines in search of an early evening cocktail. Across the city, the ever-popular **Rex Café** (Via Fiesolana 23r; tel: 055 248331; open daily 6:30 pm–3 am, mid-May to mid-Sep) is one of the best of the bars in eastern Florence for an early evening drink or a nightcap in the small hours: the interior looks rather alarming – lots of mirrors and strange lamps – but the atmosphere and clientele are easy-going.

At the other extreme are two bars on or just off Piazza di Santa Maria Novella, both of them popular with young foreigners and Italians: **Chequers** (Via della Scala 7–9r; tel: 055 287588; open Mon–Thu 7 pm–11:30 pm or later, Fri–Sat 7 pm–3 am), a raucous English-style pub and the **Fiddler's Elbow** (Piazza di Santa Maria Novella 7r; tel: 055 215056; open Sat 11 am–2 am, Sun–Fri 11 am–1 am), a small, lively "Irish pub".

In the Oltrarno, a bar aimed at the night-time crowd is **Dolce Vita** (Piazza del Carmine 6; tel: 055 284595; open daily 10 am–2 am; Tue–Sun 6 pm–2 am in winter). Forego the often over-slick interior in favour of a table outside on the piazza. The funkier **Cabiria** (Piazza Santo Spirito 4r; tel: 055 215732; open daily 8 am–1:30 am; closed Tue in winter) appeals to a more "alternative" clientele – though it opens in the day, it really comes into its own in the evening. There are tables outside in summer if you want to escape the crush and loud DJ music inside.

For something more refined and with live jazz and other music to boot, visit **Il Caffè** (Piazza de Pitti 9r; tel: 055 239 9863; open daily 11 am until late; closed Mon in winter).

CINEMA

If all you want is a film in English – a rare thing in Florence – then the **Cinema Goldoni** (Via dei Serragli 109, tel: 055 222437) usually has an English-language screening once a week.

Central Tuscany

Getting Your Bearings

Siena is second only to Florence in terms of Tuscan allure. A smaller and prettier medieval city than its rival, it is worth at least two or three days to enjoy fully its many sights – a glorious main square, ornate cathedral, magnificent art gallery and several major museums, not to mention the relaxed charm of its streets, small shops, cafés and restaurants. The appeal of the rest of central Tuscany is largely its landscape: lush hills and valleys, vineyards, farmland and meandering country roads leading to medieval gems such as San Gimignano, Arezzo and Cortona.

Its own beauty aside, Siena also makes a good base for central Tuscany, although accommodation in the city is in short supply and a largely pedestrianised centre can make access by car difficult. This said, it is perfectly placed for excursions to Chianti, a region to the north whose vineyards, villa-topped hills and pretty countryside encapsulate some of the best of Tuscany's patchwork of landscapes. You could also visit the area as part of a drive between Florence and Siena.

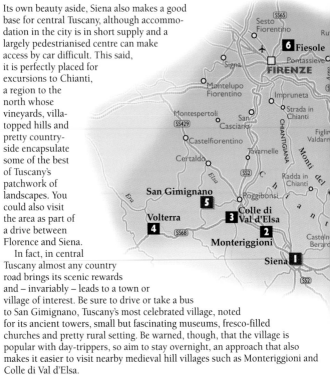

In fact, in central Tuscany almost any country road brings its scenic rewards and – invariably – leads to a town or village of interest. Be sure to drive or take a bus to San Gimignano, Tuscany's most celebrated village, noted for its ancient towers, small but fascinating museums, fresco-filled churches and pretty rural setting. Be warned, though, that the village is popular with day-trippers, so aim to stay overnight, an approach that also makes it easier to visit nearby medieval hill villages such as Monteriggioni and Colle di Val d'Elsa.

The area's other must-see towns, Arezzo and Cortona, are slightly less easy to incorporate into a logical Tuscan tour. Both are worth the detour, however – hilltop Cortona for its views, Arezzo for its famous Renaissance fresco cycle, and both for their well-preserved medieval architecture. Both towns lie some way from other Tuscan centres, but are linked to Siena by relatively good roads.

★ Don't Miss

At Your Leisure

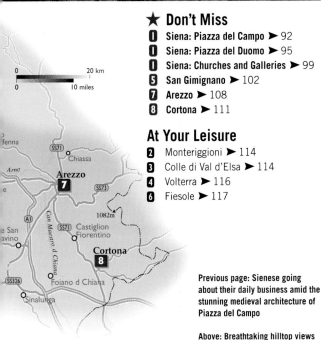

Previous page: Sienese going about their daily business amid the stunning medieval architecture of Piazza del Campo

Above: Breathtaking hilltop views from the town of Cortona

Equally, both could be seen after visiting the Chianti region or as part of a tour of southern Tuscany after Montepulciano (➤ 135). If you need to stay in either town overnight – and at a push you could see both towns in a day from Siena or Florence – Cortona has the better hotels.

A four-day tour of central Tuscany offers a varied itinerary that allows two days in Siena, the region's key city after Florence, a day in San Gimignano, in turn its most celebrated village, and a day in the smaller, art-filled towns of Arezzo and Cortona.

Central Tuscany in Four Days

Day One

Morning
Siena is Tuscany's most perfect medieval city. Start in the ❚**Piazza del Campo**, Italy's most majestic medieval square (➤ 92 below), followed by the art-filled Museo Civico (➤ 93).

Spend the rest of the morning shopping on Via di Città and other streets around the Campo.

Lunch
The Antica Trattoria Papei (➤ 123) is ideal for a good-value lunch.

Afternoon
Walk to ❚**Piazza del Duomo** (➤ 95) to see the cathedral, Baptistery, Santa Maria della Scala and Museo dell'Opera del Duomo (Buoninsegna's Maestà: Flight into Egypt, right).

Day Two

Morning
Devote the morning to the ❚**Pinacoteca Nazionale** (➤ 99). For lunch, try Le Logge or Le Al Marsili (➤ 123).

Afternoon
Leave time to see some of the less well-known ❚**churches**, especially Santa Maria dei Servi (➤ 101), and to soak up the atmosphere of the medieval streets.

Day Three

Morning
From Siena or Chianti make for **5 San Gimignano** (➤ 102), if possible
stopping off en route to spend an hour or two in **2 Monteriggioni** (➤ 114),
a perfectly preserved fortified hamlet, and in **3 Colle di Val d'Elsa** (➤ 114),
an attractive but little-visited hill town (above).

Lunch
Lunch at the Osteria del Cacere near Piazza della Cisterna (➤ 122).

Afternoon
Allow the rest of the day to see San Gimignano, where you should also
spend the night (➤ 119).

Day Four

Morning
Take the 85km (53-mile) drive east to **7 Arezzo** (➤ 108), where two hours
should be long enough to see Piero della Francesca's fresco cycle and
explore the town's captivating medieval centre.

Lunch
Try La Torrre di Gnicche for
a light meal (➤ 121).

Afternoon
Drive south to **8 Cortona** (➤ 111) to
wander in the old centre. Then visit
the town's museums (Fra Angelico's
The Annunciation, right, is in the
Museo Diocesano). Stay overnight or
drive to **Montalcino** (➤ 138) to
continue your tour of Tuscany.

Siena: Piazza del Campo

Hilltop Siena is built on three ridges, each of which corresponds roughly to a *Terzo* or "third", one of three districts into which the medieval city was divided. Close to the point where the three ridges meet stands Siena's breathtaking Piazza del Campo (or just Campo), Europe's greatest medieval square and the city's social and civic heart.

The location of the Campo was determined as much by politics as geography, for within the *terzi* were – and still are – a number of smaller districts (*contrade*). These medieval parishes commanded and continue to command fierce loyalties among their inhabitants. To avoid conflict, Siena's medieval rulers chose as the centre of the city an area that fell outside the domain of any single *contrada*, while at the same time allowing the square to be used as the stage for the Palio, a race in which the contrade's ancient rivalries are still played out (► 26).

   Not that you have to be present on race day to enjoy the Campo. The distinctive scallop-shaped arena and encircling ring of **medieval palaces** is magnificent at any time. Enjoy it first from one of the many cafés on its margins – prices are high, but the view is worth it – and then head for its chief sight, the vast Palazzo Pubblico.

The Campo's medieval palaces have a distinctive curved shape

   This palace has served as Siena's main council building for many centuries, but today also houses two important sights: the **Torre del Mangia** (1338–48), a 102m (334-foot) tower on

The city views from Torre del Mangia are as striking as the structure itself

Piazza del Campo is the place to see and be seen in Siena

its eastern side, and the **Museo Civico**, which occupies the palace's upper floors. You can climb the tower's 388 steps for staggering views, but visit the museum first so that you're fresh for its star attractions.

You enter the museum to the right off a small inner courtyard – the tower entrance is to the left – having passed the Gothic **Cappella di Piazza** (1352–1468), a distinctive arched "porch" at the base of the tower, begun by the city in 1352 to mark the passing of the Black Death four years earlier. The museum's first few rooms are unremarkable, but you soon enter a succession of salons and chambers crammed with frescoes and other works of art. The most beautiful is the **Sala del Mappamondo**, which contains two sensational paintings: on the left (with your back to the entrance) is a *Maestà* (1315), or "Madonna Enthroned", by Simone Martini, one of the greatest of the Sienese School of painters; on the opposite wall is the courtly *Equestrian Portrait of Guidoriccio da Fogliano*, which for years was also attributed to Martini but is now the subject of a controversial attribution debate among scholars. No controversy surrounds the adjoining room, the **Sala della Pace**, which

features one of Europe's finest early medieval secular fresco cycles, Ambrogio Lorenzetti's *Allegories of Good and Bad Government* (1338). The work illustrates the effects of good and bad civic rule on a city clearly modelled on Siena.

A portrait of Guidoriccio da Fogliano in the Museo Civico, attributed (controversially) to Simone Martini

TAKING A BREAK

The Piazza del Campo is lined with **cafés** and **bars** with outside tables. For a good lookout try the **Bar-Gelateria La Costerella** (no sign) at Via di Città 33 on the junction with Costa dei Barbieri and Via di Fontebranda. If you're lucky, you'll be able to sit on one of two "secret" benches overlooking the Campo.

Museo Civico
✚ 201 D3 ✉ Piazza del Campo ☎ 0577 292263; www.comune.siena.it/ museocivico ⏱ Daily 10–5:30, 7 Jan–Feb, Nov 26–22 Dec; 10–6:30, Nov 1–25, 23 Dec–6 Jan; 10–7, 16 Mar–31 Oct ✋ Expensive. Joint ticket with the Torre del Mangia available

Torre del Mangia
✚ 201 D3 ✉ Piazza del Campo ☎ 0577 292263 ⏱ Daily 10–6:15 or 7, mid-Mar to Oct; 10–4, Nov to mid-Mar. Some late opening Jul–Aug (11 pm) ✋ Moderate

---

PIAZZA DEL CAMPO: INSIDE INFO

Top tips **Parking** is difficult in central Siena, where most of the roads are closed to traffic. Use peripheral car parks and walk or catch a bus to the centre.

• Siena's **historic centre** is small and easily explored on foot. You should only need to use buses or taxis if you have travelled to the city by train. The station is about 2km (1.2 miles) from the Campo, an unpleasant uphill walk, but buses for the centre leave from the far side of the station forecourt. Tickets and information are available from a bus ticket office in the station ticket hall.

• Siena is built on a series of hills and its medieval streets are unsurprisingly uneven, so wear **comfortable shoes** for exploring the city on foot.

❶

Siena: Piazza del Duomo

Piazza del Duomo cannot rival the Campo for scale or spectacle, but in the cathedral (Duomo), the Museo dell'Opera del Duomo and the Santa Maria della Scala complex it has three of the city's most interesting and beautiful buildings together, with the cream of its many artistic treasures.

Siena began life as an Etruscan settlement and then became a Roman colony, Saena Julia. Little remains of the Roman city, though the site of the present cathedral, close to the city's highest point, was almost certainly the site of a Roman temple to Minerva. Work on the cathedral began in about 1179 and was largely completed by 1296, but in 1339 Siena's considerable medieval wealth – the result of banking and mercantile prowess – led the city to start a rebuilding project that would have made the church the largest in Europe. The Black Death of 1348, which brought economic ruin to the city, marked the end of the scheme, though you can still clearly see parts of the "new" building in the area to the right (east) of the cathedral.

The cathedral's magnificent **façade** was largely overseen by the sculptor Giovanni Pisano, and stands out even in a region where the cathedrals of Florence, Pisa and Lucca are some of the most striking in Italy. The splendour continues **inside**, starting with the floor, which consists of 56 *graffito* (incised) marble panels designed by 40 of Siena's finest artists between 1369 and 1547. Above, the many sculpted heads around the nave represent 172 popes and 36 Holy Roman Emperors.

The striped marble decoration of Siena's Duomo is a key feature of Pisan-Romanesque architecture

At the top of the left (north) side of the nave is the entrance to the **Libreria Piccolomini** (library), decorated with glorious frescoes portraying *Scenes from the Life of Pope Pius II* (1502–9) by Umbrian artist Pinturicchio. Pius, otherwise known as Enea Silvio Piccolomini, was born in Pienza (► 132). To the left of the Libreria's entrance is the sculpted *Altre Piccolomini* (1501–4), four statues of which – saints Gregory and Paul on the right, Peter and Pius on the left – are by the young Michelangelo.

Beyond the Libreria on the same side of the church is the cathedral's unmissable carved **pulpit** (1266–8), the work of Nicola Pisano and one of the greatest pieces of Italian medieval sculpture. In the left corner of the north transept, the **Cappella di San Giovanni Battista** contains more frescoes (1504) by Pinturicchio and a statue of John the Baptist (1457) by Donatello.

You can see more work by Donatello to the rear of the cathedral in the half-hidden **Battistero di San Giovanni** (Baptistery). The Baptistery's font (1417–30) includes fine bronze panels by Donatello, Lorenzo Ghiberti – Florentines both – and the leading Sienese sculptor of his day, Jacopo della Quercia. There is also an array of 15th-century frescoes by Vecchietta.

Santa Maria della Scala

The unexceptional looking building opposite the cathedral was Siena's main hospital for almost 1,000 years, until it closed as a medical centre in the 1990s. Today, its medieval interior, with entire 15th-century fresco cycles and other works of art, is open to the public. It was founded in the 11th century to offer rest and hospitality to pilgrims. Later it served many charitable functions, including looking after the city's orphans. Bequests made to the hospital enabled it to fund works of art.

Frescoes and bronze panels in the cathedral Baptistery's font

Statuary and medieval art in the Sala delle Statue in the Museo dell'Opera del Duomo

The most impressive of these is found in the **Sala del Pellegrinaio**, covered in a fresco cycle (1440) by Vecchietta, Domenico di Bartolo and other Sienese artists portraying aspects of the hospital's history. In the Sagrestia Vecchia is another fresco cycle by Vecchietta illustrating the *Articles of the Creed* (1446–9) and an altarpiece of the *Madonna della Misericordia* (1444) by Domenico di Bartolo.

Museo dell'Opera del Duomo

The first major room of this fine museum is the **Sala delle Statue**, where the walls are dotted with sculpted figures (1284–96) by Giovanni Pisano, removed from the cathedral façade. The room's masterpieces, however, are an ethereal relief of the *Madonna and Child* (1456–9) by Donatello (from one of the cathedral's doors) and a second relief of the *Madonna and Child with St Giralmo* (c1430–5) by Jacopo della Quercia.

On the first floor, La Sala di Duccio is dominated by Duccio's vast *Maestà* (1308–11), one of the greatest Italian medieval paintings, painted on two sides and with 45 minor panels.

TAKING A BREAK

The **Taverna del Capitano**, just off Piazza del Duomo (Via del Capitano 8, tel: 0577 288094), makes a good place for lunch.

PIAZZA DEL DUOMO: INSIDE INFO

Top tips You can **save money on admission** to several sights by purchasing one of three combined tickets, valid for two to seven days giving entry to a variety of sights including the Libreria Piccolomini, Baptistery, Museo dell'Opera del Duomo, Oratorio di San Bernardino, Museo Diocesano and church of Sant' Agostino.

• Don't miss the **lovely view** of Siena and the surrounding countryside from the exterior terrace of the Museo dell'Opera del Duomo.

Duccio's 14th-century *Maestà* in the Sala di Duccio, Museo dell'Opera del Duomo

Duomo
✚ 200 C2 ✉ Piazza del Duomo ☎ 0577 238048 🕓 Mon–Sat
10:30–7:30, Mar–late Aug; daily 9:30–7:30, late Aug–late Oct; Mon–Sat
10:30–6:30, Sun and public holidays 1:30–6:30, rest of year
💰 Inexpensive (includes Liberia Piccolomini); moderate late Aug–late Oct

Libreria Piccolomini
✚ 200 C3 ✉ Piazza del Duomo ☎ 0577 238048 🕓 Hours as for Duomo
💰 Inexpensive

Battistero di San Giovanni
✚ 200 C3 ✉ Piazza San Giovanni ☎ 0577 238048 🕓 Daily 9–7:30,
Mar–May, Sep–Oct; 9–7:30, Jun–Aug; 10–1, 2–5, rest of year 💰 Inexpensive

Santa Maria della Scala
✚ 200 C2 ✉ Piazza del Duomo 2 ☎ 0577 224811 🕓 Daily 10:30–6:30,
mid-Mar to Oct; 10:30–4:30, Nov to mid-Mar 💰 Moderate

Museo dell'Opera del Duomo
✚ 202 C2 ✉ Piazza del Duomo 8 ☎ 0577 283 048 🕓 Daily 9–7:30,
mid-Mar to Sep; 9–6, Oct; 9–1:30, Oct to mid-Mar 💰 Moderate

Siena: Churches and Galleries

In visiting the Museo Civico (► 93), cathedral (► 95), Ospedale (► 96) and Museo dell'Opera (► 97) you will already have seen many captivating paintings. The best collection of Sienese art, however, and the one that best enables you to follow the development of the city's distinctive school of painters, including Sassetta and Vecchietta, is housed in the city's main art gallery, the Pinacoteca Nazionale.

Pinacoteca Nazionale

Early Sienese painting owed much to Byzantine art, which was characterised by lavish use of gold backgrounds and a stylised portrayal of the Madonna and Child. Early local masters in this tradition, all of whom are represented in the gallery, were Guido da Siena, Duccio, Simone Martini and Pietro and Ambrogio Lorenzetti, brothers who died during the plague of 1348.

Later Sienese artists remained wedded to their Byzantine roots, only slowly adopting the Renaissance innovations of their Florentine rivals. The first 15th-century painters to master the new approach were Sassetta and Vecchietta, but plenty of others – notably Sano di Pietro, Giovanni di Paolo and Matteo di Giovanni – remained loyal to the old conventions.

By the 16th century, Sienese art had largely had its day, with the notable exception of Domenico Beccafumi, a Mannerist artist, and Sodoma, best known for his frescoes at Monte Oliveto Maggiore (► 130).

The lofty nave of the church of San Domenico, dedicated to Siena's patron saint, St Catherine

Churches

Many of Siena's churches can be visited as you stroll between the major sights, and those that can't – notably Santa Maria dei Servi and San Francesco – are only a few minutes' walk from the city centre (➤ 178).

The colossal brick outline of the Gothic 13th-century **San Domenico** (Piazza San Domenico) dominates the city's northern skyline. The church has strong associations with Siena-born

Christ's Crucifixion in *The Descent from the Cross* by Sodoma in the church of San Francesco

St Catherine, patron saint of the city, and with St Francis of Assisi, of Italy. The Cappella di Santa Caterina midway down the right (south) aisle has a marble tabernacle containing part of her skull and frescoes (1526) by Sodoma of episodes from her life.

The less alluring church of **San Francesco** (Piazza San Francesco) has a few patches of fresco by Sassetta and Pietro and Ambrogio Lorenzetti, but the church is worth visiting more for the separate Oratorio di San Bernardino. Inside, its beautiful upstairs chamber is distinguished by Sodoma and Beccafumi's frescoes on the *Life of the Virgin* (1496–1518).

The church of Santa Maria dei Servi lies close to Siena's old city walls

Santa Maria dei Servi (Via dei Servi), a 10-minute walk from the Campo, has several works of art and superb views of the city. The first altar on the right aisle contains a painting of the Madonna by Coppo da Marcovaldo (born 1225), a Florentine artist captured in battle by the Sienese and obliged to paint this picture as part of his ransom. There are also two grisly paintings of the Massacre of the Innocents: one by Matteo di Giovanni (1491); the other, painted 150 years earlier by Pietro Lorenzetti, in the second chapel to the right of the high altar.

Pinacoteca Nazionale
✚ 200 C2 ✉ Palazzo Buonsignori, Via San Pietro 29 ☎ 0577 281161
🕐 Mon 8:30–1:30, Tue–Sat 8:15–7:15, Sun 8:30–1:15 💶 Moderate

Oratorio di San Bernardino
✚ 201 E4 ✉ Piazza San Francesco ☎ 0577 283048 🕐 Mon–Sat 10:30–1:30, 3–5:30, mid-Mar to Oct; rest of year by request 💶 Inexpensive

SIENA'S CHURCHES AND GALLERIES: INSIDE INFO

Top tips Remember that **most churches** close for two or three hours in the middle of the day, usually from noon.
● It is sometimes possible to visit the individual small churches and museums of Siena's *contrade*. Enquire at the tourist office for details (➤ 41).
● The seven-day **"Siena Itinerari d'Arte"** pass (moderate) gives admission to the Museo Civico, Museo dell'Opera del Duomo, Baptistery, Ospedale di Santa Maria della Scala, Sant'Agostino, Oratorio di San Bernardino, Libreria Piccolomini and Palazzo delle Papesse (a gallery of modern art). Available from individual sights.

In more depth The **Palazzo Piccolomini** (Banchi di Sotto 52, tel: 0577 247145, guided visits Mon–Fri at 9:30 am, 10:30 am and 11:30 am, free) is almost unknown to most tourists, but worth a visit to see the city's archives (the oldest document dates from AD 736) and the fascinating Tavolette di Biccherna, painted wooden panels once used as covers for documents. Climb the steps from the palace's courtyard to the top floor where you will be met by a guide.

5

San Gimignano

San Gimignano is the very picture of a medieval Italian village, thanks to its crop of ancient towers – the village famously resembles a "medieval Manhattan" – and to its unspoiled streets and beautiful hilltop setting. Appearances aside, it also boasts a superb art gallery, far-reaching views and two lovely fresco-swathed churches.

The Central Squares

The best way to see the village is to start close to its southern gateway, the **Porta San Giovanni**, then walk up its main street, Via San Giovanni, to its pair of linked central squares: Piazza della Cisterna and Piazza del Duomo. The village is tiny – around 750m (half a mile) from end to end – and everything worth seeing is within easy walking distance.

A short distance up Via San Giovanni on the right you come to **San Francesco**, a deconsecrated 13th-century church that is now a food and wine shop aimed at visitors. Whether or not you want to browse, walk through to the terrace at the rear, from where there are glorious views over the countryside.

At the top of Via San Giovanni you come to the **Arco dei Becci**, a medieval arch that stands in the village's original set of walls – a second outer set of walls, incorporating the **Porta San**

The Torre Grossa offers a bird's-eye view of San Gimignano and its surrounding countryside

Giovanni, was added in the 13th century as the village grew in size. The arch opens into Piazza della Cisterna, which takes its name from the medieval well (*cisterna*) at its heart. Two of the town's major hotels are here (▶ 119), along with several good cafés and *gelaterie* (ice-cream parlours).

Adjoining the square to the north is **Piazza del Duomo**, home to the best of the village's historic sights. On its western flank stands the **Collegiata**, which served as San Gimignano's cathedral until the village lost its status as a bishopric. To its left rises the **Palazzo del Popolo** (1288), which houses the tourist office (▶ 105) and the Museo Civico.

San Gimignano's ancient towers have earned it the title of "medieval Manhattan"

Collegiata

The Collegiata probably dates from around 1056, but was altered in 1239 and then remodelled further by the architect and sculptor Giuliano da Maiano between 1460 and 1468. Little on its rather plain façade prepares you for the interior, which is almost completely covered in eye-catching frescoes. These divide into three main cycles. The rear (entrance) wall has a *Last Judgement* (1410) by the Sienese painter Taddeo di Bartolo, with *Inferno* and *Paradiso* painted on protruding walls to the left and right. Between these walls is a fresco by Benozzo Gozzoli of St Sebastian (1465), a saint often invoked during plague epidemics – one such epidemic had ravaged San Gimignano a year before the painting was commissioned.

The **second cycle** (*c*1333) on the right (south) wall is the work of either Lippo Memmi or Barna da Siena, both Sienese painters. The three tiers of paintings, some of which are damaged, portray episodes from the *New Testament*. The **cycle** (1356–67) on the opposite wall is the work of another Sienese artist, Bartolo di Fredi. Here the scenes portrayed are from the *Old Testament*, with episodes from the story of Creation depicted in the lunettes above the main wall.

Elsewhere in the church are two more artistic treasures: the **Cappella di San Gimignano** (left of the high altar), graced by an altar carved by Benedetto da Maiano (brother of Giuliano), and the **Cappella di Santa Fina**, a chapel on the right (south) side of the nave, with a lovely altar, marble shrine and bas-reliefs (1475) also by Benedetto da Maiano, and two frescoes on the life of Santa Fina, a local 13th-century saint, by the Florentine painter Domenico Ghirlandaio.

The 13th-century well at the centre of Piazza della Cisterna

Fresco cycles in the Collegiata

Museo Civico

After the Collegiata, turn your attention to the Museo Civico, which, as well as housing the town's main museum, also gives access to the **Torre Grossa** (begun 1300), the only tower in the village open to the public. San Gimignano's towers were built by local nobles for defensive purposes and as status symbols. Most Italian towns and villages once had similar towers. The reason so many survived here is a result of the 1348 Black Death, which so devastated the village that it was forced to abandon its independence and put itself under the protection of Florence. Thereafter, the power of the nobles was gone and their towers, which no longer offered a threat, could remain standing.

The museum is ranged across two floors, and opens with the **Sala del Consiglio**, or Sala di Dante, so called because it was here that Dante, then a Florentine diplomat, met members of San Gimignano's council to enlist their support. The room is dominated by a painting of the *Maestà* (1317) or "Madonna Enthroned", by Lippo Memmi, a permanent fixture, unlike other displays on this floor which are often temporary.

The core of the museum lies in four rooms on the **second floor**, filled with paintings by Florentine, Umbrian and Sienese artists such as Filippino Lippi, Pinturicchio and Coppo da Marcovaldo (▶ 101). Some of the most appealing paintings, however, are by less well-known painters, notably those detailing the lives of saints such as St Gimignano (by Taddeo di Bartolo) and St Bartholomew and St Fina (both by Lorenzo di Niccolò). Don't miss the **14th-century works** by Memmo di Filipuccio in the room on the left at the top of the stairs from the Sala del Consiglio – three wedding scenes include panels where a young couple cavort in bed and in a bath.

Church of Sant'Agostino

From Piazza del Duomo you should walk north towards the church of Sant'Agostino, either on Via San Matteo or on smaller side streets such as Via delle Romite. If you take the former route, notice **San Bartolo**, a pretty 13th-century Romanesque church on the right. Churches built by the Augustinian order (Agostini) are, as here, often near the edge of towns or villages – they were among the last of the main religious orders to build churches so the most central sites had already been occupied.

Sant'Agostino is best known for a 17-panel **fresco cycle** around the main altar on the *Life of St Augustine* (1464–5), the work of Benozzo Gozzoli. As in Florence's Cappella dei Magi (► 71), Gozzoli's work here is notable for its lovely incidental detail and vignettes of 15th-century life. The striking painting on the high altar is by Piero del Pollaiuolo and portrays the *Coronation of the Virgin* (1483), just one of several charming paintings around the walls by Florentine and Sienese artists.

The church's second major work, however, is a piece of sculpture: the **Cappella di San Bartolo**, a funerary monument immediately on the left as you enter. It contains the tomb of St Bartolo, a local 13th-century saint, and includes three reliefs (1495) of scenes from his life by Benedetto da Maiano.

Gozzoli's depiction of St Augustine as a boy in the church of Sant'Agostino

SAN GIMIGNANO: INSIDE INFO

Top tips San Gimignano becomes crowded with **day-trippers** from Florence or Siena between Easter and October. To enjoy the village at its best, stay overnight.
• A **combined ticket** is available to the Museo Civico, Torre Grossa, Cappella di Santa Fina, Museo Ornitologico, Museo Archeologico and Museo d'Arte Sacra. Details from the tourist office (tel: 0577 940008).
• If you visit by car, do not attempt to park within the village walls. There is a large **car-park** south of the village off Via Roma, a short walk from Porta San Giovanni. Other smaller car parks lie off the road which runs round the outside of the village walls. Note that San Gimignano becomes extremely crowded in summer.

Museums and Medieval Streets

Be sure to delve into some of the quieter corners. From Sant'Agostino, walk east on Via Folgore da San Gimignano to look at **San Iacopo**, a 13th-century church reputedly founded by the Knights Templar. From here, walk south to see another 13th-century church, **San Lorenzo in Ponte** (Via Santo Stefano). West of Piazza della Cisterna and Piazza del Duomo you should wander to the **Rocca** (1353), a ruined castle at the heart of a quiet public park. You may also wish to visit the **Museo d'Arte Sacra**, a museum of religious art and archaeological exhibits, and the **Museo Ornitologico**, a collection of stuffed birds. The village also has a small Museo Archeologico-Galleria d'Arte Moderna at Via Folgore 11 (open daily 11–6:30, inexpensive).

TAKING A BREAK

A good place for lunch is the **Osteria del Carcere** (➤ 122). For something slightly more expensive try **Dorandò** (➤ 122).

Collegiata and Cappella di Santa Fina
➕ 204 B3 ✉ Piazza del Duomo ☎ 0577 940008 🕐 Mon–Sat 9:30–4:30, Sun 12:30–4:40, Mar, Nov–Jan; Mon–Fri 9:30–7:10, Sat 9:30–5:30, Sun 12:30–5:30, Apr–Oct. Feb: religious services only 🎫 Moderate

Museo Civico and Torre Grossa
➕ 204 B3 ✉ Palazzo del Popolo, Piazza del Duomo ☎ 0577 990348 🕐 Daily 9:30–7:30, Mar–Oct; 10–5:30, Nov–Feb 🎫 Moderate. Combined ticket to musuem, tower and Palazzo Comunale: expensive

Sant' Agostino
➕ 204 A4 ✉ Piazza Sant'Agostino ☎ No phone 🕐 Daily 7–noon, 3–7, Apr–Oct; 7:30–noon, 3–6, Nov–Mar 🎫 Free

Museo d'Arte Sacra
➕ 204 B3 ✉ Piazza Pecori ☎ 0577 940008 🕐 Daily 9:30–7:30, Apr–Oct; 9:30–5, Nov to mid-Jan and Mar. Closed late Jan–Feb 🎫 Moderate

Museo Ornitologico
➕ 204 A3 ✉ Via Quercecchio ☎ 0577 941388 🕐 Daily 11–6, Apr–Sep; Jan–Mar and Oct–Dec may remain closed 🎫 Inexpensive

❼

Arezzo

Arezzo is best known for a fresco cycle by Piero della Francesca, but the importance of this Renaissance master-piece often overshadows the town's historic centre, an evocative medley of churches, squares, medieval streets and small museums that is as alluring as any in Tuscany.

Arezzo was first an Etruscan and then a Roman centre of some importance, and continued to thrive during the Middle Ages, when its position on vital trade routes across the Apennine mountains brought it great prosperity. Among other things, it developed as a major goldware and jewellery centre – industries that still thrive today – though the town suffered for its economic and strategic prominence when it was bombed during World War II. As a result, much of the town's outskirts are modern and unprepossessing, making the almost pristine medieval enclave at its heart all the more delightful.

Arezzo's impressive medieval Piazza Grande, with the apse of Santa Maria della Pieve on the left

The Legend of the True Cross

Much of this enclave can wait, however, until you have paid homage to **Piero della Francesca's fresco cycle** in San Francesco, an otherwise unremarkable 14th-century Gothic church. The cycle, which is painted on the walls around the high altar, portrays the *Legend of the True Cross* (1453–66), a complicated story which derived from the *Legenda Aurea* (Golden Legend), a 13th-century compendium of apocryphal tales. In essence, the paintings follow the history of the cross on which Christ was crucified, tracing the wood from the tree which grew from Adam's grave through to its use during the Crucifixion and subsequent burial and rediscovery by Helena, mother of the Roman Emperor Constantine. But while Piero della Francesca pays heed to his story's narrative, he was also particularly

concerned to explore the artistic possibilities of symmetry, space and perspective. This is one reason for the mysterious, almost unsettling quality of his paintings, and one reason why the narrative of the cycle does not follow the chronological narrative of his story. You'll notice, for example, that Piero paints two major battle scenes so that they face each other symmetrically – the large lower panels on the right and left walls.

Churches, Palaces and Gardens

After seeing the frescoes, walk the short distance to Arezzo's main central square, the steeply sloping **Piazza Grande**, filled with an eclectic mixture of buildings from different eras. The square is dominated on the left (west) side by the semicircular and arched apse of **Santa Maria della Pieve**, a fine 12th-century Romanesque church whose entrance lies around the corner on Corso Italia. Take a moment to look inside, for the interior boasts an important high altarpiece of the *Madonna and Saints* (1320) by the Sienese artist Pietro Lorenzetti. In the square's northwest corner stands the **Fraternità dei Laici**, a 15th-century palace celebrated for its Gothic door and its beautiful lunette sculptures (1434) by Bernardo Rossellino. At the top (north) side of the piazza is the **Palazzo delle Logge** (1573), dominated by a loggia designed by Giorgio Vasari, a noted painter, architect and art historian who was born in Arezzo. His former home, the **Casa Vasari** near San Domenico (► 110), is worth a quick visit to admire its beautifully decorated rooms.

A scene from Piero della Francesca's Legend of the True Cross *in the church of San Francesco*

Continue north from Piazza Grande on Corso Italia and, in a side street to the left, you'll pass a house at 28 Via dell'Orto, reputed to have been the **birthplace** of another eminent Arezzo citizen, the poet and scholar **Petrarch**. Continuing north, you

AREZZO: INSIDE INFO

Top tips Park close to the railway station or in other paying car parks **outside the town walls**. It is a 400m (quarter-mile) walk to San Francesco from the station.
● Arezzo is one of the best places in Tuscany to buy **gold jewellery**. Consult the tourist office for details of shops, workshops or factory outlets.
● You must **book ahead** to see the San Francesco frescoes (tel: 0575 352727; www.apt.arezzo.it; open Mon–Fri 9–7, Sat–Sun 9–5:30, closes at 5pm Nov–May). Visits last 30 minutes and are limited to groups of 25.

Petrarch, acclaimed poet and native son of Arezzo

come to the town's **Duomo**, whose interior has a handful of treasures: a small fresco of *Mary Magdalene* by Piero della Francesca (north aisle), the adjacent Tomb of Guido Tarlati (1330), some accomplished stained glass (1523) and sculpture (1334) and 15th-century frescoes by unknown artists in the Cappella Tarlati (last chapel off the south wall before the altar).

To the east of the Duomo stretches the Passeggio del Prato, an attractive area of parkland crowned by the **Fortezzo Medicea** (1538–60), a pentagonal castle built by the town's Medici rulers (the town fell to Florence in 1384). In the other direction, west of the Duomo, the Gothic **church of San Domenico** (begun in 1275) has a rare altarpiece (*c*1260) by Cimabue, the teacher of Giotto. To its south in Via Garibaldi stands **Santissima Annunziata**, a church that was extensively remodelled after 1460 following the miraculous tears wept by a statue of the Virgin Mary in the oratory that previously occupied the site. The museum almost on its doorstep, the **Museo d'Arte Medioevale e Moderna** (Via San Lorentino 8), has a disappointing collection of artefacts from a variety of eras, although there is fine majolica and terracotta pottery.

TAKING A BREAK

The **Caffè dei Costantini** just outside San Francesco is a good place for lunch, and the Passeggio del Prato has good picnic possibilities.

San Francesco
✚ 197 E3 ✉ Piazza San Francesco ☎ 0575 900404 🕐 Mon–Fri 9–6:30, Sat 9–5:30, Sun 1–5:30, Apr–Oct; Mon 9–5:30, Sat 9–5, Sun 1–5, Nov–Mar 💰 Church: free; Frescoes: expensive

Pieve di Santa Maria
✚ 197 E3 ✉ Corso Italia ☎ 0575 22629 🕐 Daily 8–1, 3–7:30 💰 Free

Casa di Vasari
✚ 197 E3 ✉ Via XX Settembre 55 ☎ 0575 409040 🕐 Mon and Wed–Sat 8:30–7, Sun 8:30–1 💰 Inexpensive

8

Cortona

Cortona's chief beauties are its magnificent views – its hilltop site provides a vast panorama over swathes of Tuscany and Umbria – and its picture-perfect medieval streets, as well as a handful of small churches and galleries which contain treasures out of all proportion to the town's modest size.

If you are journeying to Cortona by car, the chances are you will approach the town from Camucia on the N71, which passes **Santa Maria del Calcinaio**, an unmissable Renaissance church around 2.5km (1.5 miles) from the town's walls. It was begun in 1485 and its Greek Cross plan is strikingly similar to the church of San Biagio outside Montepulciano (► 135). The church takes its name from a lime-burner (*calcinaio*) who discovered a miraculous image of the Virgin Mary on the site. The church makes a pleasing introduction to the town.

Museums

Once inside the walls, the town centres on Piazza della Repubblica. From here, a short stroll to the northwest through Piazza Signorelli brings you to Piazza del Duomo. This is the setting for an unremarkable cathedral but a memorable gallery, the **Museo Diocesano**. The highlights are two masterpieces by Fra Angelico, who spent two years as a monk in the town's Dominican monastery. Angelico's paintings, an *Annunciation* and *Madonna and Child with Saints* (1428–30), share the gallery with paintings which would shine in any other company, notably works by Sassetta, Bartolomeo della Gatta and the Cortona-born Luca Signorelli. Don't miss the archaeological

Cortona's residents still live in preserved medieval homes

star turn, a 2nd-century Roman **sarcophagus** carved with scenes representing Dionysus battling with the Amazons, a work much admired by the Renaissance sculptors Donatello and Filippo Brunelleschi.

Cortona's second major gallery, the **Museo dell'Accademia Etrusca**, is devoted largely to the Etruscan civilisation – the town, which is considered one of the oldest in Tuscany, is thought to have been founded by the Etruscans in the 8th century BC. Exhibits include a huge 5th-century BC bronze lamp, the Lampadario Etrusco, some exquisite Etruscan jewellery, urns and vases, the contents of a partially reconstructed Etruscan tomb, an eclectic range of silverware, medieval paintings, Renaissance medallions and an impressive, if incongruous, collection of ancient Egyptian artefacts.

Fortress and Churches

From the museum the only way is up, particularly if you want to enjoy the best of Cortona's views and the attractive tangle of streets in the town's northern quarters. Prepare yourself for the climb to the **Fortezza Medicea**, a ruined fortress built on the orders of Cosimo I de' Medici in 1556. Views from here are breathtaking, and on a clear day include the hazy outline of Lake Trasimeno in neighbouring Umbria, one of Italy's largest lakes. Among the jumbled walls are remnants of the town's old Roman and Etruscan ramparts. Just below the fortress stands **Santa Margherita** (rebuilt in 1856), a large sanctuary that houses the tomb (1362) of St Margaret of Cortona, the town's much-revered patron saint.

Heading back down to the rest of the town, plan your route so that it takes you past **San Cristoforo**, a little Romanesque chapel off Piazza della Pescaia, and to **San Nicolò** on Via San Nicolò. The former is usually closed to the public but pretty to look at from outside, while a custodian should be on hand at the latter to show you a double-sided high altarpiece by Luca Signorelli. Another church worth seeking out is **San Domenico**, which features a faded exterior fresco by Fra Angelico (above the main door) and compelling works by Luca Signorelli, Bartolomeo della Gatta and Lorenzo di Niccolò Gerini.

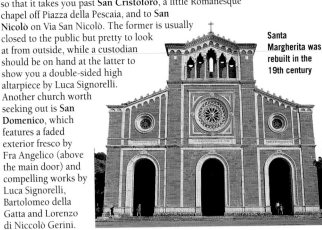

Santa Margherita was rebuilt in the 19th century

Santa Maria del Calcinaio, on the slopes below Cortona

Behind San Dominico stretch Cortona's principal public gardens, where you can begin the **Passeggiata in Piano**, a gentle 1km (0.5-mile) promenade that offers great views.

TAKING A BREAK

La Locanda del Loggiato (➤ 122) does good light lunches, or try **Tonino** for great views and an Italian atmosphere (➤ 122).

Museo Diocesano
⊕ 197 E3 ✉ Piazza del Duomo 1 ☎ 0575 62830; www.aioncultura.org
🕔 Daily 10–7, Apr–Sep; Tue–Sun 10–6, Nov–Mar 💲 Expensive

Museo dell'Accademia Etrusca
⊕ 197 E3 ✉ Piazza Signorelli 19 ☎ 0575 630415; www.accademia-etrusca.net 🕔 Tue–Sun 10–7, Apr–Oct; Tue–Sun 10–6, Nov–Mar
💲 Moderate

CORTONA: INSIDE INFO

Top tip Don't try to **park** in the centre of Cortona. Head instead for the car-parks around the town walls, aiming to park close to one of the gateways – Porta Santa Maria, Porta Colonia or Porta Sant'Agostino – that lead to Piazza della Repubblica and the town centre.

At Your Leisure

were added between 1213 and 1219, but had to be rebuilt in 1260 (when the 14 towers were added) after they were breached by the Florentines in 1244. The defences were remarkable in their own day, and earned a mention in Dante's *Inferno*, where the towers are described as resembling giants in an abyss. The relevant passage from the poem Canto XXXI, 40–44, greets you on a plaque as you enter the village, which consists of little more than a church and main square (Piazza Roma), a single street (Via Maggio) and a 4-star hotel and restaurant (➤ 119).

2 Monteriggioni

San Gimignano may be celebrated as one of Tuscany's most perfectly preserved medieval villages, but in truth it pales alongside the village of Monteriggioni. This unsullied vision of the Middle Ages comprises a ring of tower-studded walls atop a hill cloaked in olive groves that is still unmarked by modern buildings. It lies 13km (8 miles) south of the modern town of Poggibonsi, just west of the main Florence to Siena road, from which it is signposted. Like Colle di Val d'Elsa, the village is easily and quickly seen and well worth a short detour.

Monteriggioni was founded by the Sienese in 1203 as a defensive bastion to guard the northern approaches to Siena from the Florentines. The walls

Dante described the towers at Monteriggioni (below) as resembling giants in an abyss

➕ 197 D3 Monteriggioni has no visitors' centre. For information contact the Siena tourist office (➤ 41)

3 Colle di Val d'Elsa

Colle di Val d'Elsa sees relatively few visitors, most people being keen to head straight to nearby San Gimignano (➤ 102). Those who might be tempted to linger are often deterred by Colle Basso, the town's unattractive and mostly modern lower suburb. Don't be put off, however, for the old part of Colle on the hill, Colle Alto, offers quiet flower-decked lanes, old churches, views and lots of pretty medieval corners.

A labyrinth of alleyways and ramshackle medieval houses at Colle di Val d'Elsa

Navigation is easy, for once you've parked at the top of the road from Colle Basso (the SS68), Colle Alto consists of little more than a single main street, Via del Castello, that runs the length of the town's hilly ridge. Midway down, the street opens into Piazza del Duomo, where the cathedral (1603–19) on the left (north) side contains an exquisite 15th-century marble tabernacle, tentatively attributed to Mino da Fiesole. Alongside the cathedral on the left, housed in the 14th-century Palazzo Pretorio, is a small Museo Archeologico, whose exhibits are devoted mainly to finds from local Etruscan tombs. Farther down Via del Castello lies the Museo Civico e d'Arte Sacra, a small museum with a varied and pleasing collection of silverware, sculpture and medieval and Renaissance paintings.

Via del Castello becomes more medieval the farther you walk, with tempting little alleys darting off to either side. In its final section you pass Santa Maria in Canonica, a little 12th-century Romanesque church, and the Casa-Torre di Arnolfo di Cambio, so called because it is believed to have been the birthplace

of 13th-century architect Arnolfo di Cambio. Almost immediately after the tower you come to a magnificent belvedere known as the Baluardo, a vantage point which offers sweeping views over Colle Basso and the beautiful surrounding countryside.

Note that Colle is a place to shop for glassware, the town's abundant supplies of water having fostered a glass-making industry. There are a number of shops on Via di Castello and a museum, the Museo del Cristallo, at Via dei Fossi 8a (tel: 0577 924135; www.cristallo.org).

Tourist office

🏛 197 D3 ✉ Via Francesco Campana 43 ☎ 0577 922791; www.collvaldelsa .net 🕓 Mon–Sat 10–1, 2:30–7, Sun 10–1, 3–6, Apr–Oct; Mon–Sat 10–1, 3–5, Nov–Mar; closed Feb

Museo Archeologico

✉ Piazza del Duomo ☎ 0577 922954 🕓 Tue–Fri 3:30–7:30, Sat–Sun 10–noon, 3:30–6:30, Nov–Apr; Tue–Sun 10:30–12:30, 4:30–7:30, Mar–Oct 💶 Inexpensive

Museo Civico e d'Arte Sacra

✉ Via del Castello 31 ☎ 0577 923095 or 922954 🕓 Tue–Sun 10:30–12:30, 4:30–7:30 💶 Inexpensive

❹ Volterra

Volterra stands apart from the rest of Tuscany, both in its isolated position and in its rather forbidding appearance – its brooding hilltop eyrie is in marked contrast to some of the region's sunnier and more pastoral hill towns. Yet it is also a major historic town, founded by the Etruscans and home to plenty of fine medieval buildings, evocative old streets, two small galleries, and one of the region's most important archaeological museums. It is also full of shops selling alabaster, the stone having been mined and worked locally for centuries. The Ecomuseum dell'Alabastro, a small museum, plus two themed itineraries, provide background on the industry.

The town lies in the windswept volcanic hills between Siena and the Tuscan coast, well away from major roads and well off the normal tourist beat. As a result it sees relatively few visitors, which should encourage you to make an effort to include it on an itinerary – possibly as a side trip from San Gimignano or Colle, which lie about 30km (18 miles) away on the circuitous N68 road.

The town's medieval heart centres on Piazza dei Priori, a lovely ensemble of buildings which includes the Palazzo dei Priori (1208), one of Italy's oldest civic palaces, the cathedral (begun in 1120), the marble-

A preserved Etruscan tomb is just one of the hidden treasures of Volterra's rich historic past

striped 13th-century baptistery, and the Torre del Porcellino, so called because of the little boar (*porcellino*) carved alongside one of its upper windows. The cathedral's artistic highlights are a *Desposition* (1228), a group of polychrome wooden figures (in a chapel of the right, or south, transept) and the high altarpiece's marble tabernacle and flanking angels, dating from 1471, the work of Mino da Fiesole.

Just beyond the baptistery lies the Museo Diocesano d'Arte Sacra, a collection of paintings, sculptures and religious artefacts dominated by Rosso Fiorentino's painting of the *Madonna Enthroned with Saints* (1521). Fiorentino also dominates the town's art gallery and civic museum, the Pinacoteca e Museo Civico, where his otherworldly *Deposition* (1521) is one of the masterpieces of the Mannerist school of painting. Almost equally celebrated is *Gli Sposi*, or "The Married Couple", an Etruscan tomb sculpture from the Museo Etrusco Guarnacci, Tuscany's most important Etruscan museum.

Further vestiges of Volterra's Etruscan – and Roman – past can be found in the Parco Archeologico (daily 10 am–noon, 4–7 pm; free), a pretty archaeological park, or in excavations to the north of the town which have uncovered a bath complex, Roman theatre and other ruins. As ever in a Tuscan town, wander at random to soak up the medieval flavour. A good endpoint are the Balze, dramatic eroded cliffs reached through the town's western fringes.

Tourist office

➕ 196 C3 ✉ Via Giusto Turazza 2
☎ 0588 86 150; www.provolterra.it
🕐 Daily 10–1, 2–6

Museo Diocesano d'Arte Sacra

✉ Via Roma 13 ☎ 0588 86290
🕐 Daily 9–1, 3–6, mid-Mar to Oct; 9–1, Nov to mid-Mar 💶 Expensive (joint ticket with Pinacoteca and Museo Etrusco Guarnacci)

Pinacoteca e Museo Civico

✉ Palazzo Minucci-Solaini, Via dei Sarti 1 ☎ 0588 87580 🕐 Daily 9–7, mid-Mar to Oct; 9–2, Nov to mid-Mar 💶 Expensive (combined ticket with Museo Etrusco Guarnacci)

Museo Etrusco Guarnacci

✉ Via Don Minzoni 15 ☎ 0588 86347
🕐 Daily 9–7, mid-Mar to Oct; 9–2, Nov to mid-Mar 💶 Expensive (combined ticket with Pinacoteca e Museo Civico)

🔟 Fiesole

Fiesole is a small hill town about 7km (4 miles) northeast of central Florence, which makes it a popular excursion from the city, despite a comparative lack of sights in Tuscan terms. But if you have only an afternoon to spare in Florence, take a taxi or the No. 7 bus from outside the Santa Maria Novella railway station (▶ 37) for a brief glimpse of the region's countryside.

The town's main rewards are its rural, hilltop site, which provides sweeping views over Florence below and a welcome breeze in summer. Look into the cathedral on the main square, Piazza Mino da Fiesole, named after a local 15th-century sculptor who has two works in the cathedral's Cappella Salutati (right of the choir).

From the square you could climb Via San Francesco for the best views of Florence, or take a less strenuous walk to the Museo Bandini, a modest museum of ivories, ceramics and paintings, before continuing to the Area Archeologica (archaeological zone), east of Piazza Mino da Fiesole. This pretty park contains a small museum, a well-preserved 1st-century BC Roman theatre and 6th-century BC Etruscan ruins.

Farther to the south, you can visit the church of San Domenico, which contains a delicate painting by Fra Angelico of the *Madonna and Saints with Angels* (1430).

A short walk to the west of San Domenico leads to the Badia Fiesolana, an ancient abbey church with a lovely Romanesque façade.

Tourist office

➕ 197 D4 ✉ Via Portigiani 1 ☎ 055 598720; www.comune.fiesole.fi.it
🕐 Mon–Sat 9–6, Sun 10–6, Apr–Oct; Mon–Sat 9–5, Sun 10–1, 2–5, Nov–Mar

Area Archeologica

✉ Via Marini-Via Portigiani
☎ 055 59 477; 🕐 Daily 9:30–7, Apr–Sep; Wed–Mon 9:30–6, Mar, Oct; Wed–Mon 9:30–5, Nov–Feb
💶 Moderate (combined ticket with Museo Bandini)

Museo Bandini

✉ Via Dupré 1 ☎ 055 59477 🕐 Closed for restoration

Where to... Stay

Prices
Expect to pay per double room
€ under €100   €€ €100–€175   €€€ over €175

Central Tuscany contains some of the region's best-known towns and country-side. As a result, its many hotels often need to be booked weeks in advance – especially in Siena and San Gimignano.

AREZZO

Castello di Gargonza €€

Given Arezzo's dearth of good hotels, this converted medieval hamlet, complete with castle and church in attractive countryside, is a perfect solution if you wish to stay locally. It lies about 6km (4 miles) west of Monte San Savino, a village 10km (6 miles) southwest of Arezzo. The 3-star rooms must be taken for a minimum of three nights, so treat this as a base rather than a stopover: apartments and cottages in the village are available for weekly rental.

♦ 197 E3 ☒ Castello di Gargonza, Monte San Savino ☎ 0575 847054; fax: 0575 847021; www.gargonza.it ◉ Closed Nov and a period in Jan

Cavaliere Palace Hotel €€

The majority of Arezzo's hotels are aimed at business people, so don't stay here unless you have to (Cortona is a better overnight option). If you do need accommodation, the Cavaliere Palace is a 4-star hotel with 27 well-appointed rooms close to the train station, and within easy walking distance of the main sights.

♦ 197 E3 ☒ Via Madonna del Prato 83 ☎ 0575 26836; fax: 0575 21925; www.cavalierehotels.com ◉ Closed for a period in Aug

CHIANTI

Castello di Spaltenna €€€

Like many towns and villages in Chianti, Gaiole is unexceptional, but in the Castello di Spaltenna it offers one of the region's best 4-star hotels. It is set in a splendid 13th-century castle and fortified monastery, complete with towers and chapel, on a hill on the outskirts of town. The 21 rooms and eight apartments are individually furnished in a traditional style – some have fireplaces – and all have a view of the surrounding countryside. The hotel also has a first-rate restaurant (Ristorante La Pieve), fitness centre, tennis courts and swimming pool.

♦ 197 D3 ☒ Pieve di Spaltenna, Gaiole ☎ 0577 749483; fax: 0577 749269; www.spaltenna.it ◉ Hotel closed Jan to mid-Mar

CORTONA

Hotel Italia €€

The 3-star Italia has a good central position on a side street just south of Cortona's main Via Roma. The rooms are clean and well presented – but price is the main selling point here, though some rooms on upper floors enjoy good views. Much the same can be said of the 3-star Hotel Sabrina nearby (Via Roma 37; tel: 0575 630 397; fax 0575 605 763; www.emmeti.it/sabrina), though the rooms here are a touch smaller and slightly smarter in appearance.

♦ 197 E3 ☒ Via Ghibellina 5–7 ☎ 0575 630254; fax: 0575 630763; www.planhotel.com ◉ Year round

Il Falconiere €€€

The 4-star Falconiere is a beautifully restored 17th-century villa located about 3km (2 miles) outside the town walls, off the SS71 road for Arezzo. All 12 rooms are furnished in period style – some even retain original frescoes and antiques.

There is a pool and the restaurant has a terrace for outdoor dining in summer and boasts a good wine list.

🔒 197 E3 ⬛ Località San Martino a Bocena 370 ☎ 0575 612679; fax: 0575 612927; www.ilfalconiere.com ⊘ Hotel may close for a period in Nov; restaurant closed Mon, Nov–Mar

San Michele €€

This 4-star hotel is the best in town, thanks to its setting in a converted Renaissance palace. The 34 rooms all retain many original architectural features, but one room in particular, in the old tower, stands out.

🔒 197 E3 ⬛ Via Guelfa 15 ☎ 0575 604348; fax: 0575 630147; www.hotelsanmichele.net ⊘ Closed mid-Jan to Feb

MONTERIGGIONI

Monteriggioni €€€

This stylish 4-star, 12-room hotel is an enticing place in its own right: the fact that it lies at the heart of one of Tuscany's finest fortified villages only makes it all the more special. Book in advance. The rooms combine modern facilities, with air-conditioning and tasteful décor. There is a garden and swimming pool, but no restaurant. You can eat well in the moderately priced Il Pozzo restaurant (Piazza Roma 2; tel: 0577 304 127; closed Sun eve and Mon and a week in Aug).

🔒 197 D3 ⬛ Via I Maggio 4 ☎ 0577 305009; www.hotel monteriggioni.net ⊘ Closed for a period in Jan

SAN GIMIGNANO

La Cisterna €€

San Gimignano has several 3-star hotels within the village walls. The two that offer the best combination of location, facilities and relative value for money are on the same piazza. La Cisterna is tucked away in the eastern corner of Piazza della Cisterna and, with 50 rooms, is larger than the rival Leon Bianco. It opened in a medieval building in 1919 and for many years was the village's only hotel. Unlike its rival it also has a restaurant, Le Terrazze – excellent in its own right – if you want the option of half- or full-board. Room rates include breakfast.

🔒 196 C3 ⬛ Piazza della Cisterna 24 ☎ 0577 940328; fax: 0577 942080; www.hotelcisterna.it ⊘ Closed for a period between Epiphany and mid-Mar

La Collegiata €€€

If money is no object, then this extremely smart 4-star hotel offers 20 beautiful rooms set in a converted 16th-century convent, about 2km (1.25 miles) north of the town walls. Facilities include a recommended restaurant, swimming pool, air-conditioning and lovely grounds with incomparable views of San Gimignano and its towers.

🔒 196 C3 ⬛ Località Strada 27 ☎ 0577 943201; www.lacollegiata.it ⊘ Closed early Jan to early Feb

Leon Bianco €€

This 3-star hotel shares the Cisterna's perfect position just a stone's throw from the Collegiata and Museo Civico (▶ 105), but with 26 rooms it is smaller and more intimate. The rooms and common parts are bright and airy, with lots of vaulted ceilings, cool marble and terracotta floors: like the Cisterna, the building is medieval, with many of its period features preserved. Both hotels also have rooms with countryside views – rooms overlooking the piazza may suffer from late-night noise. There is no restaurant, but you can take breakfast or drinks on the pretty terrace.

🔒 196 C3 ⬛ Piazza della Cisterna 13 ☎ 0577 941 294; www.leonbianco. com ⊘ Closed for periods in Nov–Dec and Jan–Feb

Antica Torre €€

The 3-star Antica Torre is just what its name suggests – an ancient medieval tower which in the last few years has achieved an excellent word-of-mouth reputation. You will need to book well in advance to secure one of the eight pretty but moderately sized rooms in this restored 16th-century building. Try for rooms on the upper floor at the rear – they have the best views. The hotel lies about 600m (a quarter-mile) east of the Campo on a side street off Via di Pantaneto, close to the church of Santa Maria dei Servi. There is no restaurant, but breakfast is served in the medieval cellar.

✚ 201 F2 **⊠ Via Fieravecchia 7**
☎ 0577 222255;
www.anticatorresiena.it

Certosa di Maggiano €€€

This magnificent converted 14th-century abbey is one of Tuscany's finest hotels, favoured by honey-mooners and other visitors prepared to splash out on cost. The hotel, with glorious, antique-filled rooms, lies within beautiful grounds 5km (3 miles) east of Siena, so it is more a base for romance and self-indulgence than city sightseeing. Facilities include a heated swimming pool, tennis courts and heliport. Difficult to find – phone for directions.

✚ 201 off F2 **⊠ Via di Certosa 82**
☎ 0577 288180; www.certosadi maggiano.com

Hotel Duomo €€

Siena has surprisingly few good central hotels. This 23-room 3-star is the best in the mid-price range, providing a convenient base just a few minutes' walk south of the Campo and cathedral on a pretty medieval street. The carpeted rooms are clean and moderately sized but otherwise unexceptional unless you manage to secure one with views across the city. Bathrooms tend to be small. There is no restaurant, and the hotel in general, despite amiable service, has a slightly impersonal feel, largely because its rooms (reached by lift) are on the upper floors of the 12th-century building and separated from the small foyer by private accommodation. Breakfast is taken in a basement room.

✚ 200 C2 **⊠ Via di Stalloreggi 38**
☎ 0577 289088; fax: 0577 43 043;
www.hotelduomo.it

Palazzo Ravizza €€–€€€

The 18th-century Palazzo Ravizza has been owned by the same family for more than two centuries. The hotel retains much of its period appeal, thanks to its many original features, antiques and furniture. Rooms either look over a garden to the rear or, if they are high enough, over the city and a potentially noisy road to the front. The hotel is on the southwestern fringes of Siena's old centre, about 250m (270 yards) beyond the Hotel Duomo.

✚ 200 B1 **⊠ Via Piano dei Mantellini 34** **☎ 0577 280462;**
www.palazzoravizza.it

Tre Donzelle €

You will need to book well ahead to secure one of the 27 rooms in this clean and well-run 2-star hotel just off Banchi di Sotto, about a minute's walk from the Campo. Another good budget option is the spotless, 13-room, family-run Piccolo Hotel Etruria, just a few doors down the street at Via delle Donzelle 3 (tel: 0577 288088, fax 0577 288461).

✚ 201 D3 **⊠ Via delle Donzelle 5**
☎ 0577 280358, fax 0577 223933

Villa Scacciapensieri €€€

This tranquil hotel occupies a 19th-century hilltop villa about 3km (2 miles) north of the city. A tree-lined drive sets the tone for the peaceful nature of your stay. The 30 rooms and suites vary considerably, so ask to see a selection. Facilities include tennis courts, pool and restaurant, and there are gardens with views of the city and countryside.

✚ 201 off E5 **⊠ Via di Scacciapensieri 10** **☎ 0577 41441; fax: 0577 270854; www.villascacciapensieri.it**

Where to...
Eat and Drink

Prices

Expect to pay for a three-course meal for one with wine

€ under €26   €€ €26–€52   €€€ over €52

General opening times for restaurants are given, although it should be noted that these can vary based on several factors – the time of year, the arrival and departure time of the last customer, or simply the whim of the owners.

AREZZO

Antica Osteria L'Agania €

Arrive early at this busy and pleasingly eccentric restaurant as no reservations are accepted. Food is simple but expertly cooked by a group of women who have worked here for years. The décor is an eclectic mixture of old photographs, pictures, wine bottles and strings of garlic and peppers.

➕ 197 E3 ⊠ Via Mazzini 10
☎ 0575 295381 🕙 Tue–Sun
12–2.30, 7–10.30. Closed Mon (except
Jul–Aug) and a period in Jun

Buca di San Francesco €€

This central restaurant has been in business since 1929, serving simple, Tuscan staples such as thick *ribollita* (vegetable soup), *agnello* (roast lamb) and more ambitious dishes such as *pollo del Valdarno* (roast chicken flavoured with anise). The cellar dining room with its bold colours and medieval paintings is well-placed for the church of San Francesco and Piero della Francesca's fresco cycle – though this does mean it is often crowded.

➕ 197 E3 ⊠ Via San Francesco 1
☎ 0575 23271 🕙 12–2.30, 7–9.30.
Closed Mon pm, Tue, two weeks in Jul

La Torre di Gnicche €

This welcoming little venue secreted in a 14th-century *palazzo* is a mixture of wine bar and café, serving snacks, cheeses, an excellent selection of wines by the glass and a handful of simple hot dishes that include a notable *zuppa di cipolle* (onion soup).

➕ 197 E3 ⊠ Piaggia San Martino 8
☎ 0575 352035 🕙 Noon–3; 6–8
for drinks; from 8 pm for dinner.
Closed Wed, 1 week in Aug and 2
weeks in Jan

Trattoria Il Saraceno €

This inexpensive, family-run restaurant lies just a few minutes east of the church of San Francesco and offers Tuscan food of a quality you don't normally find in this price range, including *ribollita* soup and beef with porcini mushrooms. Pizzas available in the evening.

➕ 197 E3 ⊠ Via Mazzini 6a
☎ 0575 27644; www.ilsaraceno.com
🕙 12–3.30, 7–10.30. Closed Wed and
two weeks in Jan, plus two weeks in
Jul or Aug

CHIANTI

Badia a Coltibuono €€€

This well-known, exclusive restaurant is housed in the refectory of a restored 8th-century monastery. Tuscan staples as well as game such as wild boar in season are offered.

➕ 197 D3 ⊠ Badia a Coltibuono,
5km (3 miles) north of Gaiole
☎ 0577 749031 🕙 12:15–2.30
(3–4.30 snacks), 7:15–9.30. Closed
mid-Nov to Feb. Closed Mon in Mar

COLLE DI VAL D'ELSA

L'Antica Trattoria €€–€€€

This elegant but relaxed restaurant is not in the medieval part of Colle di Val d'Elsa, but on the edge of a busy, modern square in the lower town. Don't let this put you off, for the sophisticated Tuscan fare here is some of the best in the immediate region. The dining rooms are medieval in appearance – as the Antica (ancient) in the restaurant's name suggests – and the service is professional. The wine list and selection of spirits are also outstanding.

🚻 197 D3 ⊠ Piazza Arnolfo di Cambio 23 ☎ 0577 923747 ⏰ 12:30–2:30, 8–10:30. Closed Tue and two weeks in Dec and Jan

CORTONA

La Locanda del Loggiato €€

It is hard to fault the tasteful brick-vaulted medieval interior, or the restaurant's central position just off the main square, but food and service can be variable here. Come for a simple lunch and – if the weather is fine – aim to eat outdoors on the terrace.

🚻 197 E3 ⊠ Piazza Pescheria 3 ☎ 0575 630575 ⏰ 12:30–3, 7:15–11. Closed Wed and Nov

Osteria del Teatro €–€€€

A definite first choice in Cortona, thanks to its central position close to the Teatro Signorelli (hence the restaurant's name), pleasing interior – the walls are lined with photographs of actors and actresses – and good food, which may rarely strays from local staples. The *antipasto dell'osteria* is a good way to start, with lots of different tasters, followed by *ravioli ai fiori di zucca* (filled pasta with courgette flowers) or *pappardelle alle lepre*, a typical Tuscan dish of pasta ribbons with a hare sauce. It only seats 30 people, so be sure to book.

🚻 197 E3 ⊠ Via Maffei 5 ☎ 0575 630556 ⏰ 12:30–2:30, 7:30–10:30. Closed Wed, 2 weeks in Nov

Tonino €€

Tonino is big, busy, modern and noisy. Locals flock here for the views of the Val di Chiana and the famous *antipastissimo* (15 different starters) and other dishes.

🚻 197 E3 ⊠ Piazza Garibaldi 1 ☎ 0575 630500 ⏰ 12:30–3, 7:30–10. Closed Mon pm and Tue (except Jun–Oct)

SAN GIMIGNANO

Dorandò €€–€€€

The aim of this restaurant is to re-create recipes from Tuscany's Etruscan and medieval past, which may sound pretentious but the results are usually first rate. The restaurant is small – just 36 people can be served in the three small dining rooms – and enjoys an elegant medieval setting. Prices, though, are high, even by San Gimignano's standards.

🚻 196 C3 ⊠ Vicolo dell'Oro 2 ☎ 0577 941862 ⏰ 12:30–2:30, 7:30–9:30. Closed mid-Jan to Feb, Mon in winter, some Mon lunch in summer

Gelateria di Piazza €

This ice-cream parlour serves San Gimignano's best ice-cream, specialising in flavours which use only the best natural ingredients and no artificial additives.

🚻 196 C3 ⊠ Piazza della Cisterna 4 ☎ 0577 94244 ⏰ Daily 9–midnight, mid-Mar to mid-Sep: 9–8. Closed mid-Nov to mid-Feb

Osteria del Carcere €

A busy tourist destination like San Gimignano is lucky to have two *osterias*, the Carcere and the Catene, where you'll find simple surroundings, good plain food and fair prices. The Carcere is a small restaurant near the Piazza della Cisterna. You can eat simple Tuscan dishes at lunch or dinner – the *polpette* (meatballs) are especially good – or nibble *crostini* (toasts), cheese and other snacks with a glass of wine during the rest of the day.

🚻 196 C3 ⊠ Via del Castello 13 ☎ 0577 941905 ⏰ 12:30–2:30, 7:30–10:30. Closed Wed and Thu lunch

Osteria delle Catene €

In a village clogged with visitors, this pleasant *osteria* has resisted the temptation to serve low-quality tourist fare. Instead, owners Gino and Virgilio offer a variety of simple but far from boring local dishes, including *nana col cavolo nero* (duck with red cabbage) and *coniglio alla Vernaccia* (rabbit cooked with San Gimignano's Vernaccia white wine). There are also daily specials.

🛨 **196 C3** ☒ **Via Mainardi 18** ☏ **0577 941966** ⏰ **12:30–2:30, 7:30–10:30. Closed Wed, periods in Jan and Dec**

SIENA

Antica Osteria da Divo €€

It's hard to imagine a more evocative series of dining rooms than those of Da Divo, just west of the cathedral and half-excavated from one of the city's ancient walls. The unique stone and vaulted rooms, dimly lit and cosy with rich, dark fabrics, date back to the early Middle Ages,

and some contain Etruscan stones. The food is refined Tuscan fare and features such dishes as a terrine of rabbit with fresh pecorino cheese or a risotto with saffron and asparagus.

🛨 **200 B3** ☒ **Via Franciosa 25** ☏ **0577 286054** ⏰ **Daily 12:30–2:30, 7:30–10:30. Closed Tue Nov–Apr, Sun May–Oct**

Antica Trattoria Botteganova €€€

The sublime food at this formal restaurant has won many accolades, but you have to travel to enjoy it – the restaurant lies just off the SS408 road to the north of the city. Signature dishes include *tortelli di pecorino con fonduta di parmigiano e tartufo* (pasta filled with cheese and topped with truffle sauce). The same high quality is available at lunch from a more limited and lower priced menu.

🛨 **201 off E5** ☒ **Via Chiantigiana 29, off Viale Pietro Toselli** ☏ **0577 284 230** ⏰ **12:30–2:30, 7:30–10:30. Closed Sun and in Jan and Jul–Aug**

Antica Trattoria Papei €

This little *trattoria* in the market square has won deserving plaudits for good Tuscan food at reasonable prices. It also benefits from a terrace for outside dining in warm weather.

🛨 **201 D2** ☒ **Piazza del Mercato 6** ☏ **0577 280894** ⏰ **12:30–2:30, 7:30–10:30. Closed Mon**

Le Logge €€

Few Tuscan restaurants are prettier than this former medieval pharmacy just off the Campo, complete with its original wooden cabinets. The quality of the innovative food can be hit and miss: when it works, however, it's very good – a book of its recipes has even been published.

🛨 **201 D2** ☒ **Via del Porrione 33** ☏ **0577 48013** ⏰ **12:30–2:30, 7:30–10:30. Closed Sun and periods in Jun and Nov**

Al Marsili €€

Al Marsili rivals Da Divo as the best of the more expensive restaurants in

central Siena. The dining room still retains a few touches of its medieval décor, notably the brick vaulting. The food is a mixture of Tuscan staples and more ambitious dishes such as *cinghiale* (wild boar) or *faraona alla Medici* (guinea fowl with almonds, pine nuts and prunes).

🛨 **200 C2** ☒ **Via del Castoro 3** ☏ **0577 47 154;** www.risArcintealmarsili.it ⏰ **12:30–2:30, 7:30–10:30. Closed Mon**

VOLTERRA

Da Badò €

Two brothers run this popular, long-established *trattoria*, with their mother working in the kitchen. Soups such as *zuppa alla volterrana* and robust main dishes such as *cinghiale* (wild boar) are good, as are the local porcini mushrooms.

🛨 **196 C3** ☒ **Borgo San Lazzaro 9** ☏ **0588 86 477** ⏰ **12:30–2:30, 7:30–10:30. Closed Wed, Jul and the first 10 days of Sep**

Where to...
Shop

The best all-round shopping of the region is found in Siena, mainly around **Via di Città**, **Banchi di Sopra** and **Banchi di Sotto**.

SIENA

Food is the best buy, especially olive oils and *panforte*, a cake flavoured with cinnamon and other spices. Antica Drogheria Manganelli 1879 (Via di Città 71–73, tel: 0577 280002; closed Wed pm) is crammed with foods, wines and spirits in old wood cabinets. The nearby Pizzicheria di Miccoli (Via di Città 95) is almost equally attractive, and is especially good for cheeses, salamis and hams, which hang from the ceiling – ideal for picnics. You can also buy picnic provisions at La Lizza, Siena's main market, held Wednesday morning north of the city beyond Piazza Matteotti and Piazza Gramsci. For **wine**, head to the Enoteca Italiana (Fortezza Medicea, tel: 0577 288497), where the old Medici castle's cellars hold around 750 of the best Italian wines to buy.

For **gifts and household items**, visit Negozia dell'Arte(Via di Città 96, tel: 0577 286078) and Ceramiche Santa Caterina (Via di Città 74–76, tel: 0577 283098).

CHIANTI

You will pass numerous estates in the region selling wine directly to the public. For a good one-stop selection, visit **Enoteca del Gallo Nero** in Greve (Piazzetta Santa Croce 8, tel: 055 853297), which has wines by most of the Chianti Classico Gallo Nero producers plus other wines, olive oils and vinegars.

Where to...
Be Entertained

Sleepy Siena and the Chianti hills are not places teeming with night-clubs or lively bars. Entertainment in this part of the region is mostly cultural, or involves traditional pageants and festivals such as Siena's Palio (➤ 26–27). Siena also has a range of musical associations which organise classical concerts and sum-mer jazz and other music festivals. Contact the **Academia Chigiana** (tel: 0577 22091; www.chigiana.it) or the tourist office (➤ 41) for details of events, which are liable to change from year to year.

Tourist offices are also the best source of information on the plethora of small festivals devoted to food, wine, local saints and historical events across the region. Larger events – when towns are likely to be busy and almost all accommodation full – include the **Giostra del Saraceno** in Arezzo, a medieval joust held twice yearly in mid-June and the first week of September, and the **Festival di San Gimignano**, a large-scale event of opera, classical music and the arts held every year from late June to October.

Arezzo also has a major antiques fair on the first Sunday of each month, which is very popular with both collectors and browsers, and a well-regarded festival of choral music in August.

Cortona has an atmospheric crossbow competition staged in medieval dress, the Giostra dell'Archidado, which is held each year in late May.

Southern Tuscany

Getting Your Bearings

Southern Tuscany is Tuscany at its best. The pastoral landscapes south of Siena are the most beautiful in the region, gentler and more varied than those of Chianti or the mountainous region to the north – and they are dotted with a succession of ancient abbeys, fascinating historic towns and tiny hill villages.

Above: Church of Madonna di San Biagio, Montepulciano

The area to see if time is short lies immediately south of Siena. Here the landscape is that most often associated with Tuscany – olive groves, rustic stone farmhouses, rippling fields of wheat or sunflowers, and tranquil hills covered in vines or topped with lonely cypresses. Here, too, are some of the region's loveliest small towns and villages – Montalcino, famous for its red wine; Pienza, a tiny Renaissance jewel; and Montepulciano, a lofty historic redoubt with wonderful views. All three places make good overnight stops, with Montalcino the first choice, if only for its proximity to two wonderful abbeys – Sant'Antimo and Monte Oliveto Maggiore.

Farther south, beyond the Val d'Orcia (valley of the River Orcia), the landscape becomes higher, wilder and less inhabited. The best countryside clusters around Monte Amiata, southern Tuscany's highest point, a brooding mountain swathed in beech woods and circled by a small coronet of villages and hamlets. Farther south still, however, the landscape changes again, becoming flatter and, by Tuscany's exalted standards, relatively uninspiring. Large towns near the coast such as Grosseto and

Previous page: The countryside around Pienza

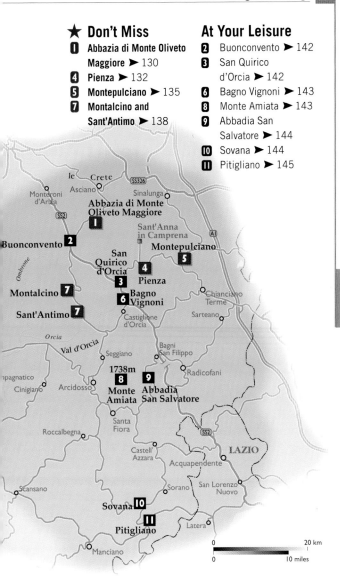

Piombino are lacklustre, while little on the coast itself merits a special journey when there is so much to see inland – the small resort of Castiglione della Pescaia and the Marina di Alberese, both within 20km (12 miles) of Grosseto, are the best options if you want an afternoon by the sea. On a short visit, the historic little village of Sovana and the spectacularly situated Pitigliano are more worthwhile – but note that both will leave you a long way south and a quite a long drive from Tuscany's other highlights.

The glorious, rugged countryside of southern Tuscany lends itself to exploration by car, starting with the Abbazia di Monte Oliveto Maggiore.

Southern Tuscany in Two Days

Day One

Morning
From San Gimignano, Montalcino or Siena drive southeast, either on the main SS2 (Via Cassia) road, or the scenic SS438 from Siena through the hills of the Crete to Asciano. From the SS2 road at Buonconvento or on the minor road south from Asciano via Montecontieri, visit ❶ Abbazia di Monte Oliveto Maggiore (► 130, right).

Lunch
Take lunch or a snack in the **abbey café** or prepare a picnic.

Afternoon
Spend an hour or so exploring ❷ Buonconvento's medieval centre (► 142) before driving to ❹ Pienza (► 132), which should occupy two or three hours. Then drive on to ❺ Montepulciano (► 135) where you can spend the night.

Day Two

Morning
Drive from Montepulciano to ❻ Bagno Vignoni (► 143), and explore the village (below), along with Castiglione d'Orcia and the other villages and lovely

countryside around Montalcino. Then go to
7 Montalcino (above) and **Sant'Antimo** (➤ 138,
right: fresco in the chancel at the abbey at
Sant'Antimo) where you can stop for lunch.

Lunch
Grappolo Blu in Montalcino makes
an ideal spot for lunch (➤ 148).

Afternoon
In the afternoon drive south to see **8 Monte
Amiata** (➤ 143) and its more rugged landscapes and villages. A longer drive takes you
to the picturesque villages of **10 Sovana**
(➤ 144, below) and **11 Pitigliano** (➤ 145).
Sovana makes a good overnight
base (➤ 149).

O

Abbazia di Monte Oliveto Maggiore

The abbey of Monte Oliveto Maggiore sits in splendid isolation on a pretty hillside amid woods of oak, pine, cypress and olive. The beauty of its setting is matched by the charm of its ancient buildings, and by the great work of art at its heart, a Renaissance fresco cycle on the Life of St Benedict by Sodoma and Luca Signorelli.

The abbey of Monte Oliveto Maggiore owes its foundation to Bernardo Tolomei (1272–1348), a member of a wealthy Sienese family who renounced his worldly life after being struck blind and experiencing visions of the Virgin Mary (the Tolomei family tombs can be seen in the church of San Francesco in Siena, ▶ 101).

The Grand Cloister at Monte Oliveto Maggiore, with frescoes by Sodoma and Luca Signorelli

Bernardo retreated with two companions to the site of the present abbey – the land was then owned by his family – and within six years began work on what, in 1320, would become a Benedictine hermitage. In 1344 Pope Clement VI recognised Tolomei and his growing band of followers as Olivetans, also known as White Benedictines, an offshoot of the Benedictines whose members sought to return to the humble roots of the order. Later Olivetans made light of this ambition, for the abbey became hugely wealthy and played a vital role in the economic and agricultural life of the surrounding region.

Artistic Highlights

Monte Oliveto is still a working abbey, and large parts of its extensive monastic buildings and grounds are closed to visitors. Its main artistic highlight, however, is fully accessible: the **Choistro Grande** (1426–43), or Grand Cloister, and its fresco cycle by Sodoma and Luca Signorelli on the life of the Benedictines' founder, St Benedict. Sodoma, a Milanese artist, completed the majority of the cycle between 1505 and 1508 – 27 panels in all – adding to the eight panels executed in 1498 by Luca Signorelli, an artist born in nearby Cortona (▶ 111). The cycle starts on the east wall to the right of the door to the

ABBAZIA DI MONTE OLIVETO MAGGIORE: INSIDE INFO

Top tips The abbey is easily visited from Buonconvento, 9km (5.5 miles) to the southwest on the SS451 road. However, you'll enjoy the **best distant view** of the abbey if you continue east on this road to the first major junction 1km (half a mile) beyond the abbey and turn right to the hamlet of Chiusure. From here you can look down on the monastery and its lovely setting.

• The abbey **closes at noon** for more than three hours, so time your visit accordingly.

abbey church. The narrative is hard to decipher unless you're well versed in the life of St Benedict, though this shouldn't spoil your enjoyment, for each of the frescoes is filled with fascinating incidental and contemporary detail. The abbey church itself, however, is disappointing, except for some breathtakingly carved and inlaid choir stalls (1503–5).

TAKING A BREAK

The abbey has a **café** for drinks, snacks and light meals, but you might also consider buying a **picnic** to eat either in the attractive abbey grounds or at a scenic spot farther along the N451 road.

Dusk falling on the abbey and its surrounding hillsides

✠ 197 D2 ✉ Near Chiusure ☎ 0577 707611 ◷ Daily 9:15–noon, 3:15–5:45 (Oct–Apr until 5); Library closed weekdays Nov–Feb ▣ Free

❹

Pienza

Pienza is one of the smallest but most memorable of all Tuscany's villages, a tiny medieval and Renaissance jewel of considerable charm set at the heart of some of the region's most beautiful countryside.

Pienza was known as Corsignano until 1459, when Enea Silvio Piccolomini – better known as Pope Pius II – decided to turn the place of his birth into a planned Renaissance city. In the event, he died before his grandiose scheme could be realised, but not before the modest hamlet had been given a cathedral filled with artworks, a handful of palaces and a grand central piazza, Piazza Pio II. This trio of sights is complemented by some wonderful views, a small but fascinating museum and two medieval churches.

A view of Pienza's cathedral from the panoramic city walls

Renaissance Vision

Pienza amounts to little more than a maze of small lanes and a main street, **Corso Rossellino**, which takes its name from Bernardo Rossellino, the architect Pius commissioned to design his model city. The Corso bisects the village from east to west, passing through the Piazza Pio II, distinguished by a Renaissance well, the **Pozzo dei Cani**, complete with twin columns and a classical frieze. This sets the tone for the rest of the square, conceived as a unified whole, and offers a tantalising glimpse of what might have been had Pius lived to realise his vision.

Pius' coat of arms – a garland of fruit – adorns the façade (1462) of the cathedral, the piazza's grand set piece. Inside, the church is dotted by five prominent paintings – all individually commissioned by Pius – by five prominent Sienese painters: the most accomplished is Vecchietta's *Assumption* with Pope Pius I

The interior of Pienza's cathedral was based on churches in Germany visited by Pope Pius II

and saints Agatha, Callistus and Catherine of Siena in the fourth chapel as you work round the church from the right.

To the right of the cathedral as you face its façade stands the **Palazzo Piccolomini**, Pius' papal residence inhabited by his descendants until 1962. Guided tours take you round many of its state apartments, notably the library, music room, dining salon and papal bedroom, all which are overflowing with books, manuscripts, rich carpets and other precious antiques (though not all are original to the palace). One of the most striking rooms is the **Sala d'Armi**, or armoury, which bristles with all manner of fearsome medieval weaponry. Equally memorable are the **views** from the rear loggia.

The Pozzo dei Cani, a Renaissance well in the Piazza Pio II

On the east side of Piazza Pio II stands the Palazzo Borgia (also known as Palazzo dei Vescovi), home to the **Museo Diocesano**, a wonderfully rich and eclectic collection of paintings, sculpture, tapestries, portrait busts and other medieval and Renaissance artefacts. First among its treasures is a beautifully embroidered 14th-century English *piviale* (cope), part of Pius' personal wardrobe.

East and West Pienza

From Piazza Pio II you could explore the little lanes to the east and especially the alleys which run along the top of the village's south-facing walls behind the cathedral – the **views** towards Monte Amiata are spell-binding. To the west, Corso Rossellino brings you to **San Francesco**, a late 13th-century Gothic church which survived Pius' redevelopment. Another fascinating survivor, the **Pieve di Corsignano**, lies 10 minutes' walk from Piazza Dante. This parish church dates from the 10th century – the custodian lives next door.

The panoramic views from Pienza's city walls are spectacular

TAKING A BREAK
Try **Falco** (busy) on Piazza Dante for good country cooking.

Duomo
🔲 197 E2 ✉ Piazza Pio II ☎ No phone ⏰ Daily 8–1, 3–7. Closed during services 🎟 Free

Palazzo Piccolomini
🔲 197 E2 ✉ Piazza Pio II ☎ 0578 748503 ⏰ Tue–Sun 10–12:30, 3–6, mid-Dec to mid-Nov. Last tours leave daily at noon and 5:30 🎟 Moderate

Museo Diocesano
🔲 197 E2 ✉ Corso Rossellino 30–Piazza Pio II ☎ 0578 749905 or 0578 749071 ⏰ Wed–Mon 10–1, 3–6:30, mid-Mar to Oct; Fri–Sun 10–6, Nov–Jan 9; Sat–Sun 10–1, 3–6, 10 Jan to mid-Mar 🎟 Moderate

PIENZA: INSIDE INFO

Top tips Pienza becomes busy with day-trippers from Florence and Siena in summer, so aim to arrive early or – better still – stay overnight: the village has a good **central hotel** (▶ 147).
• You won't be able to **park** in the centre of Pienza, but the village is so small you won't need to – leave your car outside the walls to the west near Piazza Dante or in the car-park to the north on Via Mencatelli, off Largo Roma. The Largo is on Viale Enzo Mangiavacchi, the road that runs around the outside of the walls eastward from Piazza Dante.
• If you have time, be sure to walk along the **ramparts and public gardens** west of Piazza Dante. These are outside the village proper, but offer superb views of the surrounding countryside.

In more depth Most of the countryside around Pienza is ravishing. To see some of the best, and with a further reward at journey's end, head for Sant'Anna in **Camprena**, an abbey 8km (5 miles) north, signed off the road for San Quirico. The abbey refectory has frescoes by Sodoma, whose work can also be seen at the abbey in Monte Oliveto Maggiore (▶ 130). The abbey is generally open daily in summer, but telephone 0578 748303 or check at Pienza's tourist office for current opening times.

5

Montepulciano

Montepulciano is one of Tuscany's most perfect hill towns: its high, breezy position commands sweeping views and it has art and architecture far beyond its small size, including San Biagio, one of Italy's foremost Renaissance churches. In addition, the number of visitors is still relatively low and the local Vino Nobile is one of the region's most prized wines.

The church of San Biagio, just outside Montepulciano

Montepulciano may be rewarding, but it isn't easy to explore. Built on a narrow, steep ridge, it effectively consists of one main street that climbs sharply from Piazza Sant' Agnese to Piazza Grande, the main square, before continuing up to the fortress at the top of the town – a height of some 605m (1,985 feet). So be prepared for a climb at either the start or end of your travels.

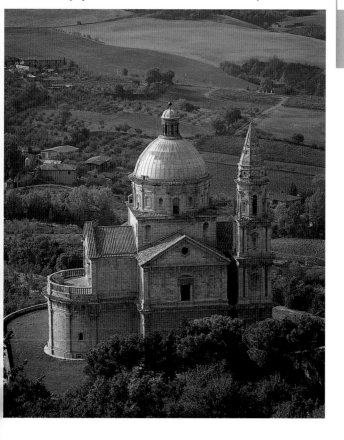

Along the Corso

This itinerary starts at Piazza Sant'Agnese, which has the advantage of making Piazza Grande the culmination of your walk. In the first square look briefly at **Sant'Agnese church**, with several 14th-century paintings. Then pass through the Porta al Prato, the town's main northern gateway, which marks the start of your walk up the **Corso**, the main street that, in one guise or another, will take you to the top of the town. In the square just inside the gate stands the **Colonna del Marzocco**, a column bearing a statue of the Marzocco, Florence's heraldic lion (➤ 64). The Florentines controlled Montepulciano from 1511, a period that saw them dispatch the architect Antonio da Sangallo the Elder to strengthen the town's defences and restore or rebuild many local palaces. This trend was continued by his nephew, Antonio da Sangallo the Younger, and later by Jacopo Vignola, one of the leading lights of early baroque architecture.

The older Sangallo was responsible for both the Porta al Prato and the Palazzo Cocconi at No 70 on the Corso. Vignola probably designed the Palazzo Tartugi (No 82) and Palazzo Avignonesi (No 91). The Corso's most striking palace, however, is the **Palazzo Bucelli** at No 73, notable for the Etruscan remains incorporated into its base (its 17th-century owner, Pietro Bucelli, was an avid collector of antiquities). A short distance past the Palazzo Cocconi, on the right, stands the 13th-century **church of Sant'Agostino** (Piazza Michelozzo), its façade remodelled around 1429 by Michelozzo, one of the Medicis' favourite architects. Opposite stands the **Torre di Pulcinella**, a medieval tower and town house – the figure of the clown, Pulcinella, strikes the hours on the clock.

The tiny figure of the clown, Pulcinella, strikes the hour on the medieval clock tower

Some 100m (110 yards) beyond this point you reach the Piazza dell' Erbe and the Renaissance Loggia del Mercato on the right. Turn right here, then take a sharp left up Via di Poggiolo. As you continue you pass the church of San Francesco (note the lovely view from the left side of the church) and then the **Museo Civico**, the town's main museum, with early paintings, medieval sculptures and other artistic fragments from as far back as the 13th century.

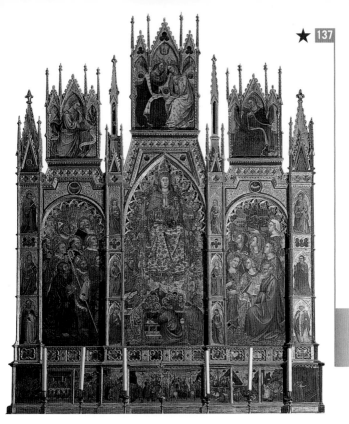

Taddeo di Bartolo's sumptuous *Assumption* on the high altarpiece of the cathedral

Piazza Grande and the Cathedral

Soon after, Via Ricci opens onto the glorious Piazza Grande, a large square dominated by the Duomo (cathedral) and an array of austere palaces. Among the latter is the **Palazzo Cantucci**, one of several places where you can sample and buy Vino Nobile di Montepulciano (▶ 24). You can also climb the tower of the Gothic 13th-century **Palazzo Comunale**, on the square's western edge – the views are far-reaching, but the opening times can be erratic: it's generally open in the morning Monday to Saturday.

The piazza's real attraction, however, is the **Duomo**. Behind its unfinished façade is one of Tuscany's greatest altarpieces, the *Assumption* (1401) by Taddeo di Bartolo. The Baptistery is filled with reliefs, terracottas and other sculptures by an array of medieval and Renaissance artists, including Andrea della Robbia and Benedetto da Maiano. Also look at Michelozzo's dismembered tomb (1427–36) of the humanist Bartolomeo Aragazzi.

TAKING A BREAK

The elegant **Caffè Poliziano** (▶ 149) or **La Grotta**, just outside town, by San Biagio, are both good places for lunch.

Museo Civico e Pinacoteca 'PF Crociani
🕂 197 E2 ✉ Palazzo Neri-Orselli, Via Ricci 10 ☎ 0578 717300 🕒 Daily 10–7, Aug; Tue–Sun 10–1, 3–7, Apr–Jul and Sep–Oct; 10–1, 3–6, rest of year 💷 Moderate

7

Montalcino and Sant'Antimo

Montalcino is yet another perfect Tuscan hill town: its breezy site offers magnificent views; it is almost completely unspoiled; it sits amid beautiful countryside; its red wines – Brunello and Rosso di Montalcino – are some of Italy's finest; and its hotels and restaurants, though few in number, are first rate. It also lies close to Sant'Antimo, the region's loveliest abbey.

The town of Montalcino is one of Tuscany's most ancient settlements, dating back to Palaeolithic or Etruscan times. Its first mention in written records in AD 814 cites it in a list of territories awarded to the abbey of Sant'Antimo by Louis the Pious, son of Charlemagne. Its finest hour came in 1555, when it was the last town in the Sienese Republic to surrender to the Florentines – Montalcino's banner still heads the procession at the Siena Palio in memory of the feat (► 26).

Exploring Montalcino

The town's most striking sight is the **Rocca** (or Fortezza), a picture-perfect 14th-century castle at the town's southern edge. Its main keep contains a busy *enoteca* (wine bar), where you can buy or sample local wine, although it is good to remember that there are nicer and less expensive places elsewhere. It's well worth paying the small fee to visit the castle battlements, which offer superb views across the Crete, a region of bare hills, to one side, and the wooded slopes of the Val d'Orcia on the other.

From the castle, head northeast on Via Panfilo and then turn left on Via dell'Oca. A short walk brings you to Piazza Garibaldi and **Sant'Egido**, a pretty old church with several fragments of

A Medici fortress crowns the hilltop town of Montalcino

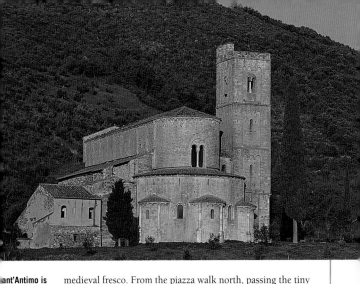

Sant'Antimo is
one of Italy's
finest
Romanesque
abbeys

medieval fresco. From the piazza walk north, passing the tiny
tourist office on the left, to the **Piazza del Popolo**, the town's
narrow main square, which is dominated by the Palazzo Comunale (1292), a fine civic palace, and a pretty café (▶ 148).

To see the splendid **Museo Civico**, the town's main museum,
walk back towards the tourist office and take the first arched
alleyway on your right. Climb the steps and then continue
straight on past the 14th-century **church of Sant'Agostino** on
your left. Have a quick look in the church, which has several
fine medieval frescoes by unknown artists, and then allow an
hour or so for the adjacent museum. Among the museum's
exhibits are lovely 14th- and 15th-century paintings by Sano
di Pietro and other Sienese

The crypt of
the 9th-century
Sant'Antimo
abbey

artists, a pair of illuminated
12th-century bibles and
a 12th-century Crucifix
from Sant'Antimo.

After seeing the museum
you should take some time to
enjoy the streets almost at
random. To the north, you
might take Via Spagni past
the Duomo – remodelled to
dull effect in 1832 – to the
**Santuario della Madonna del
Soccorso**, a large 17th-century church flanked by a park to the
right (on Viale Roma) which offers memorable views over the
Crete towards Siena.

From here you can explore the town's northern and eastern
limits, following Via Mazzini from Piazza Cavour at the bottom
of Viale Roma back to Piazza del Popolo, or taking the small
lanes east to the Fonte Castellane, a medieval washhouse, and
the nearby deconsecrated church of San Francesco.

Sant'Antimo

However long you stay in Montalcino – and the town makes
an excellent base – be certain to devote a couple of hours to
Sant'Antimo, an abbey that lies in glorious countryside just

10km (6 miles) south of the town (the abbey is signposted at the main road junction just below the Fortezza). Its beautiful situation, nestled amid a timeless pastoral landscape of olive groves and wooded hills, is reason enough to visit, but what makes the abbey still more compelling is its fascinating history and superb architecture.

Many myths surround its foundation, the most persistent being that it was created by Charlemagne, the Holy Roman Emperor, in AD 781. As Charlemagne marched his army from Rome, it's said his troops were ravaged by a mysterious disease and that the emperor promised God he would build a church if He effected a cure. While camped close to the site of the present abbey, Charlemagne was reputedly told by God in a dream to feed his men a local herb mixed with wine. The cure worked and the abbey of Sant'Antimo was duly built. The story may sound unlikely, but it is known that in 781 Pope Hadrian I presented Charlemagne with the relics of St Antimo – the very relics venerated at the abbey which took the saint's name. It's also a fact that an abbey existed in 814, when Charlemagne's son, Louis the Pious, granted it lands in a charter of that year. Pious' gift and other donations over the years made the abbey one of

The ambulatory (or walkway) around Sant'Antimo's high altar

MONTALCINO AND SANT'ANTIMO: INSIDE INFO

Top tips Do not try to park in the centre of Montalcino. The best place to leave your car is in the large car-park off Via Aldo Moro at the southern entrance to the town, below the Fortezza. From here it is just two or three minutes' walk to the town centre.

• If you have time, you could include the **abbey of Sant'Antimo** on a longer drive to Monte Amiata and the extreme south of the region (➤ 143) or through the tiny villages and hamlets of the Val d'Orcia: Castiglione d'Orcia, Rocca d'Orcia and Campiglia d'Orcia. It's also easily seen as part of a drive to Pienza (➤ 132) and Montepulciano to the east (➤ 135).

• After standing empty for some 500 years, Sant'Antimo now has a small community of French monks. **Services** in the abbey on Sunday morning often include beautiful plainsong chants.

• Some of the best prices for **Brunello or Rosso di Montalcino wines** are to be found not in the many up-market wine shops around town, but in the local Co-op supermarket at the western edge of the town, between Via Ricasoli and Via della Libertà.

In more depth Montalcino's **coat of arms** features a holm oak atop six hills, a reference to the probable derivation of the town's name – the Latin *Mons Ilcinus*, or Mount of the Holm Oak.

the richest in Tuscany, a status bolstered by its position on important pilgrimage and trade routes.

Parts of the ancient 9th-century church still exist, but most of the present church dates from a particularly large bequest in 1118, details of which are engraved on the stone around the **high altar**. The abbey authorities immediately looked to the mother church of the Benedictines in Cluny, France, and to French architects, for the design of the church, which is why its layout – a basilican plan with an ambulatory (a walkway around the altar) and radiating chapels – is unique in Tuscany and only found in a handful of other Italian churches. Both the abbey's interior and exterior are striking by any standards, a gloriously simple Romanesque building embellished with some beautiful carving; in particular, note the capital of the second column on the right of the nave, which depicts Daniel in the lions' den.

Montalcino's Fiaschetteria Italiana is an excellent place to buy wine or take a break from sight-seeing

TAKING A BREAK

Fiaschetteria Italiana is a café with a lovely interior. Or, for a more substantial meal, try the **Taverna dei Barbi** (► 148).

Tourist office

➕ 197 D2 ✉ Costa del Municipio 8 ☎ 0577 849331; www.prolocomontalcino.it ⏰ Tue–Sun 10–6

Fortezza

➕ 197 D2 ✉ Piazzale della Fortezza ☎ 0577 849211 ⏰ Daily 9–8, Apr–Oct; Tue–Sun 9–6, Nov–Mar 🏛 Castle and *enoteca*: free; Battlements: inexpensive (combined ticket with Museo Civico available)

Museo Civico e Diocesano d'Arte Sacra

➕ 197 D2 ✉ Ex-convento di Sant'Agostino, Via Ricasoli 31 ☎ 0577 846014 ⏰ Tue–Sun 10–1, 2–5:40, Nov–Mar; Tue–Sun 10–1, 2–5:50, Apr–Oct 🏛 Moderate (combined ticket with Fortezza battlements available)

Sant'Antimo

➕ 197 D2 ✉ Near Castelnuovo dell'Abate ☎ 0577 835659; www.antimo.it ⏰ Mon–Sat 10:150–12:30, 3–6:30, Sun 9:15–10:45, 3–6 🏛 Free

At Your Leisure

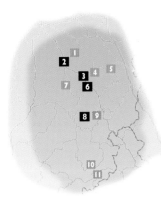

Tourist Office
197 D2 ✉ Via Soccini 32 ☎ 0577 80971

Museo d'Arte Sacra
✉ Via Soccini 18 ☎ 0577 807181
🕐 Tue–Sun 10–1, 3–7, mid-Mar to Oct; Sat–Sun 10–1, 2:30–6, Nov to mid-Mar
✋ Inexpensive

Museo della Mezzadria
✉ La Tinaia, Piazzale Garibaldi
☎ 0577 809075;
www.museomezzadria.it
🕐 Tue–Sun 10–6 ✋ Moderate

2 Buonconvento

Buonconvento, 27km (16.5 miles) south of Siena, has unattractive outskirts, but beyond these is a walled medieval centre – a brick-built redoubt forged by the Sienese as a part of their southern defences.

The town is easily and quickly seen, especially if you're on road SS2 en route for Montalcino or visiting Monte Oliveto Maggiore a few kilometres to the east (▶ 130). There's little to see or do save wandering the old streets, where you should devote most time to the Museo d'Arte Sacra, typical of Tuscany's many tiny small-town museums. Here, as elsewhere, the richness of the collection is out of all proportion to the size of the town. Highlights among the medieval Sienese paintings on display are an *Annunciation* by Andrea di Bartolo and the *Madonna del Latte*, or "Madonna of the Milk", by Luca di Tommè. The latter shows a breast-feeding Madonna, an unusual subject in Italian art but relatively common in parts of Tuscany, where several churches claimed to have reliquaries containing drops of the Virgin's milk. Also interesting is the Museo della Mezzadria, with varied displays devoted to the rural and social history of the region.

3 San Quirico d'Orcia

San Quirico is a strange mixture of the enchanting and the banal; a blend of bland modern housing, built after bomb damage in World War II, and exquisite medieval churches and Renaissance gardens. It has a rambling, forlorn feel, but is worth a brief stop on a drive between Siena (44km/ 27 miles to the north) and southern

San Quirico d'Orcia's Collegiata, with medieval carvings on its façade

Tuscany, or between Montalcino (15km/9 miles to the west) and Pienza (9.5km/6 miles to the east).

The partly walled village takes its name from San Quirico a Osenna, one of many churches that grew up on the Via Francigena, an ancient pilgrimage route between Rome and northern Europe. Today, its highlight is another church, the Collegiata, a 12th-century Romanesque gem off Piazza Chigi built on the ruins of a much older church. The Lombard-influenced carvings around the doors are exceptional, as are the interior's inlaid Renaissance choir stalls and a painting of the *Madonna and Saints* by Sano di Pietro in the north (left) transept. The choir stalls were originally from a chapel in Siena cathedral (▶ 95).

On the edge of the village, near the Porta Nuova, are the Horti Leonini (open daily dawn–dusk; free), peaceful Renaissance gardens laid out in 1580. Walk down Via Dante Alighieri to see the house at No 38, which is said to have once hosted St Catherine of Siena, and the lovely 11th-century church of Santa Maria Assunta.

Tourist Office

⊞ 197 D2 ⊠ Via Dante Alighieri 33
☎ 0577 897211;
www.comune.saquirico.it ⏰ Mon–Sat 10–1, 3:30–6:30, Apr–Oct

❻ Bagno Vignoni

Try to arrive in Bagno Vignoni early in the morning, to enjoy one of Tuscany's more magical sights in full. The hill village's main square, Piazza delle Sorgenti, is actually not a square at all but a large pool containing a natural hot spring – when the air is cool a mist rises from the warm water, drifting over the little square and its old stone buildings in an eerie shroud. The springs were known to the Romans and enjoyed by popes and saints – Catherine of Siena took the waters and Pius II built a 15th-century summer house (now a hotel) close to the square. Lorenzo de' Medici (▶ 55) also came here, the Medici having built the arcaded loggia and *piscina* (pool) that holds the spring. You can

Natural hot springs feed the pool that dominates Bagno Vignoni's main square

no longer bathe in the square, but you can soak in the waters for a fee in the nearby Hotel Posta Marcucci.

The village lies in the midst of some pretty countryside – the small lanes radiating from the central square lead into the surrounding woods and fields.

⊞ 197 D2 ⊠ Bagno Vignoni lies 1km (0.5 miles) west of the main SS2 road, from which it is signposted 5km (3 miles) south of San Quirico d'Orcia

❽ Monte Amiata

Stand on the ramparts of Pienza (▶ 132), or at many other viewpoints in central Tuscany, and one brooding and solitary peak dominates the view – Monte Amiata (1,738m/5,702 feet). Southern Tuscany has few genuine mountains, unlike the north and east of the region, but Monte Amiata's isolated position and distinctive pyramid shape – it is part of an extinct volcano – are still striking. It lies too far south of Siena and Florence for the attentions of most visitors, but can be worked into a drive from Montalcino or Pienza, or as part of a longer journey between Siena and places such as Sovana (▶ 144) and Pitigliano (▶ 145).

Views of the Tuscan countryside from the volcanic peak of Monte Amiata

On a clear day you should drive up the mountain for some staggering views – there is a road that stops at a cluster of bars. You might also want to walk in the great beech and other woods that swathe the mountain's slopes – there are plenty of marked trails suitable for short strolls or major hikes that start from the roads that ring the mountain. If you have time, you should also drive between the numerous little villages that lie on the mountain's flanks – among them, Seggiano, Arcidosso, Castel del Piano and others. None, save Abbadia San Salvatore, have any great artistic treasures, but they all have their own distinct charm.
✚ 197 D2

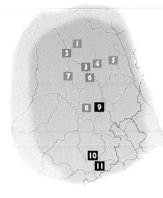

🟑 Abbadia San Salvatore

This small town takes its name from the third of the great trio of abbeys in southern Tuscany – Monte Oliveto, Sant'Antimo and San Salvatore. In the town's medieval quarter, on Via del Monastero, you'll find the abbey, which dates from about 743, making it one of Tuscany's oldest. It was reputedly founded by a Lombard king, Rachis, though much of the present building – built in Monte Amiata's distinctive brown trachite stone – dates either from 1036 (notably the crypt) or from restoration work carried out in the 13th century. The interior's Latin-cross plan, however, is widely considered the first of its kind in Tuscany. Most of the abbey's works of art were removed to Florence after the town fell to the Medici in 1559. Only the superb crypt captivates, a wonderfully austere space dominated by 35 fluted and beautifully carved columns.

Tourist Office
✚ ✚ 197 E2 ✉ Via Adua 25 ☎ 0577 775811; www.amiataturismo.it

🔟 Sovana

By Tuscany's standards, the landscape south of Monte Amiata to the border of the region of Lazio, is relatively unremarkable, with few towns and villages of note. The one exception is a pocket of countryside on Lazio's border, home to a pair of interesting villages, namely Sovana and Pitigliano.

Tiny Sovana amounts to little more than a single street, Via di Mezzo. In its day, however, the settlement was one of the region's most important centres, as the power base of the local Aldobrandeschi nobility and the birthplace of Hildebrand, who became Pope Gregory VII in 1073.

This, in part, accounts for the presence of one of Tuscany's most beautiful parish churches, the 13th-century Santa Maria, on the Piazza del Pretorio. Inside, the simple interior is dominated by lovely frescoes and a carved *ciborium* (altar canopy), a rare pre-Romanesque palaeo-Christian work from the 8th or 9th century.

The Aldobrandeschi's erstwhile presence also accounts for Sovana's Cattedrale di SS Pietro e Paolo, whose scale and splendour are out of all proportion to the size of the village. To reach it, walk down either of the two lanes that lead off Piazza del Pretorio. The building dates from different eras: many of the carvings were executed in the 8th century; most of the apse and crypt date from the 10th century; the frescoes and carvings on the capitals of the nave's columns were executed from the 12th century onwards.

Sovana also lies at the heart of an area rich in Etruscan remains. Dotted around the vicinity are many tombs, most of which are signposted on the road which leads to and from the village. Some of the best can be seen as you drive east to Sorano, 10km (6 miles) away, where part of the road runs past small niche tombs cut into the rock. Sovana also has a couple of good hotels and restaurants (➤ 149).

🔢 197 D1

⓫ Pitigliano

Pitigliano is an imposing sight from afar, its castle and medieval houses crowded on to a ridge of volcanic rock that rises sheer from the surrounding countryside. The Etruscans settled here around the 6th century BC, but the village prospered most in the 13th and 14th centuries, when it was owned by the powerful Orsini family who provided no fewer than three popes. Until World War II it also had a thriving Jewish community – a synagogue survives on Via Zuccarelli.

Beyond Piazza Garibaldi stand a large aqueduct and fortress, both completed in the 16th century by architect Giuliano da Sangallo. Inside the fortress is the Palazzo Orsini, with beautifully decorated and furnished rooms. For the most part, however, Pitigliano's main rewards come from wandering its handful of streets and admiring the views of Monte Amiata.

🔢 197 D1 ✉ Pitigliano's museums have erratic opening times: for information contact the small visitor centre on Via Roma ☎ 0564 614433 or the local council offices 0564 616322

Pitigliano's medieval houses, perched on a volcanic ridge, make an impressive sight

Where to... Stay

Montalcino and Pienza make good bases for exploring the smaller centres and superb countryside of southern Tuscany, but you need to book in advance. Montepulciano is slightly less well placed, but has far more accommodation. A variety of private rooms, *agriturismo* (▶42) and rural hotels across the region provide other alternatives. Details of these are available from local tourist offices (▶41).

MONTALCINO

Albergo Il Giglio €

This 3-star hotel just south of the Piazza Garibaldi has been a Montalcino fixture for many years, but for a while standards slipped. Renovation has now turned things around, and the hotel makes a good alternative to Dei Capitani. The 12 rooms are presented in a traditional style with period furniture, in keeping with the medieval town house in which the hotel is located. The best rooms have original frescoes and views over the countryside to the rear. There is a reasonable restaurant, though there are plenty of good alternatives in town. Breakfast is expensive, so aim to have a coffee and croissant in the Fiaschetteria Italiana instead (▶148).

➕ 197 D2 ☒ Via Soccorso Saloni 5 ☎ 0577 848 167; fax: 0577 848167; www.gigliohotel.com ☺ Closed for a period in Jan

Dei Capitani €€

This 3-star converted town house is one of the most appealing hotels in Montalcino, at the northern end of the town. All 29 rooms are comfortable and decorated in a fresh, modern style, but the best rooms are those to the rear, with wonderful views over the countryside. All rooms have telephones, air-conditioning and TVs. In summer, the terrace, small garden and panoramic bar area are a bonus, as is the small swimming pool, on a slope behind the hotel. There is no restaurant, but breakfast is served and included in the room price. A handful of parking places are available outside the hotel. Note that there are five extra rooms in a separate *dipendenza* (annexe).

➕ 197 D2 ☒ Via Lapini 6 ☎ 0577 847227; fax: 0577 847239; www.dei-capitani.it ☺ Closed mid-Jan to Feb

MONTEPULCIANO

Duomo €–€€

This family-run, 3-star hotel is a safe choice, thanks to its friendly welcome and excellent position just a few moments' walk from the cathedral and main Piazza Grande. It has 13 bright, modern and unelaborate rooms decorated with simple fabrics, marble or tiled floors and the occasional period detail.

➕ 197 E2 ☒ Via San Donato 14 ☎ 0578 757473; fax: 0578 757473; www.albergoduomolibero.it

Il Marzocco €

The 3-star Il Marzocco is the smartest hotel in Montepulciano. It occupies a 16th-century *palazzo* and has been run by generations of the same, very obliging family for more than 100 years. Its location just inside the Porta al Prato at the northern end of the Corso leaves a steep climb to Piazza Grande. The 16 rooms are simply but elegantly furnished with period furniture – the best have terraces with panoramic views. Limited private parking is available and the hotel has a reasonable restaurant.

➕ 197 E2 ✉ Piazza Girolamo Savonarola 18 ☎ 0578 757262; fax: 0578 757530; www.albergoilmarzocco.it ⊘ Closed mid-Jan to mid-Feb

La Terrazza €

There may be cheaper private rooms in town, but this 2-star is the best bet if you are looking for an inexpensive, clean hotel. It is centrally located on a quiet side street that runs south from the church of San Francesco and just a few minutes' walk from Piazza Grande.

➕ 197 E2 ✉ Via Piè al Sasso 16 ☎ 0578 757440; fax: 0578 757440; www.laterrazzadimontepulciano.com

Il Chiostro di Pienza €€€

Pienza had no central hotel until Il Chiostro opened in the mid-1990s. The superb 3-star hotel lies just off the main street and takes its name from the courtyard (*chiostro*) of the 15th-century convent from which it was converted. As befits an establishment that is part of the exclusive Relais & Châteaux group of hotels, the communal areas and 37 rooms are simple but elegant, with period furniture and tasteful fabrics.

Many original features have been retained, notably wooden ceilings, brick vaults and odd patches of frescoes. Some rooms enjoy views of the countryside, and there is also a small garden area, gym, swimming pool and restaurant. Breakfast is included in the room price. You will need to book well ahead to secure one of the more lovely rooms.

➕ 197 E2 ✉ Corso Rossellino 26 ☎ 0578 748501; fax: 0578 748440; www.relaisilchiostrodipienza.com

Corsignano €€

There is nothing wrong with the 3-star Corsignano, which for years was Pienza's only sizeable lodging, but its thunder has rather been stolen by Il Chiostro. The hotel suffers by comparison in not being within the town walls – it is located a short walk west of Piazza Dante off the main road into Pienza. The building is also modern, and the views from the 406 rooms uninspiring – those to the front look on to the road, those to the rear look on to a car-park with views of the country-side beyond. The rooms are clean and comfortable, although their décor is slightly dated. Prices are well below those of Il Chiostro, and there is a much better chance of finding space here at short notice, both a bonus. There is no restaurant, but breakfast is available and included in the room price.

➕ 197 E2 ✉ Via della Madonnina 11 ☎ 0578 748501; fax: 0578 748166; www.corsignone.it ⊘ Closed mid-Jan to Feb

Castello di Ripa d'Orcia €€

This 3-star hotel is built around a mighty *borgo* (fortified village) that dates from the 13th century. It also sits at the heart of some beautiful countryside, so peace and quiet are assured, and you can hike on marked trails that start right outside the walls. The seven rooms (available nightly), and eight apartments are large and simply furnished and can be taken on a weekly basis. Meals are available. The nearest village is San Quirico d'Orcia, 7km (4 miles) northeast.

➕ 197 D2 ✉ Via della Contea 1, Ripa d'Orcia ☎ 0577 897376; www.castellodiripadorcia.it

For other accommodation options in Sovana and near Montepulciano and Monte Amiata, see Hotel-Restaurant Etrusca, La Chiusa and Silene on pages 148–149.

Where to...
Eat and Drink

Prices
Expect to pay for a three-course meal for one with wine

€ under €26   €€ €26–€52   €€€ over €52

Cooking in southern Tuscany is generally regional and uncomplicated. Wine here is a special treat, due to three outstanding reds – Vino Nobile, Brunello and Rosso di Montalcino. General opening times are given, but note that these can vary according to the time of year, the arrival and departure time of the last customer, or just the whim of the owners.

Osteria del Leone €

This traditional-looking and often lively osteria has a simple and straightforward approach to cooking, with Tuscan basics such as tripe, soups, crostini, and pici and pappardelle pastas: it also serves hearty seasonal dishes such as wild boar, wild fennel and anatra all'uva (duck with grapes).

🚪 197 D2   ✉ Via dei Mulini 3
☎ 0577 887300   ⏰ 12:30–2:30,
7:30–10:30. Closed Mon, periods in
Nov and Feb

Fiaschetteria Italiana €

A local institution, this is the best café and bar in town, thanks to its fine 19th-century interior and central position on the main square (there are outside tables in summer). You can also buy local wine here by the glass or by the bottle.

🚪 197 D2   ✉ Piazza del Popolo 6
☎ 0577 849043   ⏰ Daily 7:30
am–midnight. Closed Thu Nov–Feb

Taverna dei Barbi €€

This smart restaurant is annexed to a Brunello vineyard 5km (3 miles) southeast of Montalcino. You can indulge in good local cooking and home-produced wines in a tasteful, rustic dining room dominated by a huge stone fireplace.

🚪 197 D2   ✉ Fattoria dei Barbi, La
Croce, Località Podernovi ☎ 0577
841200 or 0577 847117
⏰ 12:30–2:30, 7:30–10:30. Closed
Tue pm, Wed (except Aug), Jan, and
two weeks in Jul

Taverna Il Grappolo Blu €

The cool, stone-walled medieval interior of this informal restaurant has two small dining rooms with space for just 35 people, so be sure to book. It's located in a stepped alley off the main Via Mazzini. The pasta dishes are especially good and also often innovative – watch for some fiery sauces with plenty of garlic and chillies – and the wine list is good, including wines from the Caparzo and Castello Romitorio vineyards. Service, however, can be a bit slow at busy times.

🚪 197 D2   ✉ Via Scale di Moglio 1
☎ 0577 847150   ⏰ Daily 12:30–2:30,
7:30–10:30

Silene €€

People come from miles around to eat at Silene, tucked away just outside Pescina, one of the tiny villages ringing the summit of Monte Amiata. The cooking makes use of ingredients from the local area –

mushrooms, asparagus, roebuck, boar, truffles, snails and much more. There's nothing rustic about the refined cooking, however. The seven rooms in the adjoining 3-star hotel need to be booked in advance, as does a place in the restaurant for dinner or Sunday lunch.

➕ 197 D2 ⊠ Signed from Pescina, 4km (2.5 miles) east of Seggiano ☎ 0564 950805; fax: 0564 950553 ⏰ 12:30–2:30, 7:30–10:30. Closed Mon

MONTE OLIVETO

Da Ottorino €

This informal restaurant-pizzeria lies about 9km (5.5 miles) north of the abbey at Monte Oliveto Maggiore, on the outskirts of Asciano. It occupies an old farmhouse – you eat in the converted stables or at tables outside – signed off the road towards Rapolano Terme. You can feast on succulent hams and warm crostini (toasts) as starters, pastas such as pici con pancetta e fagioli (with pancetta and beans) and, for main courses, simply grilled cuts of meat such as vitella con funghi (veal and mushrooms) and arista con le melanzane (pork with aubergines). Also pizzas. No credit cards.

➕ 197 D2 ⊠ Via Sante Marie 114, Asciano ☎ 0577 718770 ⏰ 12:30–2:30, 7:30–10:30. Closed Mon and 2 weeks in Jul

MONTEPULCIANO

Caffè Poliziano €

The best café in Montepulciano, with an art nouveau interior and good cakes, snacks and Vino Nobile wines by the glass. There is a more formal restaurant for fuller meals.

➕ 197 E2 ⊠ Via di Voltaia nel Corso 27–9 ☎ 0578 758 615 ⏰ Bar: daily 7 pm–midnight; Bar-restaurant: daily 12:30–2:30; Restaurant: daily 7:30–10:30

La Chiusa €€€

The small village of Montefollonico, 8km (5 miles) northwest of Montepulciano, is home to this former mill and award-winning hotel-restaurant (the hotel has 14 high-priced rooms). Meals are also expensive but outstanding. Dishes might include crespelli ai funghi (pancakes filled with mushrooms) or agnello da latto al rosmarino (tender lamb with rosemary). Booking is essential.

➕ 197 E2 ⊠ Via della Madonnina 88, Montefollonico ☎ 0577 669668; fax: 0577 669593 ⏰ 12:30–2:30, 7:30–10:30. Closed Tue and mid-Jan to mid-Mar

Osteria Borgo Buio €–€€

This restaurant is housed in 14th-century wine cellars and adorned with numerous antiques. Food is simple and Tuscan: vegetable tartlets among the starters and coniglio ripieno (stuffed rabbit) or polpettone (meatballs) with vegetables and pistachios as entrées.

➕ 197 E2 ⊠ Via di Borgo Buio 10 ☎ 0578 717497 ⏰ Thu–Mon 12:30–2:30, 7:30–10:30, Tue–Wed 7:30–10:30

PIENZA

Latte di Luna €€

This family-run trattoria near the centre of the village has simple but appetising food: try the daily specials or local pici all'aglione (pasta in garlic and tomato sauce). Be sure to book, especially in summer if you want to eat outdoors.

➕ 197 E2 ⊠ Via San Carlo 2–4 ☎ 0578 748606 ⏰ 12:30–2:30, 7:30–10:30. Closed Tue and periods in Feb and Jul

SOVANA

Hotel-Ristorante Etrusca €€

A simple but beautiful interior in a building dating from 1241 provides the elegant setting for this restaurant. The 12 rooms in the adjoining 3-star hotel provide an excellent base for exploring the Tuscan countryside.

➕ 197 D1 ⊠ Piazza del Pretorio 16 ☎ 0564 616183/614193 ⏰ 12:30–2:30, 7:30–10:30. Closed Wed

Where to...
Shop

The best buy here is wine, from Montalcino (Brunello di Montalcino and Rosso di Montalcino) or Montepulciano (Vino Nobile di Montepulciano). Olive oils, honey and cheese are also noted specialities.

MONTALCINO

Montalcino is full of shops selling wine and gourmet foods. One of the cheapest places is the Co-op supermarket off Via Ricasoli, and one of the nicest the **Fiaschetteria Italiana** in the Piazza del Popolo (▶ 148). Many vineyards sell directly to the public, but most require appointments (details from the tourist office). One that doesn't is the

Fattoria dei Barbi (La Croce, 8km/ 5 miles southeast of Montalcino; tel: 0577 841111; open daily).

PIENZA

Pienza is renowned for its *pecorino* (sheep's cheese). Much cheese is brought from elsewhere, however, so read the labels. A good shop is **La Cornucopia** (Piazza Martiri della Libertà, tel: 0578 748150), or you can visit local producers such as **Silvana Cugusi**, 10km (6 miles) away off the SS146 road for Montepulciano at Via della Boccia 8 (tel: 0578 757558).

MONTEPULCIANO

Contucci (Via del Teatro 1, tel: 0578 757006; open daily) is a central outlet for Vino Nobile. The **Enoteca Oinochoe** (Via di Voltaia nel Corso 82, tel: 0578 757524) sells wine by leading local producers. For olive oil, visit Piazza Pasquino 9, an outlet for a co-operative of 650 olive-growers.

Where to...
Be Entertained

Southern Tuscany offers very little in the way of nightlife, but the area has numerous pageants and festivals devoted to food and wine, particularly in summer and early autumn. Contact tourist offices for details, or look for posters.

MONTALCINO

The start of the hunting season is celebrated with the **Torneo dell' Apertura della Caccia** (second Sun in Aug), with processions and archery competitions in medieval costume. A similar event is the Sagra del Tordo (last Sun in Oct).

PIENZA

The **Fiera** (first Sun in Sep) is a celebration of the town's cheese and includes a medieval street market and fair. At the main morning Mass on most Sundays you can hear monks singing plainsong at Sant' Antimo abbey (▶ 140).

MONTEPULCIANO

The key festival is the **Bravio delle Botti** (last Sun in Aug), a barrel-rolling race between the town's eight districts, with processions and vast banquets.

The **Feast of the Assumption** (14–16 Aug) is celebrated by the *Bruscello*, a series of plays and concerts in the town's squares.

Northern Tuscany

Getting Your Bearings

Northern Tuscany does not have the many small historic villages and hill towns of southern Tuscany, nor as much of the pretty pastoral countryside found elsewhere – the landscapes here are dominated by forested and marble-streaked mountains – but in Lucca and Pisa it has two cities that stand comparison with any in Italy, and the region's two most compelling urban centres after Florence and Siena.

Lucca is unmissable – an urbane and immediately likeable city. Pisa is far less charming, but in the Leaning Tower and its surrounding buildings it has one of the most beautiful medieval ensembles in Italy. The two cities are only a few kilometres apart, but Lucca is by far the better place to stay.

Whereas Pisa was badly bombed during World War II, leaving much of the city with a modern architectural veneer, Lucca is almost completely unspoiled. Clasped within a ring of walls, its grid of cobbled streets, dating back to Roman times, is thickly scattered with Romanesque churches, museums, galleries, gardens and, in the words of the American novelist Henry James, "everything that makes for ease, for plenty, for beauty, for interest and good example." Lucca is also a city in which it is a pleasure to wander at random or to join the locals and ride around by bicycle (there are several rental outlets).

Pisa, on the other hand, is a much larger city and one that concentrates its historic treats in one or two key areas. Chief of these is the Campo dei Miracoli, or "Field of Miracles", a large grassy piazza that provides the stage not only for the famous Leaning Tower, but also for the less celebrated but almost equally beautiful cathedral and Baptistery. Elsewhere, the city's charms are confined to one or two galleries and isolated churches.

Outside these two cities, northern Tuscany's rewards are mostly rural and

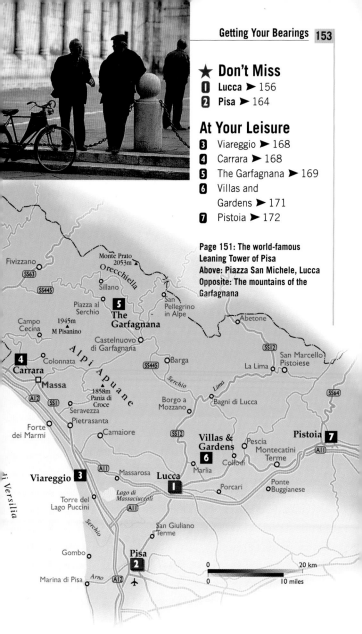

**Page 151: The world-famous Leaning Tower of Pisa
Above: Piazza San Michele, Lucca
Opposite: The mountains of the Garfagnana**

Fivizzano
(SS63)
(SS445)
Monte Prato 2053m
Orecchiella
Sillano
Piazza al Serchio
5 The Garfagnana
San Pellegrino in Alpe
Abetone
Campo Cecina
1945m
M Pisanino
Castelnuovo di Garfagnana
(SS445) Barga
La Lima
San Marcello Pistoiese
(SS12)
(SS12)
4 Carrara
Colonnata
Alpi Apuane
Serchio
Limo
(SS64)
Massa
(A12) (SS1)
1858m Pania di Croce
Seravezza
Pietrasanta
Borgo a Mozzano
Bagni di Lucca
Forte dei Marmi
Camaiore
(SS12)
Villas & Gardens
6
Pescia
Collodi
Montecatini Terme
Pistoia 7
(A11)
Versilia
Viareggio 3
Massarosa
(A11)
Lucca
1
Marlia
Porcari
Ponte Buggianese
Torre del Lago Puccini
Lago di Massaciuccoli
(A11)
di Versilia
Serchio
San Giuliano Terme
Gombo
Pisa
2
Marina di Pisa
Arno (A12)

0   20 km
0   10 miles

cenic. Around Lucca lie a medley of villas and gardens, while to the north is he Garfagnana region, defined by the Alpi Apuane mountains noted for Carrara narble mines, and the wild, forested slopes of the Orecchiella. These offer great lriving or walking opportunities, with lots of marked trails, or you can enjoy a cenic train ride through the area. For those who fancy an afternoon on a beach, 'iareggio is a traditional seaside resort, while Pistoia, one of Tuscany's least vis-ted historic towns, offers yet more in the way of art and architecture.

Three days are plenty to see Pisa and Lucca, with time left over to devote either to Lucca's villas and gardens or to the varied countryside of the Garfagnana. If you are flying to Pisa, see the city when you arrive and then drive to Lucca, where you can then stay for two nights.

Northern Tuscany in Three Days

Day One

Morning

Travel to – or wake up in – **1 Lucca** (► 156), booking a hotel for two or three nights (► 173). Visit the **tourist office** (► 41) and then walk to Piazza San Michele to see the church of San Michele in Foro and Casa di Puccini (► 156). Have coffee at Caffè di Simo (► 175) then visit the Duomo (left) and its sights.

Lunch

Have lunch at Da Leo (► 175), or buy a picnic to eat on Lucca's town walls.

Afternoon

Continue exploring the eastern and northern parts of Lucca, visiting **Piazza del Mercato**, **Museo Nazionale di Villa Guinigi**, **Casa Guinigi** and the churches of **Santa Maria Forisportam**, **San Frediano** and **San Pietro Somaldi**. In the late afternoon, explore the shops on Via Fillungo. Have dinner at Buca di Sant'Antonio (► 174).

Day Two

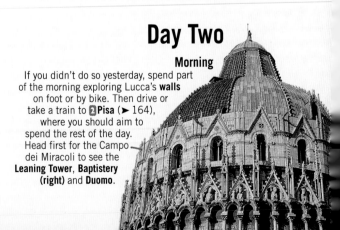

Morning

If you didn't do so yesterday, spend part of the morning exploring Lucca's **walls** on foot or by bike. Then drive or take a train to **2 Pisa** (► 164), where you should aim to spend the rest of the day. Head first for the Campo dei Miracoli to see the **Leaning Tower, Baptistery (right)** and **Duomo**.

See the **Museo dell'Opera del Duomo,** with its renowned sculptures by Giovanni Pisano now or after lunch. If you like markets, note that you'll need to to visit Pisa's main **Mercato Vettovaglie** (➤ 176) when you arrive, as it closes in the afternoon.

Lunch

Have lunch at La Mescita (➤ 175) or Osteria dei Cavalieri south of the Campo.

Afternoon

Visit the Museo dell'Opera and admire Piazza dei Cavalieri (above) before visiting the **church of Santa Maria della Spina** and one or both of Pisa's **main museums** (➤ 166). Break for tea, coffee or a snack in Pasticceria Salza (➤ 175). If you want to shop, head for Borgo Stretto (➤ 176) after about 4 pm, when many shops re-open after the afternoon break.

Return to Lucca for dinner, or for a treat stop at the Gazebo restaurant at the Locanda L'Elisa hotel (➤ 173) on the road between the two cities.

Day Three

Spend the morning either exploring more of Lucca or drive out of the city to see some of the **6 villas and gardens** in the countryside nearby (➤ 171, Villa Torrigiani, below). From here you could visit **7 Pistoia** (➤ 172), which would leave you well placed for reaching Florence or Siena. Alternatively, devote the day to the **5 Garfagnana** (➤ 169), driving up the Serchio valley, perhaps seeing the Orecchiella mountains before crossing the Alpi Apuane. Depending on time and inclination, you could see **4 Carrara** (right) and its marble mines (➤ 168) or spend an hour or two on the beach at **3 Viareggio** (➤ 168). Note, though, that the 30km (18.5-mile) drive down the coast from Carrara is not particularly attractive.

❶

Lucca

Lucca is the most intimate and charming of Tuscany's cities, a civilised and untroubled backwater where neither the pace of life nor the appearance of the medieval streets and squares seems to have changed over the centuries. Preserved within a redoubtable oval of walls, the city is full of exquisite churches, fascinating museums and galleries, and plenty of quiet corners and flower-hung lanes.

Medieval buildings abound in Piazza San Michele

Piazza San Michele

Lucca's heart is Piazza San Michele, the site of the old Roman forum, or *foro*, hence the name of San Michele in Foro, the beautiful **Romanesque church** at the piazza's centre. The church was begun in 1070 but never finished, the result of a financial shortfall caused by the vast sums of money lavished on its façade. One of Italy's most dazzling church exteriors, it is an intricate medley of tiny loggias, blind arcades and countless decorated columns; the decoration and distinctive striped marble walls are repeated in churches around the city. The architectural style was borrowed from Pisa – it is often known as Pisan-Romanesque – and developed during the course of Pisa's trading links with the Orient (► 165). Few of these exotic influences found their way into the church's austere interior, however, where the only outstanding work of art is a late 15th-century painting by Filippino Lippi of *Saints Jerome, Sebastian, Roch and Helena* (at the end of the south nave).

A few moments' walk away from Piazza San Michele lies the **Casa di Puccini**, birthplace of Giacomo Puccini (1858–1924), the composer responsible for operas such as *Tosca*, *La Bohème* and *Madame Butterfly*. His former home is now given over to a music academy and a small museum filled with artefacts connected with the composer – old scores, costume designs, portraits and the piano on which he composed his last opera, *Turandot*. A couple of streets to the west, on Via San Paolino, stands the baroque church of San Paolino, unremarkable save for the fact that Puccini served as organist here in his youth.

From Piazza San Michele you should head south on either Via Vittorio Veneto or Via Beccheria to **Piazza Napoleone**, named after Napoleon Bonaparte, who presented the city to his sister, Elisa Baciocchi, during his campaigns in Italy at the beginning of the 19th century. The large building on the square's western flank is the **Palazzo della Provincia** (1578–1728), erstwhile home of Lucca's ruling councils. Behind the palace rises San Romano, an impressive medieval church that has been under restoration for many years. A short walk east of Piazza Napoleone brings you to Piazza San Martino, the stage for Lucca's magnificent cathedral, the **Duomo di San Martino**.

The Duomo

The cathedral was begun in 1060 on or close to the site of several earlier churches, though work on its glorious façade, a close facsimile of San Michele, was only completed around 1241. The façade's squashed appearance – the third of its three arches is decidedly smaller than its neighbours – came about because it had to be squeezed alongside the bell-tower to its right, the lower half of which (built originally as a defensive redoubt) was already in place when work on the façade began.

The exterior's most important works of art are the **13th-century reliefs** on and around the three principal doors. Noted Pisan sculptor Nicola Pisano was responsible for the carvings on the left-hand door – an *Annunciation*, *Nativity*, *Adoration of*

The Archangel Michael crowns the façade of San Michele in Foro

the Magi, and for the *Deposition* in the lunette above the door. The carvings between the doors are attributed to Guidetto da Como, the architect responsible for much of the façade: they portray episodes from the Life of St Martin (San Martino) and a series of narrative scenes depicting the labours of the Twelve Months of the Year – look out for December's pig-sticking.

The distinctive arched façade of the cathedral

The cathedral's **interior** has some equally notable works of art. One of the most eye-catching is the **Tempietto** (1482–5), an octagonal chapel midway down the nave, designed by local sculptor Matteo Civitali (1435–1511) to house the *Volto Santo* (Holy Face), a cedar-wood Crucifix reputed to be an exact likeness of Christ carved by Nicodemus, an eyewitness to the Crucifixion. Scholars believe it is a 13th-century copy of an 11th-century copy of an original 8th-century statue, but pilgrims still venerate the image.

Three of the labours associated with the Twelve Months of the Year above the main portal of the cathedral

Civitali was responsible for other interesting works around the cathedral, notably the Altare di San Regolo (1484) or Tomb of St Regolus, an early bishop of Lucca

(on the wall right of the high altar), and the Tomb of Pietro da Noceto (1472), secretary to Pope Niccolò V. The **Tomb of Illaria of del Carretto** (1408) is a sublime funerary monument by the Sienese sculptor Jacopo della Quercia, which portrays the body of Illaria, wife of Paolo Guinigi, member of a dynasty that ruled medieval Lucca for decades. The dog at her feet is a symbol of her faithfulness. The tomb is housed in the sacristy off the south aisle (small fee).

The sacristy admission also admits you to the **Museo della Cattedrale** on Piazza Antelminelli, home to a collection of paintings, sculptures and religious artefacts, and the **church of Santi Giovanni e Reparata**. Excavations in this ancient church in the northwest corner of Piazza San Martino have uncovered remnants of Roman buildings, parts of Lucca's first medieval cathedral, and two 5th- and 8th-century baptisteries.

The Walls and East of the Town

The streets near the cathedral are a convenient point from which to climb up to Lucca's tree-lined **walls** (1544–1645), part or all of which you should walk or cycle along at some

work by Fra Bartolommeo in the Museo Nazionale di Villa Guinigi

point during your visit – they enclose the city for a distance of 4.2km (2.5 miles) The walls were built to counter the threat from Florence and to replace older medieval walls made redundant by advances in weaponry: in the event, they never had to be defended in earnest and were converted into the present-day promenade in the 19th century.

From the cathedral it also makes sense to explore Lucca's eastern fringes, which contain a small assortment of worthwhile sights. The first is **Santa Maria Forisportam** ("St Mary Outside the Gates"), an unfinished 13th-century Pisan-Romanesque church which takes its name from the fact that it once lay outside the limits of the Roman and medieval city. It stands at the intersection of Via della Rosa and Via Santa Croce. To its southeast lies the **Giardino Botanico**, Lucca's pretty and peaceful botanical garden, while to the east on or close to Via Santa Croce and Via Elisa is a **quartet of small churches**: SS Trinità, San Ponziano, San Gervasio and San Michelotto. The last stands close to the entrance of the Villa Bottini, also known as the Villa Buonvisi, whose Italianate gardens are worth a visit.

North of the villa is the **Museo Nazionale di Villa Guinigi**, a major city museum housed in a palace built for the Guinigi family in 1418. It has a large and eclectic collection of paintings, sculpture, textiles, Roman and Etruscan archaeological displays, silverware and important works by the painter Fra Bartolommeo and the sculptor Matteo Civitali, the latter best known for his work in the cathedral. Look out, too, for the lovely cathedral choir stalls (1529) decorated with inlaid wood images of Lucca. A few steps west of the entrance to the museum on Via della Quarquonia lies **San Francesco**, a huge 13th-century church noteworthy only for a few frescoes.

A more captivating church lies a little farther west, the Romanesque **San Pietro Somaldi**. It dates from the 12th

Piazza Anfiteatro is built over an old Roman amphitheatre

he 12th-entury osaic of the scension at an Frediano

century, but was built over a Lombard chapel raised as early as 763. Walk south from here and pick up Via Guinigi, one of Lucca's most evocative old streets, and less than 200m (220 yards) from San Pietro stands the **Casa Guinigi**, another rambling palace built for the Guinigi family. Its key feature is a medieval tower, the 44.25-metre (48-yard) **Torre Guinigi**, unmistakable by virtue of the holm oaks growing from its battlements. It is well worth climbing the tower for some wonderful views over the medieval rooftops. The city once had 250 similar towers.

Piazza Anfiteatro to San Frediano

Retrace your steps north on Via Guinigi and turn left on Via Antonio Mordini and then first right on the little alley that leads into **Piazza Anfiteatro**. The piazza's oval shape corresponds exactly to the outline of the Roman amphithe-atre which once stood here. Much of the stone from the arena was ran-sacked in the 12th century to build Lucca's churches and palaces, but fragments of the structure still exist embedded in the piazza's buildings.

From the square's northern edge it is just a few steps across Lucca's main street, Via Fillungo, to **San Frediano** (1112–47), Lucca's third most important church after San Michele and San Martino. The façade is unusual for its 13th-

he 12th-entury Fontale ustrale font in an Frediano

century mosaic of the Ascension, while the interior is distinguished by a 12th-century carved font, the **Fontale Lustrale**. Behind and to the left of these is a chapel containing the uncorrupted body of St Zita, a 13th-century Lucca-born maid who became the patron saint of servants. Also admire the fine frescoes (1508–9) on a variety of subjects by the little-known Amico Aspertini in the **Cappella di Sant' Agostino**.

Via Fillungo takes you south from San Frediano back to Lucca's heart, but by following a more circuitous route you can also take in other sights around the north and west. The closest of these to San Frediano is the **Palazzo Pfanner** (1667), where the 18th-century gardens – but not the palace – are open to the public. Almost alongside are the 14th-century church of Sant' Agostino and the chapel of San Salvatore in Muro. Farther west stands the Museo Nazionale di Palazzo Mansi, a rambling museum which makes up for a lack of genuine masterpieces by the richness and variety of its decorated apartments, tapestries, fabrics, carpets, precious *objets d'art* and fine furniture.

TAKING A BREAK

One of the best cafés is **Caffè di Simo** (➤ 175), which has a delightful 19th-century interior.

The elaborate gardens of Palazzo Pfann

LUCCA: INSIDE INFO

Top tips The best way to visit Lucca is by **train** – the station is a few moments' walk from the city walls. If you arrive by car, you may find a parking space at Piazzale Giuseppe Verdi. Otherwise, park outside the walls and walk to the centre.

• It is well worth **renting a bike** in Lucca: unusually for Italy, which is devoted to the motor car, locals largely get around on bicycles and you can follow suit, to explore the town and to ride around the ramparts. There are several rental outlets around the city, including the visitor centre and Piazza Santa Maria.

• A **combined ticket** to see the cathedral sacristy, the Museo della Cattedrale and Santi Giovanni e Reparata church is much cheaper than buying individual tickets for each sight.

San Michele

✚ 202 C3 ✉ Piazza San Michele ☎ No phone ⏰ Daily 7:40–noon, 3–6. Closed during services 💵 Free

Casa di Puccini

✚ 202 B3 ✉ Corte San Lorenzo 9, Via di Poggio 30 ☎ 0583 584028
⏰ Daily 10–6, Jun–Sep; Tue–Sun 10–1, 3–6, Oct–May 💵 Inexpensive

Duomo di San Martino

✚ 203 D2 ✉ Piazza San Martino ☎ 0583 490530 ⏰ Cathedral: Daily 7–6/7, May–Sep; 7–5, Oct–Apr. Sacristy: Mon–Fri 9:30–5:45, Sat 9:30–6:45, Sun 9 am–10 am and 1–5:45, Apr–Oct; Mon–Fri 9:30–4:45, Sat 9:30–6:45, Sun 9 am–10 am, 3–5, Nov–Mar 💵 Cathedral: free; Sacristy: inexpensive; Combined ticket with Museo della Cattedrale and Santi Giovanni e Reparata: moderate

Museo della Cattedrale

✚ 203 D2 ✉ Piazza Antelminelli 5 ☎ 0583 490530 ⏰ Daily 10–6, Apr–Oct; daily 10–2, Nov–Mar (Same hours for Santi Giovanni e Reparata) 💵 Inexpensive

Museo Nazionale di Villa Guinigi

✚ 203 F4 ✉ Via della Quarquonia ☎ 0583 496033 ⏰ Tue–Sat 8:30–7, Sun 8:30–1 💵 Moderate (combined ticket with Palazzo Mansi: expensive)

Torre Guinigi

✚ 203 D3 ✉ Via Sant'Andrea ☎ 0336 203221 ⏰ Daily: call for times 💵 Inexpensive

San Frediano

✚ 202 C4 ✉ Piazza San Frediano ⏰ Mon–Sat 8:30–noon, 3–5, Sun 10:30–5. Closed during services

Palazzo Pfanner

✚ 202 C4 ✉ Via degli Asili 33 ☎ 0583 954029 ⏰ Daily 10–6, Mar–Oct; by appointment Nov–Feb 💵 Palazzo: moderate. Gardens: inexpensive

Museo e Pinacoteca Nazionale di Palazzo Mansi

✚ 202 A3 ✉ Via Galli Tassi 43 ☎ 0583 55570 ⏰ Tue–Sat 8:30–7, Sun 8:30–1:30 💵 Moderate (combined ticket available with Villa Guinigi)

2

Pisa

Pisa is so closely associated with one dramatic building – the Leaning Tower – that it's all too easy to overlook the city's glorious cathedral and Baptistery, not to mention an idiosyncratic little church, an evocative medieval piazza and its trio of art-filled museums.

For centuries Pisa was one of Italy's greatest cities. An Etruscan and then a Roman colony, it prospered throughout the Middle Ages, reaching the peak of its power in the 11th to 12th centuries, when its maritime prowess yielded the riches that would help finance the Leaning Tower and many other buildings. Naval defeats and the loss of its harbour to silt then led to a waning influence and after 1406, when Florence assumed control of the city, it became little more than a centre of science and learning.

Campo dei Miracoli

Today's visitors are denied much of the city's former glory, however, for a great deal of the old city was destroyed by World War II bombing in 1944. Pisa is therefore something of an

Pisa's Duomo, flanked by the famous Leaning Tower

anomaly in a region famed for its medieval patina, as post-war rebuilding means that both the city's suburbs and much of what should be its historical core have a bland, modern appearance. The great exception is the **Campo dei Miracoli** ("Field of Miracles"), a grassy sward that survived the bombs and is home not only to the celebrated Leaning Tower, but also to the Duomo (cathedral), Baptistery and a medieval cemetery, the Camposanto.

Decisive intervention by scientists and engineers during the 1990s means that the **Leaning Tower** – which had threatened to collapse – now appears to be safe. The fame of the tower has long overshadowed the Baptistery and Duomo, which rank among Tuscany's most outstanding medieval buildings.

The **cathedral** was begun in 1064, well before the cathedrals of Florence (1296) and Siena (1179), a hint as to the relative wealth of Pisa at the time. Its ornate marble-striped exterior, in particular the tiny columns and arcades of the façade, provided the model for similar Pisan-Romanesque churches across central Italy, notably in Lucca, Siena and Florence. The style developed in the wake of Pisa's trading links with the Orient, which brought the city into contact with the architecture of the Middle East and eastern Mediterranean.

Before entering the cathedral, take time to admire the **Portale di San Ranieri** (1180), a door that once provided the building's main entrance but which now lies behind the right (south) transept facing the Leaning Tower. Its bronze panels portray stories from the *New Testament*, while its architrave is made up of Roman friezes and reliefs salvaged from an earlier building dating from the 2nd century.

Sadly, many of the cathedral's interior treasures were destroyed by fire in 1595, though at least two masterpieces survived: one, the apse mosaic of *Christ in Majesty* (1302) by Cimabue, the second a superlative carved **pulpit** (1302–11) by Giovanni Pisano, one of several medieval Pisan artists whose work influenced Italian sculpture for centuries.

The work of Giovanni and another of these sculptors, Nicola Pisano, adorns the circular **Baptistery** (begun 1152), the beautiful circular building a short distance from the cathedral. Both men were responsible for much of the delicate carving that embellishes the building's exterior, added between 1270 and 1297, though it is the work of Nicola, in the shape of another breathtaking pulpit (1260), that holds centre stage inside the Baptistery's largely plain interior. A sculptor from northern Italy, Guido Bigarelli da Como, was responsible for the other main highlight, an inlaid font dating from 1246.

Some idea of how close Pisa came to losing these treasures in 1944 can be gained by visiting the **Camposanto**, a medieval cemetery contained within a large Gothic cloister on the Campo's northern edge. In its day, the cloister was decorated with one of Tuscany's most important fresco cycles, but an incendiary bomb destroyed all but a handful of the precious frescoes below. One or two panels survived, along with a variety of carved tombs and headstones from different eras. Various *sinopie*, the rough sketches often found beneath frescoes, were also salvaged, and are now displayed in the Museo delle Sinopie on the southern side of the Campo.

Nicola Pisano's beautiful Baptistery pulpit

Pisa's Museums

Other items saved from the bombing, or otherwise removed from the buildings of the Campo, are housed in the **Museo dell'Opera del Duomo**, in the square's southeast corner.

Pisa's other principal museum, the **Museo Nazionale di San Matteo**, lies 1.5km (1 mile) east of the Campo dei Miracoli. If you want to walk here, head first for Piazza dei Cavalieri, a square ringed by medieval buildings, pausing in Piazza Vettovaglie, home to a lively market held every morning except Sunday. Via Dini leads from Piazza dei Cavalieri to Borgo Stretto, where you'll find Pisa's most interesting shops. A left turn at the street's southern end by the River Arno takes you along Lungarno Mediceo to Piazza San Matteo and the museum. Among its great works are a bronze bust of San Lussorio by Donatello and fine paintings by Masaccio, Simone Martini, Fra Angelico and Gentile da Fabriano. More paintings, ceramics and decorative arts are in the **Museo Nazionale di Palazzo Reale** farther west.

Just across the river, on Lungarno Gambacorti, stands the 14th-century **Santa Maria della Spina**. It was built by a merchant who had obtained a "thorn" (*spina*) from Christ's Crown of Thorns, hence its name and the deliberately spiky appearance of its exterior carvings.

TAKING A BREAK

Pasticceria Salza on Borgo Stretto, is ideal for lunch, or for a more formal meal try the **Osteria dei Cavalieri** (► 175).

PISA: INSIDE INFO

Top tips If you are **flying** in or out of Pisa (▶ 36), consider visiting the city's sights – which can be seen in a couple of hours – on the day you arrive or depart.
● One-way systems and parking restrictions make it difficult to visit central Pisa and the Campo dei Miracoli by car. One option is to visit the city from Lucca (▶ 156) by **train**. It's a 15-minute walk from the station to the Campo dei Miracoli, or you can take a taxi or city bus No 1 from the station forecourt.
● For the Duomo, Baptistery, Museo dell'Opera and Camposanto, a choice of **combined tickets** (moderate–expensive) is available. To **prebook tickets** (compulsory) to the **Leaning Tower** visit www.opapisa.it (at least 16 days in advance) or go to the ticket office next to the tourist office. For further information call 050 560547.

Duomo, Baptistery, Museo dell'Opera, Camposanto

🞤 196 B4 ✉ Campo dei Miracoli ☎ 050 560921; www.duomo.pisa.it; Leaning Tower visits 050 560547; www.opapisa.it
🕐 Tower: daily 8:30–8:30, Apr–Sep; 9:30–5, Nov–Feb; 9–7, Mar and Oct; 8:30 am–11 pm, mid-Jun to mid-Jul. Guided visits only. Duomo: Mon–Sat 10–1, 3–5, Sun 1–5, Jan–Feb and Nov–Dec; Mon–Sat 10–6, Sun 1–6, Mar; Mon–Sat 10–8, Sun 1–8, Apr–Sep; Mon–Sat 10–7, Sun 1–7, Oct. Baptistery: daily 10–5, Jan–Feb; 9–6, Mar; 9–7, Apr and Oct; 10–5, Nov–Dec.
Camposanto/Museo dell'Opera: opening hours as for Baptistery (except daily 8–8, Apr–Sep; 9–7, Oct) 🎟 Inexpensive (combined tickets available: expensive)

Museo Nazionale di San Matteo

🞤 196 B4 ✉ Piazza San Matteo ☎ 050 541865 or 050 971 1395
🕐 Tue– Sat 8:30–7, Sun 8:30–1 🎟 Moderate (combined ticket with Palazzo Reale: expensive)

Museo Nazionale di Palazzo Reale

🞤 196 B4 ✉ Piazza Carrara, Lungarno Pacinotti 46 ☎ 050 926511
🕐 Mon–Fri 9–2:30, Sat 9–1:30 🎟 Moderate (combined ticket with Museo Nazionale: expensive)

The Palazzo dei Cavalieri (left) and Santo Stefano in Piazza dei Cavalieri

At Your Leisure

❸ Viareggio

The coastal town of Viareggio does have things to see – a handful of art nouveau buildings on the palm-lined seafront for a start – but virtually no one comes here for the sights. Rather they are here for the beach, which is one of the best on a tract of coast known as the Riviera di Versilia that stretches north to the Ligurian border. Much of this coastline is lacklustre or worse – the chic resort of Forte dei Marmi is an honourable exception – which is why the ordered, late 19th-century elegance of Viareggio is so attractive. Many of the visitors here are Florentines escaping the city for the day – the resort is a little over an hour by road or rail from Tuscany's landlocked capital.

There is plenty of sand on the long, broad beach, but it is divided up between *stabilimenti bagnari* (bathing concessions), which means you have to pay to use the beach. Payment may sound invidious, but it does mean

that the sand is groomed and kept clean and it also allows you to use sunloungers, showers, changing rooms and other facilities.

Viareggio is also crammed with inexpensive hotels, as well as numerous pizzerias, fish restaurants, shops and nightlife.

Tourist office
🚹 196 B4 ✉ Viale Carducci 10
☎ 0584 962 233; www.versilia.turismo. toscana.it 🕐 Mon–Sat 9–2, 3–7:30, Sun 9–1

❹ Carrara

Carrara has long been synonymous with one thing – marble. The town's distinctive ivory- and milky-grey coloured stone has been quarried from the nearby Alpi Apuane for thousands of years, and been prized by sculptors from Michelangelo – the stone for the statue of *David* came from here – to Henry Moore.

It is well worth driving the short distance from the town to see some of the quarries and the staggering scale of the mining operation. Platforms at

Viareggio is popular with Florentines trying to escape the summer heat in the city

The Alpi Apuane mountains, celebrated for their marble since Roman times

the roadside enable you to watch operations during working hours. Some of the most accessible quarries are at Colonnata, 8km (5 miles) east of the town, but those at Fantiscritti (5km/3 miles to the northeast on a twisting road via Miseglia) are more impressive. Another twisting road, the 446d to the north, offers sensational views, particularly where the road cuts eastward to climb to Campo Cecina at over 1,500m (4,920 feet).

Unlike its near neighbour to the south, Massa, another marble town, Carrara is an attractive place in its own right. At its hill-encircled heart is Piazza Alberica, a gracious square flanked by pretty coloured medieval houses; the 11th- to 14th-century Pisan-Romanesque Duomo is a few moments' walk to the northeast in Piazza del Duomo.

Tourist office
➕ 196 B4 ✉ Viale Vespucci 24, Marina di Massa ☎ 0585 240 063 ⏰ Mon–Sat 9–1, 3–7, Sun 10–noon, Easter–Sep; Mon–Sat 9–1, 3–5, Oct–Easter

🖪 The Garfagnana
The Garfagnana is the name give to a region to the north of Lucca. It centres on the valley of the River Serchio, which divides two beautiful sets of mountains: to its west rise the Alpi Apuane, a rugged and spectacular range of upland meadows, fast-flowing rivers and jagged peaks (the highest point is Pania di Croce at 1,858m/6,094 feet).

To the east lie the forested and more rounded slopes of the Orecchiella – less spectacular to look at, but still no less

wild, beautiful or lofty (the highest point is Monte Prato at 2,053m/ 6,733 feet). Both areas are protected nature parks (*parchi naturali*).

The valley and the mountains are well worth exploring if you have a car. If you don't have transport, then a quaint railway runs from Lucca up the valley and through the mountains to Aulla (connections to La Spezia) near the Tuscan border with Liguria. You could sit back on the train and admire the scenery as far as Piazza al Serchio, then catch a return train to Lucca.

If you're driving up the valley, it's as well to know that the first 20km (12.5 miles) or so from Lucca are fairly uninspiring – only beyond the village of Borgo a Mozzano does

Garzagnanza is just one of the typical Tuscan villages clustered around the Garfagnana mountain region

the scenery begin to improve. You might detour slightly to visit Bagni di Lucca, a quiet but elegant 19th-century spa 27km (16.5 miles) from Lucca that has played host to visitors such as Lord Byron, Shelley and Robert and Elizabeth Barrett Browning.

The best detour, however, is to Barga, a pretty hill village 5km (3 miles) from the valley road that has a wonderful 10th-century cathedral.

Castelnuovo di Garfagnana, 14km (8.5 miles) farther up the valley, is the region's largest town, and is best used as a departure point for drives into the mountains to the east and west. If you have time, almost any minor road has its scenic rewards, but a good loop into the Orecchiella takes you on the minor road to the north (with sensational views en route) to the hamlet of San Pellegrino in Alpe (1,524m/5,000 feet), where there is an excellent folk museum, the Museo Etnografico Provinciale. From here the road climbs to 1,600m (5,250 feet) at Foce dei Radici and then curves back to Castelnuovo via Castiglione di Garfagnana (a total round-trip of 50km/ 31 miles). For a scenic taste of the

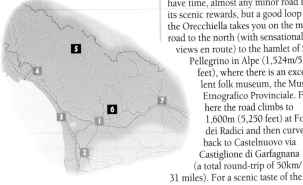

Alpi Apuane, take the minor road west over the mountains either to Massa or Seravezza.

Both the Alpi Apuane and Orecchiella are laced with marked hiking trails, though you should note that many of the better walks in the Apuane start from trailheads in villages such as Levigliani on the western side of the mountains. Unlike much of Tuscany, there are also plenty of large-scale maps for walking available locally. For more information, contact the tourist office in Lucca (► 41) or park centres in Castelnuovo for the Alpi Apuane (Piazza delle Erbe 1, tel: 0583 644242) or, for the Orecchiella, the isolated centre 7km (4 miles) north of the hamlet of Corfino on the minor road to Sillano (tel: 0583 619098 or 0583 644911).

Museo Etnografico Provinciale

🔲 196 B4 ✉ Via del Voltone 14
☎ 0583 649072 🕐 Daily 9:30–1, 2:30–7, Jul–Aug; Tue–Sun 9:30–1, 2:30–7, Jun–Sep; Tue–Sat 9–1, Sun 9–noon, 2–5, Oct–Mar; Tue–Sat 9–1, Sun 9–noon, 2–5, Apr–May
💲 Inexpensive

Villas and Gardens

The countryside round Lucca has many houses and grounds open to the public.

One of the most sumptuous is the Villa Reale, a 14th-century villa about 14km (8.5 miles) northeast of Lucca close to the village of Marlia. Only the gardens are open to the public. The grounds were mostly laid out in the 17th century, but modified in the 19th century by Elisa Baciocchi, the sister of Napoleon Bonaparte. Just 200m (220 yards)

away is a lesser but still charming villa, the Villa Grabau, where both the grounds and ground floor of the building are open to the public.

Of more note is the Villa Torrigiani, or Villa Camigliano, about 8km (5 miles) east of Marlia, a 16th-century villa with baroque and rococo gardens dating from a later period. Just 2km (1.5 miles) away lies the Villa Mansi, 11km (7 miles) northeast of Lucca near the village of Segromigno in Monte. The 16th-century villa is distinguished by its statue-covered façade, while the grounds are a wonderful combination of English-style parkland and Italianate gardens. For further information: www.villelucchesi.net

Villa Reale

🔲 196 C4 ✉ Via Fraga Atta, Marlia
☎ 0583 30 108 or 0538 30 009
🕐 Tue–Sun, guided tours hourly 10–noon and 3–6, Mar–Nov; Dec–Feb by appointment 💲 Moderate

Elegant statuary decorates the baroque gardens of Villa Torrigiani

The Piazza del Duomo, the stage for a magnificent Campanile (bell-tower), 14th-century Gothic Baptistery and art filled cathedral, is not to be missed.

Highlights in the latter include the *Dossale di San Jacopo* (1287–1456), a stunning silver altarpiece that weighs more than a tonne and contains 628 individual figures.

Three churches in the town are also worth visiting: San Bartolommeo, San Giovanni Fuorcivitas and Sant'Andrea, largely for their 13th- and early 14th-century carved pulpits; the best is Giovanni Pisano's pulpit (1301) in Sant'Andrea.

Try to see the Chiesa del Tau, famed for its 14th-century frescoes by local artists, and the Spedale del Ceppo, a 13th-century hospital noted for its 16th-century Della Robbia frieze of coloured and glazed terracotta.

Villa Grabau

✚ 196 C4 ✉ Via di Matraia 269, Marlia ☎ 0583 406098 🕐 Wed–Sun 10–1, 2:15–6:15, Tue 2:15–6:15 (except Jul–Aug, 3–7), Easter–Oct; Sun 11–1, 2–5:30, Nov–Easter 👋 Garden: Moderate; Villa and garden: expensive

Villa Torrigiani

✚ 196 C4 ✉ Via del Gomberaio 3, Camigliano, off the SS 435 ☎ 0583 928041 🕐 Daily 10–1, 3–7, Mar to mid-Nov; mid-Nov to Feb by appointment 👋 Expensive

Villa Mansi

✚ 196 C4 ✉ Via delle Selvette 242, Segromigno in Monte ☎ 0583 920234 or 0583 920096; www.villa-mansi.it 🕐 Tue–Sun 10–1, 3–6, Apr–Oct; Tue–Sun 10–1, 3–5, Nov–Mar. Closed Dec 23–Jan 7 👋 Expensive

7 Pistoia

Pistoia would be a must-see historic town in almost any region other than Tuscany, where there are so many outstanding towns and villages. One reason it isn't is its surroundings, which are largely built-up and uninspiring, and another is its position, which is on the main road and railway line between two more tempting centres: Florence and Lucca.

Push past Pistoia's outskirts, however, and you'll find a fine medieval and Renaissance heart.

Tourist office

✚ 196 C4 ✉ Piazza del Duomo 4 ☎ 0573 21 622; www.comune.pistoia.it 🕐 Tue–Sun 9–1, 3–6

Glazed terracotta decoration above the main entrance to Pistoia's superb medieval cathedral

Where to... Stay

Prices

Expect to pay per double room

€ under €100   €€ €100–€175   €€€ over €175

You generally need to book hotels in Lucca and Pisa well in advance. The resort of Viareggio has a vast array of accommodation in all price categories. Lucca also has a range of private rooms – contact the tourist office for details (▶ 41).

La Luna €€

This family-run 3-star hotel has 29 rooms arranged in two 17th-century palaces that face each other across a sleepy courtyard. All rooms have telephones and TVs, and there is a wide variety of styles, with some larger suites and apartment-type rooms available. There is no restaurant, but (an expensive) breakfast is available.

➕ 202 C4 ✉ Via Fillungo-Corte Compagni 12 ☎ 0583 493634; www.hotellaluna.com 🚫 Closed Jan

Locanda L'Elisa €€€

This luxury 5-star hotel – part of the Relais & Chateaux group – is in a league of its own, and provides a romantic option if you wish to indulge yourself. The former home of Napoleon's sister, Elisa Baciocchi, the neo-classical villa is 4.5km (3 miles) south of Lucca on the road to Pisa. It has just two rooms and eight sumptuous suites, all beautifully decorated in 18th-century style and adorned with a stunning collection of antiques and period furniture: all rooms have views of the villa's park or gardens. There's a large swimming pool and a noted restaurant, Il Gazebo (open to non-patrons), set in an English-style conservatory, which offers refined versions of both Lucchese and Tuscan dishes.

➕ 202 off B1 ✉ Via Nuova–Strada Statale del Brennero 1952 ☎ 0583 379737; www.locandaelisa.it 🚫 Closed for periods in Nov, Dec, Jan and Feb. Restaurant closed Sun

Piccolo Hotel Puccini €

This charming, small 3-star hotel is the first choice in Lucca's centre. Just a few minutes from Piazza San Michele, it occupies a peaceful 15th-century Renaissance palace close to the birthplace of composer Giacomo Puccini (▶ 156). The hotel is capably and enthusiastically run – the owners speak some English – and the 14 cosy rooms, some of which have views of the small square and Puccini statue outside, are bright and tasteful. Limited private parking is available, but must be requested in advance. There is no restaurant, but a Continental breakfast is available.

➕ 202 B3 ✉ Via di Poggio 9 ☎ 0583 55421; www.hotelpuccini.com

Villa La Principessa €€€

This 4-star hotel is the less expensive of Lucca's two leading out-of-town options. It lies close to its rival, the Locanda L'Elisa, about 4.5km (3 miles) south of Lucca on the twisting road to Pisa (the road is also known as the Via Nuova). Parts of the hotel building date back to 1320, when a palace was built for Castruccio Castracani, one of Lucca's most powerful medieval nobles. Most of the present building and its attractive grounds, however,

Where to...
Eat and Drink

Prices
Expect to pay for a three-course meal for one with wine
€ under €26   €€ €26–€52   €€€ over €52

General opening times for restaurants are given, although it should be noted that these can vary based on the time of year, the arrival and departure time of the last customer, or simply the whim of the owners.

LUCCA

Buca di Sant'Antonio €€
The Buca lies in a half-hidden alley just off the southwest corner of Piazza San Michele and has long been the best of the city's central restaurants. As befits an establishment founded in 1787, the service is formal and the cooking is based on Lucchese traditions. Dishes might include *tordelli Lucchesi* (pasta filled with borage, beef, pork and nutmeg); *zuppa di farro* (vegetable soup made with a wheat-like grain); *capretto allo spiedo* (spit-roasted kid goat) and *semifreddo Buccellato*, a mixture of cream and wild berries.

🗺 202 B3 ✉ Via della Cervia 3 ☎ 0583 312199 🕐 12:30–2:30, 7:30–10:30. Closed Sun pm, Mon and a period in Jul

---

date from the 18th century. There are 40 spacious rooms and suites, all with TVs, telephones and air-conditioning, decorated in elegant 18th-century Parisian style with a selection of period and reproduction furniture and antiques. Breakfast is the only meal served.

🗺 202off B1 ✉ Via Nuova-Strada Statale del Brennero 1616 ☎ 0583 370037; fax: 0583 379136 🕐 Closed Nov–Mar

PISA

Hotel Amalfitana €
This 2-star hotel is a reasonable choice in a convenient and central position about midway between the river and the Campo dei Miracoli, just south of the Orto Botanico (Botanical Garden, ▶ 164). The 21 rooms are all clean and modern and are equipped with telephones, televisions and air-conditioning.

Parking is also available There is no restaurant, but breakfast, is served in the modern dining area.

🗺 196 B4 ✉ Via Roma 44 ☎ 050 29000; www.hotelamalfitana.com

Royal Victoria €€
Pisa has virtually no high-class hotels, so this hotel stands out. Its welcoming service and sedate, if old-fashioned style, are just what you would expect of an establishment that has been owned by five generations of the same family since 1839. Its position on the banks of the Arno, between the station and Campo dei Miracoli, is convenient for Borgo Stretto and Piazza dei Cavalieri, central Pisa's main shopping street and piazza respectively. The Leaning Tower and other sights are 10 minutes' walk away. The 48 rooms are clean and comfortable, with or without private bathroom, and there are also three- and four-bed rooms. Parking is available for a fee.

🗺 196 B4 ✉ Lungarno Pacinotti 12 ☎ 050 940111; www.royalvictoria.it

Caffè di Simo €

This is Lucca's loveliest old café, thanks to a fine belle époque interior of brass, marble and mirrors. Puccini is just one of the famous names to have sampled its cakes, pastries, coffee and snacks. The ice-cream here is also some of the best in Lucca.

202 C3 ✉ **Via Fillungo 58**
☎ **0583 496234** ⊙ **8:30–8.**
Closed Mon

Da Leo €

The family-run Da Leo is not the place to come for a quiet and intimate dinner. It is a lively and informal Italian restaurant with just two dining rooms (one large, one tiny) which are invariably crammed with voluble locals tucking into simple and fairly priced Tuscan food such as home-made pasta, grilled meats, soups and stews. The building is medieval, but the décor has the postwar period look of the type of restaurant you might once have found across Italy in the 1950s.

Not much English is spoken, but the staff are helpful and welcoming. No credit cards are accepted.

202 C3 ✉ **Via Tegrimi 1** ☎ **0583 492236** ⊙ **12:30–2:30, 7:30–10:30. Closed Sun pm**

La Mora €€€

Michelin inspectors have rewarded La Mora's sublime Lucchese and Garfagnana cooking with a coveted star, but to sample dishes such as pigeon or rare local specialities such as anguilla (eel) you need to travel 8km (5 miles) northwest of Lucca to the hamlet of Ponte a Moriano. Booking is advised.

203 off D5 ✉ **Via Sesto di Ponte a Moriano 1748** ☎ **0583 406402** ⊙ **12:30–2:30, 7:30–10:30. Closed Wed and periods in Jan and Jun**

La Mescita €

This is just the place if you want to mix with students, university professors and other locals in a homely,

central and inexpensive trattoria. Menus change daily to reflect what is available from the Vettovaglie market stalls nearby, but always reflect local traditions – dishes might include pappardelle con fiori di zucca (pasta strips with courgette flowers), wild fennel and ricotta salad, or baccala bollito con i ceci (boiled salt cod with pulses). The choice of cheese is excellent. The setting is attractive – the vaulted ceilings date from the 15th century – and the atmosphere warm and lively. The only drawbacks are the restaurant's popularity, so book or arrive early.

196 B4 ✉ **Via Cavalca 2, corner of Piazza delle Vettovaglie** ☎ **050 544294** ⊙ **7:30–10:30. Closed Mon and part of Aug**

Pasticceria Salza €

This is the most celebrated and frequented of Pisa's smart cafés. It has been in the same family since the 1920s. The double-fronted shop is located on the city's main shopping street and is ideal for coffee, sandwiches (more than 40 varieties), cakes, snacks or an evening apéritif. Hot sandwiches and a few simple pasta dishes are available at lunch in a separate waiter-service room to the rear. No credit cards.

196 B4 ✉ **Borgo Stretto 46** ☎ **050 580144** ⊙ **Tue–Sun 7:45 am–8:30 pm**

Osteria dei Cavalieri €€€

The two dining rooms of this long-established osteria occupy part of a medieval tower and town-house. A wide range of Tuscan food at reasonable prices is available, including à la carte options such as manzo con fagioli e funghi (beef with beans and mushrooms), plus set meals based around fish, meat or vegetables. The restaurant is conveniently located in the city, just a few moments' walk south of the main Piazza dei Cavalieri.

196 B4 ✉ **Via San Frediano 16** ☎ **050 589858** ⊙ **Mon–Fri 12:30–2, 7:45–10, Sat 7:45–10. Closed Aug**

Where to... Shop

LUCCA

The best shopping streets for shoes, clothes, china and other goods are Via Fillungo and Via del Battistero.

Olive oil from Lucca is considered some of the best in Italy. It is available from supermarkets and food stores (*alimentari*). **Taddeucci** (Piazza San Michele 34, tel: 0583 494933; closed Thu), is a wood-panelled bakery; try local specialities such as *buccellato*, flavoured with aniseed and raisins. For handmade chocolates visit **Caniparoli** (Via San Paolino 96, tel: 0583 53456l, closed Mon) and for quality shoes, bags, and clothes, visit **Cuoieria Fiorentina** (Via Fillungo 155, tel: 0583 491139). For wine go to **Vini Liquori Vanni** (Piazza del Salvatore 7, tel: 0583 491902; www.enoteca-vanni.com, closed Mon and Sun).

The **Mercato del Carmine** in Piazza del Carmine is held every morning except Wednesday and Sunday. A craft market takes place in Piazza San Giusto over the third weekend of the month.

PISA

In Pisa, most of the up-market stores cluster on Borgo Stretto and Corso Italia. The food market, **Mercato Vettovaglie**, is held every morning (7–1:30) except Sunday in Piazza delle Vettovaglie, and there is an antiques market off Borgo Stretto on the second weekend each month.

For chocolates, seek out **De Bondt** (Via Turati 22–Corte San Domenico, tel: 050 501896; closed Sun and Mon). For excellent cheeses, oils, wines and snacks, visit **Gastronomia a Cesqui** (Piazza delle Vettovaglie 38, tel: 050 580269, closed Wed pm, and Sun).

Where to... Be Entertained

LUCCA

Lucca's major festival is the **Luminara di Santa Croce**, a torchlit procession bearing the Volto Santo, the city's most sacred relic, around the streets (14 Sep). This takes place in conjunction with the **Settembre Lucchese**, a series of classical music and other events at various venues (Sep–Oct). A similar illuminated festival, the **Luminaria di San Paolino**, takes place on 11–12 July to commemorate Lucca's patron saint. Other music festivals include the **Estate Musicale Lucchese** (Jul), concerts held in Piazza Anfiteatro and other venues, and the **Stagione Lirica**, operatic performances (Sep–Nov) at the Teatro del Giglio (tel: 0583 46531).

Opera invariably includes works by Lucca's most famous son, Puccini.

PISA

Pisa's main festival is the **Festa di San Ranieri** (16–17 Jun), which involves candlelit processions. This is followed the next day by a rowing regatta in medieval dress to celebrate Pisa's patron saint and recall its former maritime prowess, then the Gioco del Ponte, a tug-of-war in medieval costume held on the city's Ponte di Mezzo (last Sun in Jun).

Visit the tourist office or consult local papers for details of events, particularly if you want to catch one of the occasional concerts in the cathedral or outdoors in Campo dei Miracoli on summer evenings.

Walks & Drives

1 SIENA
Walk

This walk takes you through the heart of old Siena, starting in the north of the city and wending its way south past medieval churches and palaces to the Campo, one of Italy's finest squares. It then winds through the city's less-visited southern quarters, to culminate in the spectacular piazza containing the cathedral and Spedale di Santa Maria della Scala.

DISTANCE 2km (1.2 miles) **TIME** 2–3 hours
START POINT Piazza San Domenico 🚩 200 B4
END POINT Piazza del Duomo 🚩 200 C2

1–2

Start your walk in **Piazza San Domenico**, home to the church of the same name,

see frescoes by Sodoma (▶101). With your back to the church, take Via della Sapienza east from the piazza (note the view of the Duomo to the right), ignoring Via del Paradiso on the left. A further 100m (110 yards) on the right is the **Biblioteca Comunale degli Intronati**, a library founded in 1759 in what was probably Via del Paradiso in what was probably a 13th-century hospital. It contains more than 500,000 books and other documents, including precious letters by St Catherine of Siena and many noted medieval Sienese painters and architects. Just beyond, at the next minor crossroads, is the **church of San Pellegrino alla Sapienza**, built in 1767 over the site of a much older chapel.

Continue straight on at the church to emerge on Banchi di Sopra, a major street that follows the course of the Via Francigena in the city, an ancient pilgrimage route between Rome and northern Europe. Ahead is **Piazza Salimbeni**, home to a trio of fine palaces: Palazzo Tantucci (1548) on the left, the 13th-century **Palazzo Salimbeni** to the rear, and the **Palazzo Spannocchi** (1470) to the right. The Salimbeni family were important bankers and traders in silk and grain, while Ambrogio Spannochi was the treasurer to the Sienese Pope Pius II. A 75m (82-yard) diversion left on Banchi di Sopra brings you to the **church of Santa Maria delle Nevi** (erratic opening hours), known for its wonderful high altarpiece, the *Madonna della Neve* (1477), by Matteo di Giovanni.

3–4

Retrace your steps (south) on Banchi di Sopra. After 175m (190 yards) look for the **church of San Cristoforo** on the left. Romanesque in origin, it was rebuilt in the late 18th century after earthquake damage. Opposite is the **Palazzo Tolomei**, part of the original fortress home of the Tolomei, one of the most powerful of Siena's medieval dynasties of bankers and merchants. It is the oldest surviving private residence in the city, dating to at least 1205. Note the statue of the she-wolf on the street. Continue south to the junction with Banchi di Sotto and Via di Città and the Loggia della Mercanzia (1428–44), an attractive Gothic three-arched loggia. Little alleys to either side take you into **Piazza del Campo** (▶ 92).

4–5

Admire the Campo, possibly from one of its many cafés, then walk to its east side to exit either by Vicolo dei Pollaiuoli or Via dei Rinaldini. Both bring you to Banchi di Sotto, where you should turn right. Immediately on your right stands the **Palazzo Piccolomini**, a majestic palace begun in 1469. Inside, on an upper floor, is the little-known Archivio di Stato (State Archive), open to the public and full of fascinating works of art (▶ 101). Beyond the palace is the **Loggia del Papa** (Loggia of the Pope), built in 1462 on the orders of the Tuscan-born Pope Pius II (Enea Silvio Piccolomini). Take the right fork in front of the loggia and follow it round to the junction with Via del Porrione, named after the Latin "emporium", or "place of the market", as Roman markets once stood nearby.

5–6

Cross Via del Porrione and walk through the arch down Vicolo delle Scotte, passing Siena's **Sinagoga** (synagogue) on the right, the heart

Taking a Break

The **Nannini** café at Banchi di Sopra 95–99 is a good place for a break.

At the corner of Via Sant'Agata and Via della Cerchia is **Il Vinaio dell'Eremita** (tel: 0577 49490; closed Sun), a simple, brick-vaulted wine bar that is perfect for a snack or light meal.

Map labels: Nazionale · San Giuseppe · San Pietro · Sant'Agostino · VIA GIOV. · VIA S. AGATA · SAN PIETRO · CERCHIA · TARTUCA · VIA DELLA · VIA DI CASTELVECCHIO · VIA DI STALLOREGGI · Arco delle Due Porte · VIA DEL ROSSO DI SANSA · ANSA · 6

of the city's Jewish ghetto, created in 1571 by Cosimo I de' Medici. Turn left on Via di Salicotto, then first right to emerge on the Piazza del Mercato. Cross the square and bear right to pick up Via del Mercato and then turn left almost immediately to follow Via Giovanni Dupré. Note the many evocative alleys leading off this street. At the church of San Giuseppe on the left take Via Sant'Agata straight on to a gravel area on your left and the 13th-century **church of Sant'Agostino**, with paintings by Sodoma and Ambrogio Lorenzetti (➤ 97).

6–7

Head through the arch to Via San Pietro and the church of San Pietro (set back on your right) and the red-brick **Pinacoteca Nazionale** beyond (➤ 99). Just before the church turn sharp left on Via di Castelvecchio (an easily missed alley) and bear right to Via di Stalloreggi. Turn left to the Arco delle Due Porte, an arch that formed part of the city's 11th-century walls, passing a house on the left (Nos 91–3) where Duccio painted his famous *Maestà* (➤ 97). Turn right after the arch and follow the peaceful Via del Fosso di

San Ansano to Piazza della Selva, where either Via Franciosa or Via Girolamo lead to Piazza del Duomo or Piazza San Giovanni. In the latter you can see the Battistero di San Giovanni (Baptistery) and then walk up the steps to your right to see the **Duomo** (cathedral), Santa Maria della Scala and **Museo dell'Opera del Duomo** (➤ 95).

Looking down on Siena's Piazza del Campo from the top

2 CHIANTI
Drive

This drive takes you through the heart of Chianti, the name given to much of the region between Florence and Siena. An often wild landscape, it is characterised by rolling hills, rich farmland, heavily wooded slopes, isolated villas and numerous vineyards. Many minor and often circuitous roads run across the region. A good way of getting to Siena from Florence is to follow the Chiantigiana (the SS222), a designated scenic "wine" road that runs for 65km (40 miles) between the two cities.

DISTANCE 110km (68 miles) **TIME** 1 day
START POINT Siena ⊞ 197 D3
END POINT Siena ⊞ 197 D3

Top Tip
Distances may not look great on a map, but Chianti's roads are winding and slow, so allow more time than might seem necessary when exploring the region.

1–2
Begin your tour in Siena by driving to the start of the SS222 (Chiantigiana) road; follow the main road west from Siena's railway station for about 2km (1.2 miles) and you will see signs for the SS222, also listed as the "*Raccordo Siena-Firenze*" (the main dual-carriageway between Siena and Florence), and **Castellina in Chianti**. Within just a few minutes of picking up the SS222 the scenery begins to improve, setting the tone for much of the drive, where the beauty and variety of the landscape takes precedence over historic towns and other "sights". After 6.5km (4 miles) you pass through the hamlet of Quercegrossa (literally "Large Oak") – much of Chianti's forests are made up of oak woods – followed by 7.5km (4.5 miles) of undulating road which brings you to another tiny hamlet, **Fonterutoli**.

Chianti's most familiar views are its hills, dotted with the world-renowned vineyards

Chianti's grapevines cover the region's landscapes

2–3

From here it's about 4km
(2.5 miles) to **Castellina in Chianti**.
Castellina's name – which means
the "little castle" – offers a clue
to its former strategic importance. For many centuries the
town stood at the border
between the territories of

often changed hands –
hence the presence of the
town's fortress. Castellina
was also the headquarters
of the Chianti League, a
military alliance of
Chianti's three main towns
– Gaiole in Chianti,
Castellina in Chianti and
Radda in Chianti – set up
by Florence at the begin-
ning of the 13th century.
Its symbol was the *Gallo
Nero* (Black Cockerel),
now used by one of the
leading consortia of local

wine producers. Stop to look at the town's *Via
delle Volte*, an unusual vaulted street that runs
around the old town walls. From the northern
edge of Castellina take the SS429 road for
Radda in Chianti (10km/6 miles), ignoring the
left fork for Greve in Chianti after about 1km
(0.5 miles). Take a detour 2km (1.2 miles)
south on a minor road from the centre of the
village to San Giusto in Salcio.

3–4

A parish church already documented in 1018,
San Giusto in Salcio is one of Chianti's oldest
places of worship. Return to Radda and follow
the main road east out of the village, taking
a left turn at the major junction after 3.5km
(2 miles). Drive for 6km (4 miles) down this
road to a junction of five roads, where a turn
to the left takes you to the 11th-century
abbey **Badia a Coltibuono** (1km/0.5 mile).

4–5

Return to the five-road junction
and turn right to follow the main
road south to **Gaiole in Chianti**,
a town with unexceptional outskirts but a pretty main street.
Continue south through the
town on the main road

summer, one of Chianti's oldest wine estates. Whether or not you buy anything, the views from here are breathtaking.

5–6

From the junction below the Castello di Brolio take the SS484 road south. After 7.5km (4.5 miles) you come to a crossroads, where a left turn takes you to **San Gusme**, a medieval hamlet with good views. Return to the junction and continue south to **Castelnuovo Berardenga** (4.5km/3 miles), Chianti's most southerly village, and on to the main 326 road 3km (2 miles) beyond. Turn right on the SS326 towards Siena (17km/10.5 miles), perhaps detouring right at Santa Maria a Dofana to **Montaperti**, site of Siena's great victories over Florence in 1260.

(3km/2 miles) to the junction with the 408 to Radda, then turn left and drive for another (3km/2 miles) to the next major junction. Turn left towards San Regolo and after 5km (3 miles) you come to a junction with signs for the 12th-century **Castello di Brolio** (tel: 0577 747104 or 0577 747156, open daily in

Taking a Break

Chianti has only a few towns suitable for refreshment breaks, so a picnic can be a good idea. Passengers will be able to sample wine at a variety of the region's many estates, all of which are well signposted from the road (▶ 20) – drivers should be aware that drink-driving laws in Italy are as strict as in the rest of Europe. The **Antica Trattoria La Torre** on Piazza del Comune 15 in Castellina in Chianti (tel: 0577 740236; closed Fri and 1–15 Sep; moderate) is a simple and popular trattoria run by the Stiaccini family since 1895.

Radda in Chianti has an elegant restaurant for lunch if you didn't stop at Castellina: Il Vignale at Via XX Settembre 23 (tel: 0577 738094; closed Thu and Jan–Feb; expensive).

San Regolo has a relaxed, little restaurant for a late lunch or early dinner, Trattoria San Regolo (tel: 0577 747136; closed Mon).

Castelnuovo has a nice wine bar, Bengodi (Via della Società Operai 11; tel: 0577 355116; closed Mon; inexpensive for light meals).

3 SOUTHERN TUSCANY

Drive

This drive takes you through the historic small towns and villages south of Siena and some of the richest and most archetypal landscapes in Tuscany.

DISTANCE 175km (108 miles) **TIME** 2 days
START POINT Siena ✚ 197 D3
END POINT Pienza ✚ 197 E2

1–2

Start in **Siena**, taking the ring road (SS326) to the eastern side of the city. About 5km (3 miles) from the centre, take the SS438 road, a right turn off the SS326. This runs for about 21km (13 miles) to **Asciano** through the Crete, an area of bare clay hills that in summer are swathed in fields of wheat, flax and sunflowers. Asciano has several

best of which is the Museo d'Arte Sacra, home to important medieval paintings: for more information contact the town's tourist office (Corso Matteotti 18; tel: 0577 719510; closed Nov–Apr).

2–3

From the centre of Asciano take the minor road southeast signed to San Giovanni d'Asso. After 8km (5 miles) turn right at Montefresco and follow another scenic minor road for 3km (2 miles) through Chiusure to the junction with the SS451. Turn left and after 1km (0.5 mile) turn left again to the **Abbazia di Monte Oliveto Maggiore** (▶ 130),

admire the frescoes by Sodoma and Signorelli in the main cloister and perhaps take a break in the abbey café. Return to the SS451, turn left and drive 9km (5 miles) to **Buonconvento** (▶ 142), where the tiny brick-built old centre and art gallery is worth a brief exploration.

3–4

In Buonconvento turn south on the SS2, the Via Cassia, and after 2km (1.2 miles) take the right fork signed to **Montalcino** (14km/9 miles), allowing at least an hour to explore (▶ 138). At the

Taking a Break

The café at the **Abbazia di Monte Oliveto Maggiore** (▶ 130) is a good place for a snack break. **Fiaschetteria Italiana** wine bar or **Taverna Il Grappolo Blu restaurant** in Montalcino (▶ 148) are recommended places for lunch.

central road signed for Castelnuovo dell'Abate and the **abbey of Sant'Antimo** (➤ 139). The abbey is set in stunning countryside, but is closed between 12:30–3 and 10:45–3 on Sunday. Continue southeast beyond

to the junction at **Ansidonia**. Where you head next will depend on where you started, how much time you have, and where you are spending the night. If time is short, a left turn here takes you via the villages of **Castiglione d'Orcia** and **Bagno Vignoni** (➤ 143) to **San Quirico d'Orcia** (➤ 142), all three of which are worth at least a half-hour exploration. From San Quirico you can return to Siena on the SS2. If you have time, however, take the 146 east to **Pienza** (➤ 132). From here it is 13.5km (8 miles) along the SS146 to Montepulciano, but you might also consider the pretty (and part gravel) road from the east of Pienza to Montepulciano via the walled hamlet of **Monticchiello**.

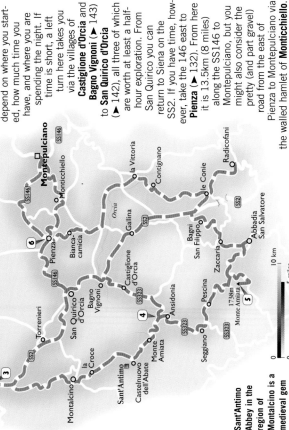

Sant'Antimo Abbey in the region of Montalcino is a medieval gem

The seemingly empty countryside around Montepulciano is typical of much of southern Tuscany

4–5

From Ansidonia, a right turn on the SS323 leads to Seggiano (6km/4 miles), beyond which you should turn left for Pescina. After another 5km (3 miles) – and the start of glorious beech and other woods that flank the slopes of Monte Amiata – you come to a junction where you should turn left. About 2km (1.2 miles) beyond is another junction, where a right turn leads after 5km (3 miles) almost to the summit of **Monte Amiata** itself (1,738m/5,700ft) (➤ 143), the highest point in southern Tuscany. The views on a clear day are breathtaking.

5–6

Backtrack from the summit, take a downhill right turn and drive to **Abbadia San Salvatore** (➤ 144). See the abbey here then drive on the only road north from the town towards Zaccaria, beyond which a left fork leads to the SS2 (7.5km/4.5 miles) via the small spa

village of **Bagni San Filippo**. To the southeast towers the fortress village of **Radicofani**, visible from much of the immediate region. Be sure to drive the 9.5km (6 miles) to see the village if you have time – to reach it turn right on the SS2 and then almost immediately left. The medieval village has two simple **churches,** San Pietro and Sant'Agata, at its heart. From here, return towards the SS2, which takes you to **San Quirico d'Orcia** (➤ 142), or follow prettier minor roads from Le Conie. These head north past Contignano and La Vittoria to Pienza.

Top Tip

The small summer-only tourist office in Radicofani is at Via R Magi 25 (tel: 0578 55684; open Mon–Sat 8–2).

Practicalities

GETTING ADVANCE INFORMATION

Websites
- Official Tuscany website: www.turismo.toscana.it
- Official Florence website: www.firenzeturismo.it
- www.uffizi.firenze.it
- www.terresiena.it

- Alitalia: www.alitalia.it
- Italian Arts and Culture Ministry: www.beniculturali.it
- Florence Service Provider: www.fionline.it
- Italian State Railways: www.trenitalia.it

Florence Tourist Offices
Via Cavour 1r
☎ 055 290832/833
Borgo Santa Croce 29r
☎ 055 234 0444
Piazza della Stazion 4a
☎ 055 212245

BEFORE YOU GO

WHAT YOU NEED

- ● Required
- ○ Suggested
- ▲ Not required
- △ Not applicable

Some countries require a passport to remain valid for a minimum period beyond the date of entry – contact their consulate or embassy for details.

	UK	Germany	USA	Canada	Australia	Ireland	Netherlands	Spain
Passport/National Identity Card	●	●	●	●	●	●	●	▲
Visa	▲	▲	▲	▲	▲	▲	▲	▲
Onward or Return Ticket	○	○	●	●	●	○	○	○
Health Inoculations (tetanus and polio)	▲	▲	▲	▲	▲	▲	▲	▲
Health Documentation (▶ 192, Health)	●	●	▲	▲	▲	●	●	▲
Travel Insurance	○	○	○	○	○	○	○	○
Driver's Licence (national)	●	●	●	●	●	●	●	●
Car Insurance Certificate	●	●	●	●	●	●	●	○
Car Registration Document	●	●	●	●	●	●	●	○

WHEN TO GO

Florence

High season   Low season

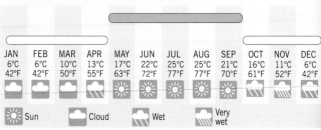

JAN	FEB	MAR	APR	MAY	JUN	JUL	AUG	SEP	OCT	NOV	DEC
6°C	6°C	10°C	13°C	17°C	22°C	25°C	25°C	21°C	16°C	11°C	6°C
42°F	42°F	50°F	55°F	63°F	72°F	77°F	77°F	70°F	61°F	52°F	42°F

☀ Sun   ☁ Cloud   🌧 Wet   🌧 Very wet

Temperatures shown above are the **average daily maximum** for each month.
The best times of the year for good weather are May, June, July, August and September. July and August can be extremely hot and uncomfortable in the cities, although temperatures are lower and more bearable in the Tuscan countryside. Thunderstorms are possible in summer and through September and October.
Winters (January–February) are short and cold, and snow is possible on higher ground, particularly the mountainous region of Northern Tuscany.
Spring starts in March (later in the mountains), but March and April can be humid and sometimes very rainy.
Autumn weather is mixed, but often produces crisp or warm days with clear skies.

In the UK
ENIT
. Princes Street
London
W1R 2AY
☎ (020) 7408 1254

In the US
ENIT
630 Fifth Avenue,
Suite 1565, New York,
NY 10111
☎ (212) 245 4822/3/4

In Australia
Italian Consulate
Fourth Floor
46 Market Street Sydney
NSW 2000
☎ (02) 9262 1666

GETTING THERE

By Air Tuscany is served by two airports: Pisa's Galileo Galilei airport and the smaller Amerigo Vespucci (Peretola) airport just outside Florence. Most European carriers fly to Pisa, but only small jets can use Peretola. Flights to Bologna's Guglielmo Marconi airport can also be useful for Florence and northern Tuscany (► 38).

From the UK British Airways and several charter companies, including the low-cost airline Ryanair, fly to Pisa. Meridiana flies to Florence. The flight time from London to Pisa is two hours.

From the US There are no direct non-stop flights to Pisa or Florence from the US. US carriers fly either to Milan (Malpensa) or Rome (Fiumicino): there are connecting flights from both airports to Pisa, but it is easier to take a train or drive from Rome. Flying time to Rome is 8–10 hours from east coast USA, 11 hours from the west coast.

From Australia and New Zealand Qantas and Air New Zealand fly to Rome or Milan (see "From the US" above). Flying time from Australia's east coast is 21 hours, and 24 hours from New Zealand.

By Rail Numerous fast and overnight services operate to Florence and Pisa from most European capitals. The Italian State Railway, Trenitalia (still often referrd to by its old name, the Ferrovie dello Stato), offers high-speed trains between major Italian cities, and connecting services from both Florence and Pisa to the other major towns in Tuscany. Ticket prices are usually the same or more than equivalent air fares.

TIME

Italy is on GMT+1, making it one hour ahead of the UK, six hours ahead of New York and nine hours ahead of Los Angeles from November to March. Daylight Saving Time adds one hour to these figures between April and October.

CURRENCY AND FOREIGN EXCHANGE

Currency The euro is the legal currency of Italy. Euro notes are issued in denominations of 5, 10, 20, 50, 100, 200 and 500. Coins are denominations of 1, 2 and 5 euro cents and 10, 20 and 50 gold-coloured euro cents. In addition there is a 1 euro coin with a silver centre and gold surround and 2 euro coin with a gold centre and silver surround. Euro coins carry a common European face, and each member state decorates the reverse of the coins with their own motif. All coins and notes are accepted in all member states.

Exchange Most major travellers' cheques – the best way to carry money – can be changed at exchange kiosks (*cambio*) at the airports, Santa Maria Novella railway station in Florence and in exchange offices near major tourist sights. Many banks also have exchange desks, though lines can be long. Most major credit cards (*carta di credito*) are accepted in larger hotels, restaurants and shops, but cash is often preferred in smaller establishments. Most cities and main towns have ATM machines which accept foreign-issued cards.

TIME DIFFERENCES

GMT
12 noon

Florence
1 pm

Rest of Italy
1 pm

Germany
1 pm

USA (NY)
7 am

WHEN YOU ARE THERE

CLOTHING SIZES

UK	Rest of Europe	USA	
36	46	36	
38	48	38	
40	50	40	
42	52	42	Suits
44	54	44	
46	56	46	
7	41	8	
7.5	42	8.5	
8.5	43	9.5	
9.5	44	10.5	Shoes
10.5	45	11.5	
11	46	12	
14.5	37	14.5	
15	38	15	
15.5	39/40	15.5	
16	41	16	Shirts
16.5	42	16.5	
17	43	17	
8	34	6	
10	36	8	
12	38	10	
14	40	12	Dresses
16	42	14	
18	44	16	
4.5	38	6	
5	38	6.5	
5.5	39	7	
6	39	7.5	Shoes
6.5	40	8	
7	41	8.5	

NATIONAL HOLIDAYS

1 Jan	New Year's Day
6 Jan	Epiphany
Mar/Apr	Easter Monday
25 April	Liberation Day
1 May	Labour Day
2 June	Republic Day
15 Aug	Assumption
1 Nov	All Saints' Day
8 Dec	Immaculate Conception
25 Dec	Christmas Day
26 Dec	St Stephen's Day

In addition, some towns and cities have special saints' days and other holidays when businesses may close. In Florence the main city holiday is 24 June (St John's Day).

OPENING HOURS

○ Shops   ● Post Offices
● Offices   ◐ Museums
● Banks   ◐ Pharmacies

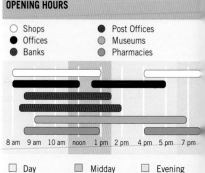

8 am   9 am   10 am   noon   1 pm   2 pm   4 pm   5 pm   7 pm

☐ Day   ☐ Midday   ☐ Evening

Shops Mon/Tue–Sat 8–1, 4–8, Mon 4–8 with seasonal variations. Many stores in major cities open all day.
Offices Mon–Fri 8–noon, 12:30–5.
Banks Mon–Fri 8:30–1:30; major branches may open Saturday and longer weekday hours.
Post offices Mon–Fri 8:15–2 or 7, Sat 8:15–noon or 2.
Museums Varies but often Tue–Sat 9–7, Sun 9–1.
Pharmacies Mon–Sat 8:30–1 and 4–8. In Florence, the railway station's pharmacy and Molteni, Via dei Calzaiuoli 7r, are generally open 24 hours.
Churches 7–noon, 4:30–7. Closed during services.

EMERGENCY 113

POLICE 113 or 112

FIRE 113 or 115

AMBULANCE 113 or 118

PERSONAL SAFETY

Tuscany is generally safe – pickpockets are the main worry in Florence or busy tourist areas – but it's still wise to take commonsense precautions:

• Carry money and valuables in a belt or pouch.
• Close bags and hold them across your front.
• Wear your camera – never put it down on a café table.
• Leave valuables and jewellery in the hotel safe.
• Never leave luggage or other possessions in parked cars.
• Guard against pickpockets, especially in buses, markets and busy shopping or tourist areas.
• Avoid parks late at night.

Police assistance:
 113 from any phone

TELEPHONES

Telecom Italia (TI) payphones are on streets and in bars, tobacconists and restaurants. Most take coins or a phone card (*scheda telefonica*), available from post offices, shops and bars. Tear the corner off the card first.
To dial another number in Florence while there dial the area code then the number. Cheap rate is Mon–Sat 10 pm– 8 am. Hotels usually add a surcharge to calls from rooms. Dial 170 to make reverse charge calls. Dial 12 for operator or directory enquiries.

International Dialling Codes
Dial 00 followed by

UK:	44
USA/Canada:	1
Irish Republic:	353
Australia:	61
Germany:	49

POST

Florence's central post office (*ufficio postale*) is at Via Pellicceria 3. Stamps (*franco-bolli*) can be bought from post offices and *tabacchi*. Mail boxes are red or blue with two slots: one for city mail (*Per La Città*) and one for all desti- nations (*Altre Destinazioni*).

ELECTRICITY

Current is 220 volts AC (50 cycles). Plugs are two-round-pin Continental types; UK, North American and Australasian visitors will need an adaptor. North American visitors should check whether 110/120-volt AC appliances require a voltage transformer.

TIPS/GRATUITIES

Tipping is not expected for all services and rates are lower than in other countries. As a general guide:

Pizzerias	Nearest €2.50 or €5
Trattorias	Nearest €2.50 or €5
Smart restaurant	10–15% or discretion
Bar service	Discretion
Tour guides	Discretion
Taxis	To the nearest €0.50
Porters	€0.50 to €1 per bag
Chambermaids	€0.50 to €1 per day

CONSULATES and EMBASSIES

 UK
☎ 055 284133 or
06 4220 0001

 USA
☎ 055 266951
or 06 46741

 Ireland
☎ 06 697 9121

 Australia
☎ 06 852721

 Canada
☎ 06 445981

HEALTH

 **Insurance** It's essential to take out full travel insurance cover when visiting Tuscany. Nationals of EU countries can obtain medical treatment at reduced cost with the EHIC (European Health Insurance card). However, it is advisable to take out private insurance.

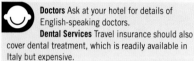 **Doctors** Ask at your hotel for details of English-speaking doctors.
Dental Services Travel insurance should also cover dental treatment, which is readily available in Italy but expensive.

Weather Minor health worries in Tuscany include too much sun, dehydration or mosquito bites: drink plenty of fluids and wear sunscreen and a hat in high summer. Insect repellent may be useful if you have to sleep in rooms with windows open in summer. Tuscany does have poisonous snakes (*vipere*), although bites are generally only fatal if you have an allergic reaction.

 Drugs Prescriptions and other medicines are available from pharmacies (*farmacie*), indicated by a large green cross.

 Safe Water All tap water is safe. So, too, is water from public drinking fountains unless marked "*Acqua Non Potabile*". Mineral water is cheap and widely available.

CONCESSIONS

Senior Citizens (over 65) are entitled to free entrance into state museums and galleries if they are residents of a European Union country.

Students under 18 are also entitled to free entrance into state museums.
For both concessions, you will need to carry some form of identification, such as a passport, as proof of age and nationality.

TRAVELLING WITH A DISABILITY

Medieval centres are difficult for those using wheelchairs, but many pavements now have dropped kerbs and many areas are traffic-free. In Florence, newer buses (grey-green in colour) are wheel-chair accessible as is the "D" electric bus. Many museums have dedicated ramps, lifts and toilets. Tourist offices carry pamphlets with information on accessibility of hotels and attractions in the region.

CHILDREN

Most hotels, bars and rest-aurants will be very welcoming to children, but few have baby-changing facilities. You will need to be extremely careful with young children on Florence's busy streets.

TOILETS

Few Tuscan towns have good public toilets. Most bars have toilets but standards are poor. Men's toilets are signed *Signori*, women's are *Signore*.

CUSTOMS

The import of wildlife souvenirs sourced from rare or endangered species may be either illegal or require a special permit. Before purchase you should check your home country's customs regulations.

SURVIVAL PHRASES

Yes/no **Sì/non**
Please **Per favore**
Thank you **Grazie**
You're welcome **Di niente/prego**
I'm sorry **Mi dispiace**
Goodbye **Arrivederci**
Good morning **Buongiorno**
Goodnight **Buona sera**
How are you? **Come sta?**
How much? **Quanto costa?**
I would like... **Vorrei...**
Open **Aperto**
Closed **Chiuso**
Today **Oggi**
Tomorrow **Domani**
Monday **lunedì**
Tuesday **martedì**
Wednesday **mercoledì**
Thursday **giovedì**
Friday **venerdì**
Saturday **sabato**
Sunday **Domenica**

DIRECTIONS

I'm lost **Mi sono perso/a**
Where is...? **Dove si trova...?**
  the station **la stazione**
  the telephone **il telefono**
  the bank **la banca**
  the restroom **il gabinetto**
Turn left **Volti a sinistra**
Turn right **Volti a destra**
Straight on **Vada dritto**
At the corner **All'angolo**
the street **la strada**
the building **il palazzo**
the traffic light **il semaforo**
the intersection **l'incrocio**
the signs for...
  le indicazione per...

IF YOU NEED HELP

Help! **Aiuto!**
Could you help me, please?
  Mi potrebbe aiutare?
Do you speak English? **Parla inglese?**
I don't understand **Non capisco**
Please could you call a doctor
  quickly? **Mi chiami presto un
  medico, per favore**

RESTAURANT

I'd like to reserve a table
  Vorrei prenotare un tavolo
A table for two please
  Un tavolo per due, per favore
Could we see the menu, please?
  Ci porta la lista, per favore?
What's this? **Cosa è questo?**
A bottle of/a glass of...
  Un bottiglia di/un bicchiere di...
Could I have the bill?
  Ci porta il conto

ACCOMMODATION

Do you have a single/double room?
  Ha una camera singola / doppia?
with/without bath/toilet/shower
  **Con/senza vasca/gabinetto/
  doccia**
Does that include breakfast?
  E'inclusa la prima colazione?
Does that include dinner?
  E'inclusa la cena?
Do you have room service?
  C'è il servizio in camera?
Could I see the room?
  E' possibile vedere la camera?
I'll take this room **Prendo questa**
Thank you for your hospitality
  Grazie per l'ospitalità

NUMBERS

0	**zero**	12	**dodici**	30	**trenta**	200	**duecento**
1	**uno**	13	**tredici**	40	**quaranta**	300	**trecento**
2	**due**	14	**quattordici**	50	**cinquanta**	400	**quattrocento**
3	**tre**	15	**quindici**	60	**sessanta**	500	**cinquecento**
4	**quattro**	16	**sedici**	70	**settanta**	600	**seicento**
5	**cinque**	17	**diciassette**	80	**ottanta**	700	**settecento**
6	**sei**	18	**diciotto**	90	**novanta**	800	**ottocento**
7	**sette**	19	**diciannove**	100	**cento**	900	**novecento**
8	**otto**	20	**venti**			1000	**mille**
9	**nove**			101	**cento uno**	2000	**duemila**
10	**dieci**	21	**ventuno**	110	**centodieci**		
11	**undici**	22	**ventidue**	120	**centoventi**	10,000	**diecimila**

MENU READER

acciuga anchovy
acqua water
affettati sliced cured meats
affumicato smoked
aglio garlic
agnello lamb
anatra duck
antipasti hors d'oeuvres
arista roast pork
arrosto roast
asparagi asparagus
birra beer
bistecca steak
bollito boiled meat
braciola minute steak
brasato braised
brodo broth
bruschetta toasted bread with garlic or tomato topping
budino pudding
burro butter
cacciagione game
cacciatore, alla rich tomato sauce with mushrooms
caffè corretto / macchiato coffee with liqueur/spirit, or with a drop of milk
caffè freddo iced coffee
caffè lungo weak coffee
caffellatte milky coffee
caffè ristretto strong coffee
calamaro squid
cappero caper
carciofo artichoke
carota carrot
carne meat
carpa carp

casalingo home-made
cassata Sicilian fruit ice-cream
cavolfiore cauliflower
cavolo cabbage
ceci chickpeas
cervello brains
cervo venison
cetriolino gherkin
cetriolo cucumber
cicoria chicory
cinghiale boar
cioccolata chocolate
cipolla onion
coda di bue oxtail
coniglio rabbit
contorni vegetables
coperto cover charge
coscia leg of meat
cotoletta cutlets
cozze mussels
crema custard
crostini canapé with savory toppings or croutons
crudo raw
digestivo after-dinner liqueur
dolci cakes / desserts
erbe aromatiche herbs
fagioli beans
fagiolini green beans
fegato liver
faraona guinea fowl
facito stuffed
fegato liver
finocchio fennel
formaggio cheese
forno, al baked
frittata omelette
fritto fried
frizzante fizzy
frulatto whisked

frutti di mare seafood
frutta fruit
funghi mushrooms
gamberetto shrimp/prawn
gelato ice-cream
ghiaccio ice
gnocchi potato dumplings
granchio crab
gran(o)turco sweetcorn
griglia, alla broiled
imbottito stuffed
insalata salad
IVA Value Added Tax (VAT)
latte milk
lepre hare
lumache snails
manzo beef
merluzzo cod
miele honey
minestra soup
molluschi shellfish
olio oil
oliva olive
ostrica oyster
pancetta bacon
pane bread
panna cream
parmigiano parmesan
passata sieved or creamed
pastasciutta dried pasta with sauce
pasta sfoglia puff pastry
patate fritte chips
pecorino sheep's milk cheese
peperoncino chilli
peperone red / green pepper
pesce fish
petto breast
piccione pigeon

piselli peas
pollame fowl
pollo chicken
polpetta meatball
porto port wine
prezzemolo parsley
primo piatto first course
prosciutto cured ham
ragù meat sauce
ripieno stuffed
riso rice
salsa sauce
salsiccia sausage
saltimbocca veal with prosciutto and sage
secco dry
secondo piatto main course
senape mustard
servizio compreso service charge included
spuntini snacks
succa di frutta fruit juice
sugo sauce
tonno tuna
uova strapazzate scambled egg
uovo affrogato / in carnica poached egg
uovo al tegame / fritto fried egg
uovo alla coque soft-boiled egg
uovo alla sodo hard-boiled egg
vino bianco white wine
vino rosso red wine
vino rosato rosé wine
verdure vegetables
vitello veal
zucchero suga
zuppa soup

Atlas

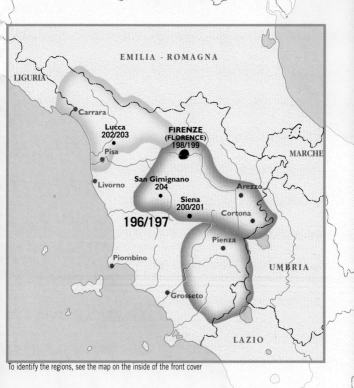

EMILIA - ROMAGNA

LIGURIA

- Carrara
- Lucca 202/203
- Pisa
- FIRENZE (FLORENCE) 198/199
- Livorno
- San Gimignano 204
- Siena 200/201
- Arezzo
- Cortona
- Pienza
- Piombino
- Grosseto

196/197

MARCHE

UMBRIA

LAZIO

To identify the regions, see the map on the inside of the front cover

Regional Maps

International boundary	Built-up area
Regional boundary	City
Major route	Major town
Motorway	Large town
Main road	Town, village
Other road	Featured place of interest
National park	Place of interest

City Plans

Pedestrian area	Information
Railway	Important building
City wall	Featured place of interest

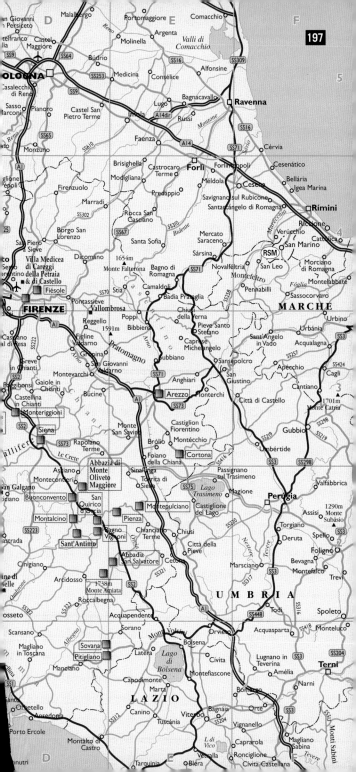

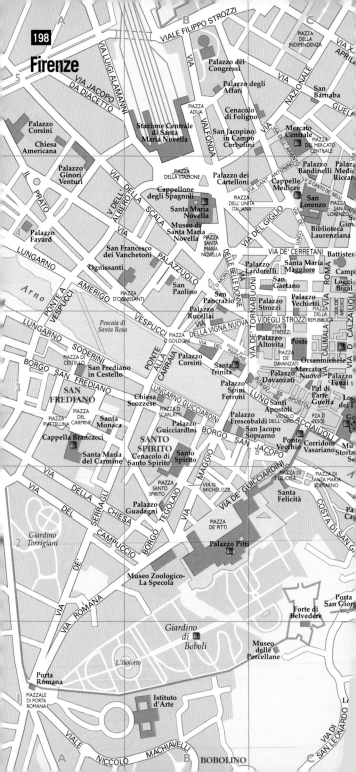

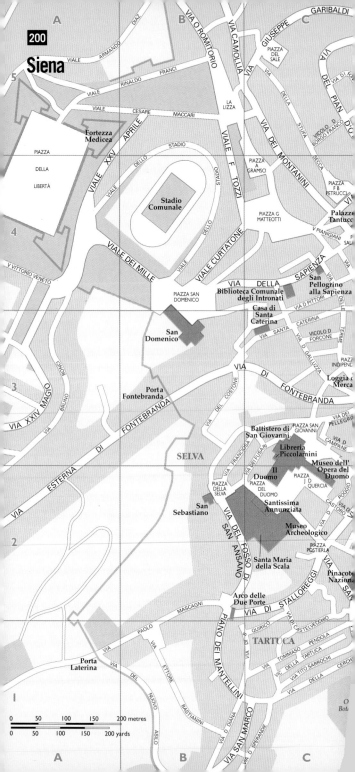

Siena

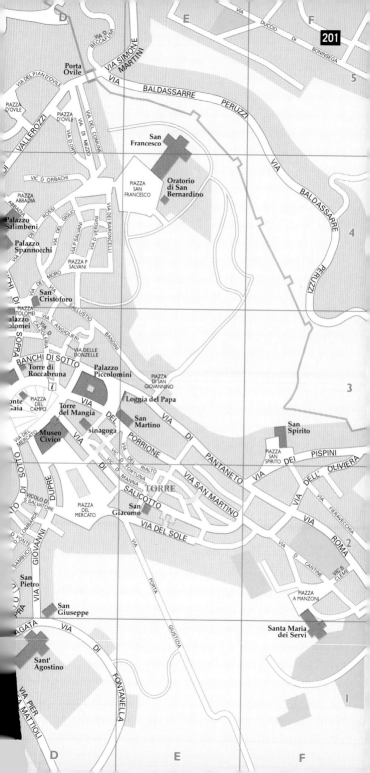

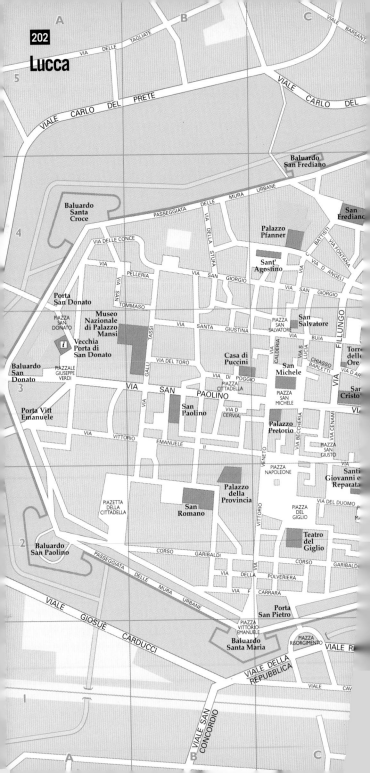

Lucca

VIA DELLE TAGLIATE

VIALE BARSANT

VIALE CARLO DEL

VIALE CARLO DEL PRETE

PASSEGGIATA DELLE MURA URBANE

Baluardo
San Frediano

Baluardo
Santa
Croce

VIA DELLA STUFA

San
Frediano

VIA DELLE CONCE

Palazzo
Pfanner

VIA BATTISTI

VIA FONTANA

VIA SAN GIORGIO

VIA
PELLERIA

VIA SAN TOMMASO

Sant'
Agostino

VIA D. ANGELI

Porta
San Donato

VIA SANTA GIUSTINA

VIA SAN GIORGIO

PIAZZA
SAN
DONATO

Museo
Nazionale
di Palazzo
Mansi

VIA GALLI

VIA TASSI

PIAZZA
SAN
SALVATORE

San
Salvatore

VIA BUIA

VIA FILUNGO

i

Vecchia
Porta di
San Donato

VIA DEL TORO

Casa di
Puccini

VIA CALDERIA

VIA S. LUCIA

CHIASSO
BARLETTI

VIA D. AR

Torre
delle
Ore

Baluardo
San
Donato

PIAZZALE
GIUSEPPE
VERDI

VIA DI POGGIO

San
Michele

San
Cristo

VIA SAN PAOLINO

PIAZZA
CITTADELLA

PIAZZA
SAN
MICHELE

VIA

Porta Vitt
Emanuele

San
Paolino

VIA D
CERVIA

VIA BECCHERIA

VIA CENAMI

VIA VITTORIO EMANUELE II

Palazzo
Pretorio

PIAZZA
SAN
GIUSTO

VIA VENETO

PIAZZA
NAPOLEONE

Santi
Giovanni e
Reparata

Palazzo
della
Provincia

VIA DEL DUOMO

PIAZZETTA
DELLA
CITTADELLA

San
Romano

VIA VITTORIO

PIAZZA
DEL
GIGLIO

Baluardo
San Paolino

PASSEGGIATA DELLE MURA URBANE

CORSO GARIBALDI

VIA DELLA

Teatro
del
Giglio

CORSO GARIBALDI

POLVERIERA

VIALE GIOSUE CARDUCCI

VIA F CARRARA

Porta
San Pietro

PIAZZA
VITTORIO
EMANUELE

PIAZZA
RISORGIMENTO

VIALE R

Baluardo
Santa Maria

VIALE DELLA
REPUBBLICA

VIALE

CAV

VIALE SAN CONCORDIO

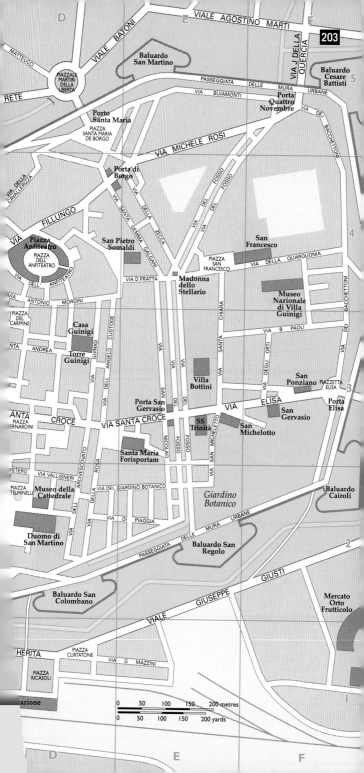

VIALE AGOSTINO MARTI

VIALE BATONI

VIA J DELLA QUERCIA

Baluardo
Cesare
Battisti

Baluardo
San Martino

PIAZZALE
MARTIRI
DELLA
LIBERTA

RETE

MATTEUCCI

PASSEGGIATA DELLE MURA URBANE

VIA BUIAMONTI

Porta
Quattro
Novembre

Porto
Santa Maria

PIAZZA
SANTA MARIA
DE BORGO

VIA MICHELE ROSI

VIA DEI BACCHETTONI

VIA DELLA CAVALLERIZZA

Porta di
Borgo

VIA DEL FOSSO

FILLUNGO

San Pietro
Somaldi

VIA SANTA GEMMA GALGANI

VIA DELLA ZECCA

San
Francesco

Piazza
Anfiteatro

PIAZZA
DELL'
ANFITEATRO

PIAZZA
SAN
FRANCESCO

VIA DELLA QUARQUONIA

VIA D FRATTA

VIA DELL' ANFITEATRO

Madonna
dello
Stellario

Museo
Nazionale
di Villa
Guinigi

VIA DEI BACCHETTONI

ANTONIO MORDINI

PIAZZA
DEL
CARMINE

Casa
Guinigi

VIA B PAOLI

VIA SANTA CHIARA

VIA DEGLI ORTI

ANTA

ANDREA

Torre
Guinigi

VIA DEL CUSTODE

VIA GUINIGI

VIA DELL' ANGELO

VIA SAN

VIA DEL

VIA DEL FOSSO

Villa
Bottini

San
Ponziano

PIAZZETTA
ELISA

Porta
Elisa

Porta San
Gervasio

VIA ELISA

San
Gervasio

SANTA

PIAZZA
BERNARDINI

CROCE

VIA SANTA CROCE

VIA NICOLAO

VIA SAN MICHELETTO

VIA SANTA MICHELETTO

SS
Trinità

San
Michelotto

Santa Maria
Forisportam

VIA DELLA ROSA

VIA ARCIVESCOVATO

STERO

VIA VALLISNERI

Baluardo
Cairoli

PIAZZA
TELMINELLI

Museo della
Cattedrale

VIA DEL GIARDINO BOTANICO

VIA DELLA

Giardino
Botanico

VIA DI PIAGGIA

Duomo di
San Martino

PASSEGGIATA DELLE MURA URBANE

Baluardo San
Regolo

Baluardo San
Colombano

VIALE GIUSEPPE GIUSTI

Mercato
Orto
Frutticolo

HERITA

PIAZZA
CURTATONE

VIA G MAZZINI

PIAZZA
RICASOLI

azione

| 0 | 50 | 100 | 150 | 200 metres |
| 0 | 50 | 100 | 150 | 200 yards |

D   E   F

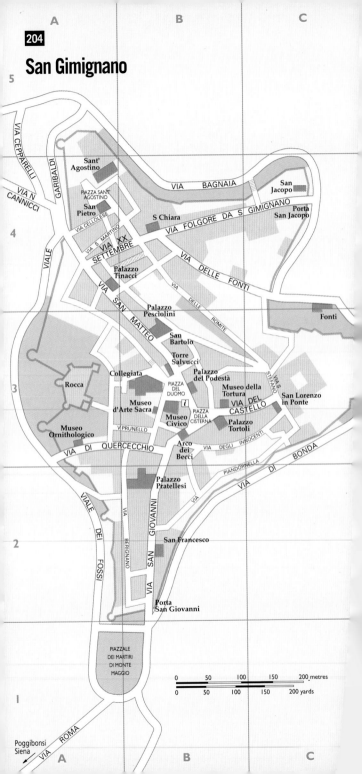

San Gimignano

VIA CEPPARELLI

VIA N CANNICCI

GARIBALDI

Sant' Agostino

PIAZZA SANT AGOSTINO

San Pietro

VIA CELLOLESE

VIA BAGNAIA

San Jacopo

Porta San Jacopo

S Chiara

VIA FOLGORE DA S. GIMIGNANO

VIALE

VIA S. MARTINO

VIA XX SETTEMBRE

Palazzo Tinacci

VIA DELLE FONTI

VIA SAN MATTEO

VIA DELLE ROMITE

Palazzo Pesciolini

Fonti

San Bartolo

Torre Salvucci

Collegiata

Rocca

Palazzo del Podestà

Museo della Tortura

VIA S. STEFANO

VIA DEL CASTELLO

San Lorenzo in Ponte

PIAZZA DEL DUOMO

Museo d'Arte Sacra

i

Museo Civico

PIAZZA DELLA CISTERNA

Palazzo Tortoli

Museo Ornithologico

V. PRUNELLO

VIA DI QUERCECCHIO

Arco dei Becci

VIA DEGLI INNOCENTI

PIANDORNELLA

VIA DI BONDA

VIALE DEI FOSSI

VIA BERIGNANO

VIA SAN GIOVANNI

Palazzo Pratellesi

VIA

San Francesco

Porta San Giovanni

PIAZZALE DEI MARTIRI DI MONTE MAGGIO

| 0 | 50 | 100 | 150 | 200 metres |
| 0 | 50 | 100 | 150 | 200 yards |

Poggibonsi Siena

VIA ROMA

Picture credits

The Automobile Association wishes to thank the following photographers and libraries for their assistance the preparation of this book.

Front and back cover: (t), AA Photo Library/Clive Sawyer; (ct), AA Photo Library/Ken Paterson; (cb), AA Photo Library/Ken Paterson; (b), AA Photo Library/Ken Paterson; Spine, AA Photo Library/Ken Paterson.

AKG, London 10t, 11t, 11b, 17t, 17b; THE ARTARCHIVE 2(i), 5, 15b, 26, 68/9; BRIDGEMAN ART LIBR LONDON 13t, 14/5 b/g and 16 b/g) (Detail) Santa Croce, Florence, Italy; 14t Palazzo Medici-Riccardi, Florence, Italy; 14b Santa Croce, Florence, Italy; 15t San Francesco, Arezzo, Italy; 53c Cappelle Medicee, Florence, Italy; 56 Chapel of the Princes, San Lorenzo, Florence, Italy; 58 Santa Maria Novella, Florence, Italy; 63 Bargello, Florence, Italy; 66/7 Santa Croce, Florence, Italy; 90t (Detail) Museo dell'Opera del Duc Siena, Italy; 91b Museo Diocesano, Cortona, Italy; 94 Palazzo Pubblico, Siena, Italy; 98 Museo dell'Opera Duomo, Siena, Italy; 100 Pinacoteca Nazionale, Siena, Italy, 106 Sant'Agostino, San Gimignano, Italy; 108 San Francesco, Arezzo, Italy; 159 Villa Guinigi, Lucca, Italy; MARY EVANS PICTURE LIBRARY 6, 7, 8, 9 10b, 13b; EYE UBIQUITOUS 27; GETTYONE/STONE 115; RONALD GRANT ARCHIVE 12t; JOHN HESELTINE 129b, 133t; IMAGES COLOUR LIBRARY 20b, 22/3, 114; MARKA 28, 29b, 30t, 30b, 97, 99, PICTURES COLOUR LIBRARY 26/7, 33, 89, 112; REX FEATURES LTD 12b; WORLD PICTURES LTD 3 91t, 162, 167, 168, 177.

The remaining photographs are held in the Association's own photo library (AA PHOTO LIBRARY) and taken by SIMON MCBRIDE with the exception of the following:
JERRY EDMANSON 93, 110, 154t, 155t, 160, 191br; KEN PATERSON 23b, 25bl, 25br, 29t, 34, 92/3b, 10 143, 144, 145, 170, 181, 182; CLIVE SAWYER 2(iii), 2(iv), 3(i), 3(ii), 6/7, 16b, 19, 20t, 24, 49, 53b, 64, 75, 87, 96, 105, 108, 111, 112/3, 116, 125, 126, 135, 137, 141, 151, 152, 153, 154b, 155c, 155b, 156, 15 158t, 158b, 161t, 161b, 164/5, 165, 166, 169, 171, 172, 191t, 191bl.

SPIRAL GUIDES

Questionnaire

Dear Traveler

Your comments, opinions and recommendations are very important to us. So please help us to improve our travel guides by taking a few minutes to complete this simple questionnaire.

Send to: Spiral Guides, MailStop 66, 1000 AAA Drive, Heathrow, FL 32746–5063

Your recommendations...

We always encourage readers' recommendations for restaurants, nightlife or shopping – if your recommendation is added to the next edition of the guide, we will send you a FREE AAA Spiral Guide of your choice. Please state below the establishment name, location and your reasons for recommending it.

_____

_____

_____

_____

_____

Please send me AAA Spiral_____

(see list of titles inside the back cover)

About this guide...

Which title did you buy?

_____ AAA Spiral

Where did you buy it? _____

When? mm/ y y

Why did you choose a AAA Spiral Guide? _____

_____

_____

_____

Did this guide meet your expectations?

Exceeded ☐   Met all ☐   Met most ☐   Fell below ☐

Please give your reasons _____

_____

_____

_____

continued on next page...

Were there any aspects of this guide that you particularly liked?

_____

_____

_____

_____

Is there anything we could have done better?

_____

_____

_____

_____

About you...

Name (Mr/Mrs/Ms) _____

Address _____

_____

_____ Zip_____

Daytime tel nos. _____

Which age group are you in?

Under 25 ☐   25–34 ☐   35–44 ☐   45–54 ☐   55–64 ☐   65+ ☐

How many trips do you make a year?

Less than one ☐   One ☐   Two ☐   Three or more ☐

Are you a AAA member? Yes ☐   No ☐

Name of AAA club _____

About your trip...

When did you book? m m / y y   When did you travel? m m / y y

How long did you stay?_____

Was it for business or leisure?_____

Did you buy any other travel guides for your trip? ☐ Yes   ☐ No

If yes, which ones?_____

_____

Thank you for taking the time to complete this questionnaire.